The Keys to Prosperity

OTHER BOOKS BY THE SAME AUTHOR

The Elements of Statistical Method. 1911 (Macmillan Co.)

Exercises in Statistical Method. 1913 (Published by Author)

The Valuation of Urban Realty for Purposes of Taxation
1914 (University of Wisconsin)

The Wealth and Income of the People of the United States
1915 (Macmillan Co.)

Income in the United States
(Joint Author) 1922 (National Bureau of Economic Research)

Employment Hours and Earnings in Prosperity and Depression
1923 (National Bureau of Economic Research)

Trends in Philanthropy. 1928 (National Bureau of Economic Research)

Economics in Rhyme. 1928 (Gorham Press)

The National Income and Its Purchasing Power
1930 (National Bureau of Economic Research)

Index Numbers Elucidated. 1930 (Longmans Green & Co.)

The Causes of Economic Fluctuations. 1938 (Ronald Press)

THE KEYS
TO PROSPERITY

By

WILLFORD I. KING

Economics-Professor Emeritus
New York University

New York
Constitution and Free Enterprise Foundation
Publishers
1948
Distributed by
Committee for Constitutional Government, Inc.
Bartholomew Building, New York 17, N. Y.

PRINTED IN THE UNITED STATES OF AMERICA
RUMFORD PRESS
CONCORD, NEW HAMPSHIRE

Dedicated to those Liberals who wish to conserve the old until something better is discovered, and to those Conservatives who are ready to adopt the new as soon as its superiority is established

PREFACE

IN THE SAME YEAR that America declared its independence, that monumental work, *The Wealth of Nations,* was published in England. Its author was Adam Smith — "the father of economics." What an amazing man he was! Before he wrote, no systematic treatise on economics existed. But, by gathering material from a thousand sources, by observing painstakingly, and by reasoning precisely, he was able to set forth clearly the essentials which must underlie national prosperity.

One hundred and seventy-one years have passed since Adam Smith finished his masterpiece, and the field of economics has been explored by thousands of inquiring minds, yet surprisingly few of the principles which he laid down have been overturned. In the main, they stand as firm as the Rock of Gibraltar.

The principal result of the extensive research conducted since Smith's day has been to fill in gaps and round out his conclusions. Some of the most important additions to the fundamentals set forth in *The Wealth of Nations* have resulted from pure deductive reasoning. Others have been made possible by the accumulation of masses of statistical data and by the developments of new statistical techniques. Major advances have occurred in our understanding of the principles governing population, interest rates, the relationship of prices to money and credit, the workings of monopoly, and cyclical movements in economic phenomena. It therefore seems desirable again to have restated the basic essentials underlying national prosperity — in this restatement utilizing the pertinent contributions of science made during the years between 1776 and 1948. Such is the task essayed by the present writer in preparing this volume.

In this undertaking, it has seemed necessary to clear away a great tangle of misconceptions and fallacies under which economic truths have been buried so deeply that it has required a trained eye to detect them. It is hoped that this task has been done thoroughly enough to enable the reader to distinguish readily the true from the false.

The author wishes to express his appreciation of the valuable help given to him by the members of his family, by Mr. Fred Sexauer, and by Dr. Orval Watts. He is especially indebted to Mr. Norman Lombard, who read the entire manuscript with meticulous care and offered numerous suggestions which eliminated many weaknesses. The steady encouragement given by Dr. Edward A. Rumely has been a constant inspiration.

WILLFORD I. KING

Douglaston, New York,
January 20, 1948

Table of Contents

List of Tables

List of Charts

The Keys to Prosperity

Chapter I

INTRODUCTION

Practically all progress in this world of ours has been due to the fact that thinkers have dreamed dreams in which they have seen better things, and have then proceeded to devise ways and means of making these visions real. One of the most common of these dreams has pictured a land in which the masses live in comfort rather than in poverty, and in which progress is ever upward — never being interrupted by periods of depression and unemployment. Thousands have sought to make such dreams come true, but everywhere they have been confronted by locked doors bearing such signs as Ignorance, Prejudice, Custom, Tradition, and Inertia. Before these doors to the land of dreams can be opened it is necessary to secure the right keys. But they are mixed in among thousands of other keys, many of which fit Pandora's box rather than the gates to the land of progress. How can we recognize the keys to prosperity? This book has been written in an attempt to make such recognition easier.

That locating the keys to prosperity is no simple matter is evidenced by the length of time during which the quest has continued. From Adam's day down to the present, almost everyone has been engaged in trying to find freedom from want, and to build for himself at least minimum safeguards against the vicissitudes of life. Yet, after all these centuries, the desired security is far from being attained.

One of the chief obstacles to the attainment of such security has, of course, been war. In recent decades, wars have tended to become world-wide in scope. With the development of the atomic bomb and allied devices, it seems not improbable that, if a third world war occurs, it will wipe out most important cities and industrial equipment, and cause as complete a reversion to primitive life as that described by H. G. Wells in his prophetic book *The War in the Air*.

In view of this situation, it becomes evident that any and all plans for maintaining security for the people of any nation must be based upon the assumption that, in the near future, a world government, strong and wise enough to prevent war, will be established and made effective.

The *immediate* cause of World War II was, of course, lust for power on the part of two men — Adolf Hitler and Benito Mussolini. However, it seems improbable that either could have gained control of his nation had his way not been paved by certain malign economic forces, the operations of which will be discussed in later chapters. Manifestly, therefore, such forces play no minor rôle in world affairs.

If the United Nations do cooperate and prevent the destruction of civilization, it seems safe to say that the thinking people of the world will continue to be interested in the question of how to prevent nations from falling periodically into those "Sloughs of Despond" known as depressions. The thesis

1

of this book is that such breakdowns of our economic machinery are wholly unnecessary.

Ever since the publication of *The Wealth of Nations,* economists have been setting up easily read signs pointing out the road to general prosperity. That our nation — the nation having the most abundant natural resources, the most ingenious people, and the highest degree of education of any country in the world — should stand in constant dread of a wave of mass unemployment shows how we have ignored the application of simple, sound economic principles to our everyday problems, even while we have been utilizing almost incredibly intricate mechanical devices and chemical processes. To the traditional man from Mars it would seem unbelievable that such a supposedly progressive nation should know of no way of keeping its industries active except to go to war. He would, of course, infer that the mechanics of operating an economic system smoothly are so intricate that no one has yet been able to fathom them.

This conclusion would, however, be far from the truth, for many of the fundamental principles were clearly elucidated by Adam Smith nearly two centuries ago, and subsidiary principles have been gradually worked out and explained by later economists. At present, it is just as feasible to write a reliable manual on the correct operation of our economic system as to write one on the correct operation of a steam engine. The difficulty is to find operators who are willing to study the manual and follow the rules laid down.

In recent years, the problem of successful operation of our economic mechanism has been complicated by the appearance of a mass of literature written by charlatans posing as economists, and both ordinary citizens and government officials have, of course, found it extremely difficult to distinguish between economic science and economic quackery. Under the circumstances, it is perhaps not surprising to find the nation flooded with books, pamphlets, and articles giving advice, running all the way from the thoroughly sound to the extremely bizarre, on how to assure "permanent" prosperity. Some demand complete freedom of competition. Others believe in a carefully planned and controlled economy.

Advocates of planning assert vehemently that the only way to prevent the advent of depression is to prepare now the blueprints for the economy of the future. They contend that, to assure "full employment," considerable governmental control of industry is imperative. Their opponents reply that planning and governmental control mean regimentation, muddling, and general inefficiency, and that the only effective way to maintain full employment is to restore complete freedom of enterprise and remove all hindrances to investment. When the planners retort that the great depression of "the Thirties" developed fully under a regime in which enterprise was relatively free and investment unrestricted, the advocates of *laissez faire* commonly dodge the issue by boasting of the remarkable progress which the nation has made under free competition and by deriding as weaklings those who prefer security to opportunity. By so doing, the proponents of free enterprise place themselves in a lamentably weak position before the bar of public opinion, for most Americans feel that our nation is great enough to give to its citizens *both* security and opportunity. As its title suggests, the thesis of this book is that, in this particular case, the view of the majority is correct.

However, past experience seems to prove that, under complete *laissez faire,* both security and prosperity are decidedly intermittent rather than "permanent." It follows that, if prosperity is to be stabilized, there must be some planning and a certain amount of governmental control. Does this, however, mean that enterprise must necessarily give up a significant part of its freedom of action? Does it signify that consumers must be regimented? Does it imply continuance of bureaucracy and loss of liberty? These are some of the questions dealt with in the following pages.

One thing seems certain. Regulation cannot be expected to produce salutary results unless those responsible for the regulatory process understand exactly what forces give rise to poverty and depression and what devices can be used to overcome these forces. The purpose of this book is to present in simplified form some of the fundamental facts and principles involved. Emphasis is laid upon the latter, much of the factual material being purely illustrative.

Careful study indicates that among the factors which must be considered are the supply of natural resources, population, the birth rate, money, circulating credit, the process of exchange, income, demand, purchasing power, the price level, saving, investing, hoarding, price fixing, taxation, and the volume of employment. An attempt will be made to show how all of these forces interact with each other in our economic mechanism. Especial attention is directed to the question of whether we actually have had "over-saving," "under-spending," "hoarding," and "under-investing." It is hoped that the reader will thus be aided in finding the keys which unlock the gates to lasting prosperity.

Chapter II

POPULATION AND RESOURCES

Origin of Goods

Prosperity means either the receipt of or the possession or enjoyment of an abundance of *goods*. The term *good*, as used in economics, refers to any thing or service which is capable of directly or indirectly satisfying a human want. The want may be wise or foolish, social or anti-social. Regardless of any ethical implications, the thing which is wanted is called a *good*.

Goods may be either *gifts of nature* such as, for instance, wild fruits, game, natural forests, rivers, seas, sunshine, mountain scenery, fresh air, minerals, tillable land, or building sites, or they may be *products of nature acted upon by man's efforts* — for example, buildings, machines, tools, grain, livestock, textiles, clothing, automobiles, furniture, foodstuffs, electric current, or the services of a cook, waiter, or lawyer. *Direct* goods are those which serve us directly. Examples are food and clothing. *Indirect* goods serve us only indirectly. Such is the case with factories, tools, raw materials, etc., and also with things like stocks, bonds, notes, and money. The last mentioned are wanted because they represent claims to services or things.

It is often said that man creates goods. In reality, all that he can do is to move things from place to place. Nature must do the rest. The equipment, tools, and machines which he uses in the productive process are themselves nothing but the materials of nature modified by man's efforts.

The Quest for Prosperity

The quest for prosperity began with the appearance of life on our planet. At first, plants strove to obtain the sunshine and carbon dioxide which they must have to live. Later, animals fought to secure an adequate supply of plant food. Much later, man began his struggle for the sustenance, shelter, clothing, and other goods which he deemed essential to a state of well-being.

Through nearly all of the long period which has elapsed since man first appeared on earth, the prime requisite upon which his attention has been focused has been food. The problem of avoiding starvation is still the major concern of at least half the population of our planet.

Freedom from Want

Those of us who have never traveled outside of the domains of Uncle Sam or his Canadian neighbor frequently have no comprehension whatever of what *want* has generally meant to the common people of most nations. Our friends and neighbors want a new car, new furniture, and new clothes to replace articles that are looking a trifle shabby or *passé*; they want more spacious and modern homes, more luxurious foods and drinks, longer and more costly vacations; but almost never are they troubled by the problem of getting food enough to satisfy hunger, and shelter and clothing adequate to

4

keep out the cold. Hence, we are prone to infer that the same situation exists today almost everywhere, and has, in fact, been the rule at most times and most places.

Nothing could be further from the truth. The situation prevailing north of the Rio Grande today is characteristic only of the most favored nations in the most favored century of the earth's history. It is probably not going too far to say that, before the discovery of America, there was never a time in any sizable nation in which the majority of the people did not *live at the subsistence level.* But just what does *"living at the subsistence level"* signify? It means that, in years when crops were good, the majority had enough food to satisfy their hunger, but that, in years when crops were short, most people were hungry much of the time, and that many died from diseases of malnutrition or actual starvation.

Thomas R. Malthus

Everyone everywhere took it for granted that such was the natural lot of the common man. Furthermore, until that learned English clergyman, Thomas Robert Malthus (1766–1834), the outstanding economist of his generation, evolved his famous laws of population, practically everyone believed that nothing could be done about it. His *Essay on the Principle of Population*, published first at the close of the Eighteenth Century, may, then, be looked upon as a new gospel — the first real message of hope that John and Mary Doe might attain freedom from want.

As in the case of most great prophets, Malthus was misunderstood by many of the people of his time — and, even yet, the full significance of his message is commonly overlooked. He was denounced and reviled as a harbinger of gloom, but the fact remains that he was the first to point out a path by which the common man might escape from the bondage of poverty.

Just what great truths did Malthus work out and bring to the attention of the public?

The Law of Diminishing Returns

He knew that food was a basic need — that people could not survive without it. He also was familiar with *the law of diminishing returns* — the principle of which is familiar to every farmer, even though he has never heard of an economic law. In essence, this law records the observed fact that the output of farm products cannot be increased proportionally as more labor is used on a given piece of land. Thus, if, on a 160-acre wheat farm, one farmer could produce 2,000 bushels of wheat, it is possible that two men might be able to increase the crop to 3,200 bushels; three men might bring it up to 4,000 bushels; four men to 4,600 bushels; and five men to not more than 5,000 bushels — in brief, the more men working on the farm, the less would be the wheat produced per man. While one man on the farm would produce 2,000 bushels of wheat, five men on the same farm would turn out but 1,000 bushels each, that is per capita production would be reduced to one-half of what it would be with but one man on the farm. Furthermore, on the typical 160-acre wheat farm, the probabilities are that a hundred men, using their best endeavors, could not raise production much above the 6,000 bushel mark. The principle just illustrated for wheat applies with equal force to every known crop. Evidently, then, the more people that try to draw their living from any given farm, the less will be the food supply available for each family.

Limits on the World's Food Supply

One of the unfortunate facts which humanity must face is that the supply of usable land is definitely limited; indeed, all the land on earth, including deserts and mountains, adds up to but fifty odd million square miles, and of this area not more than ten million square miles constitute reasonably good farm land. The Mississippi Valley farmer feels that he needs a full quarter-section to support his family decently. On this basis, there is room on the earth for only 40,000,000 prosperous farm families. At five persons to the family this would mean 200,000,000 people on farms. To support the 2,000,000,000 people living on our planet, it would therefore be necessary for each of these farm families to feed itself and nine other families — not too easy a task.

The reader of popular pseudo-scientific literature is likely to assume that, as time passes, new methods of producing crops can be depended upon to prevent the development of any serious shortages in food supply. Unfortunately, the facts do not support such an optimistic line of reasoning. It is doubtful that Chinese farmers today get larger yields per acre than did their ancestors of forty centuries ago. Even in the United States, the headquarters for inventive genius, statistics show that, during the past seventy years — the period for which we have dependable records — science has been able to increase average acre productivity but moderately. The correctness of this statement is indicated by the following figures showing average yields per acre:[1]

Period	Corn	Wheat	Oats	Cotton	Potatoes
1866–1875	25.6 bu.	12.3 bu.	26.5 bu.	163 lbs.	86.9 bu.
1935–1944	28.5 bu.	15.3 bu.	30.7 bu.	243 lbs.	125.8 bu.

While our experiment stations have been successful in originating better strains of plants, better methods of cultivation, and more scientific ways of using insecticides and fertilizers, their efforts have been largely offset by diminution in soil fertility, by the washing away of large amounts of our rich topsoil, and by the necessity of using poorer and more arid land in order to meet the food and clothing requirements of our growing population.

While, of course, Malthus had at hand no volumes of statistics such as are available today, his wide reading led him to believe that the opportunity for expanding the food supply of the world by increasing acre yields was not great. The chief prospect of securing more food for humankind lay in opening up the fertile virgin lands in unsettled regions, and, after all, such arable areas amounted to but a few millions of square miles. The earth's surface could not be stretched, and no one had discovered any method of making it rain in the vast arid areas comprising such a large fraction of it.

[1] *Statistical Abstract of the U. S. 1944-5*, pp. 685-7.

The Tendency of Population to Expand

In striking contrast to this rigidity of land supply stood the unlimited tendency of population to expand. As he studied the various nations of the world, he found that, everywhere, human beings yielded to the innate urge to procreate their kind. Everywhere, the typical working-class mother gave birth to from five to a dozen children. In most regions, however, on the average, only two of these children would grow up, marry, and have children of their own, all the others perishing in wars or accidents, succumbing to disease, or dying of malnutrition or starvation. Under such circumstances, the population did not increase, but remained roughly stationary generation after generation.

However, he found that there was a striking exception to this rule in the case of new settlements in relatively unpopulated regions. In such areas (for example the American Colonies), land was plentiful, hence food was abundant, and diseases of malnutrition did not destroy human life. Moreover, population was scattered, and hence epidemics did not spread rapidly. Wars were not particularly destructive of human life. Therefore, most children survived to maturity, and the population grew at a very rapid rate, in some instances actually doubling in fifteen years or less.

He was much impressed by the potentialities of such a proportionate rate of population growth — and well he might be. If we apply that proportionate rate of increase to the 4 millions of people then in the United States and continue it up to the present time, we find that our population would now (1948) be around 4 billions, some 28 times our actual number, and far more than the present population of the entire earth. Had all populations in all nations increased since Malthus' time at the speed he noted for the American Colonies, the world's population would now be at least a trillion. Such a population would mean that each of our hypothetical forty millions of farm families would have to produce food enough to support 25,000 people — the population of a small city — a manifestly absurd impossibility.

The Malthusian Principles

After years of study of the habits, customs, and histories of peoples in all parts of the earth, Malthus arrived at certain broad generalizations which are approximated by the following propositions:

1. Everywhere, population, if not restrained by lack of food or otherwise, increases rapidly in geometric ratio, doubling every 15 to 25 years.
2. Because of the law of diminishing returns, the inexpansibility of the supply of arable land, and the non-feasibility of increasing rapidly average acre crop yields, it is impossible for the food supply to continue for long any such proportionate rate of increase as doubling every 15 to 25 years.
3. Therefore, the high birth rate commonly existing, by causing population to press persistently upon the food supply, usually reduces the people to misery.

His *Essay* was largely devoted to illustrations showing that the need for food sets an absolute limit upon population growth. If a nation does not import food, and produces only food enough to keep 100,000,000 people alive, it follows that, when the population rises to that limit, it can go no further, and, thereafter, for every birth there must be a death; in other words, the death rate must equal the birth rate. Malthus made plain that three *positive checks* unite to arrive at this inexorable result. These checks are famine, pestilence, and war. Warlike nations fight with one another for available food, and enough people may perish in the war to make the food supply adequate to keep alive those surviving the fray. More peaceful peoples are first weakened by malnutrition, and then either fall prey to epidemics or suffer many deaths from actual starvation.

Had Malthus gone no further than to describe the nature of the positive checks, he would have rendered but a minor service to mankind. His great contribution to humanity was the startling pronouncement that a way existed to lift the masses out of the slough of hunger in which they had been mired from time immemorial — that way was to exercise the preventive check on population — in other words to lower the birth rate. Were the birth rate sufficiently reduced, the population would gradually diminish, food would eventually become abundant, and the first essential of prosperity for the masses would be attained.

Malthus showed in his *Essay* that, in many sections of the world, attempts had been made to restrict population growth, but that such attempts had usually met with but limited success. It did not appear that any great nation had ever been able to prevent the masses from multiplying to such an extent that they sank to the level of bare subsistence.

While Malthus made clear as crystal the principle that the only possibility of lessening the poverty of the masses lay in reducing their birth rate, there is little to indicate that he expected his message to be heeded. His painstaking studies showed that, through the centuries, the common people had multiplied up to the number permitted by the food supply. At times, terrible epidemics such as the Black Death had decimated the populations of large areas, and, for a short time thereafter, the survivors would live in relative plenty; but, within a few decades, the high existing birth rate, accompanied by a reduced death rate, would again build the population up to the food supply, and the masses would be as miserable as ever.

Malthus saw the remarkable effects upon production which had resulted from applying the steam engine to machinery, yet, at the time of his death (1834), most of the common people of Europe still endured the same hand-to-mouth precarious existence that had characterized the long ages before the Industrial Revolution. The gains from all discoveries, from all inventions, had been overwhelmed by "the devastating torrent of children."

Elevation of Standards of Living

Yet, in America, at the very time when Malthus was studying and writing, a leaven was at work which was destined eventually to make his fondest dreams come true. The probabilities are, however, that he never realized its portent. But neither did anyone else. What was it? How did it operate?

When white settlers first came to North America, they found a land so vast and a soil so fertile that, despite the rapidity of their multiplication, good land was available either for the taking or at nominal cost. From the time when the Pilgrims landed at Plymouth, this situation prevailed almost continuously for two and a half centuries. As a result, food was so abundant as to amaze immigrants to America. For the first time in their lives, these immigrants were able to secure readily all the nourishing food that they cared to consume.

Since the abundance of good land made ample food so easy to get, even ordinary farmers or mechanics had time to think of things other than how to keep the wolf from the door. They imitated the gentry and built for themselves attractive homes fitted with comfortable and even artistic furniture. More important still, they began to demand training in "the three R's," and this demand resulted in the establishment of a system of elementary schools, accompanied by academies and colleges open to the unusually studious. As generation followed generation, the things necessary to gratify these newly acquired tastes came to be regarded not as luxuries, but as prime necessities; in other words, they became part of the *standards of living* of typical Americans.

At this point, it is necessary to differentiate clearly between an individual's *scale of living* and his *standard of living*. The term "scale of living" is merely a name describing the broad characteristics of the individual's way of life. It includes the quality of his meals, the conveniences of his dwelling, the up-to-dateness of his clothing, and the expensiveness of his amusements. Usually its altitude is determined by what the income of the family will buy. Since, typically, it merely reflects the individual's income, the use of the term adds to our stock of economic concepts nothing of fundamental importance. Careless writers, however, continually confuse this with "the standard of living" — a concept of outstanding significance.

While the *scale* of living is something objective which can be observed by others, a person's *standard* of living is purely mental or subjective. The *standard of living* of an individual is defined by economists as being "the aggregate of wants taking precedence over marriage and a family." That is, it includes all those services and material goods which, to the given individual, seem so fundamental to a decent existence that, before they will be given up, he or she will abstain from marriage and will refrain from increasing the size of his or her family. The *standard of living* therefore dominates the actions of the individual in the most vital of all matters. As a result, it seems safe to say that the prosperity of any given nation is generally influenced more by the prevailing level of the standards of living of its inhabitants than by all other forces combined. Unless a man is exceptionally wealthy, if his standard of living is high, he will find it impossible to gratify his expensive tastes unless he keeps his family small. The result is that, where people generally have high standards of living, the birth rate is low, population does not press upon the food supply, and most of the inhabitants are well fed and prosperous.

A man may sink into poverty or attain prosperity without affecting much his *standard* of living. Between 1607 and World War I, many millions of immigrants arrived in America from Europe. The typical newcomer had a very low standard of living. Perhaps he worked hard, gained wealth, built a big house, and lived on the fat of the land; in other words, his *scale* of living rose greatly. Even so, his *standard* of living probably remained about as low as when he first arrived; that is, he still considered a large family more important than his recently acquired luxuries. Therefore, his family probably contained from five to a dozen children.

These children, however, soon came to consider essential the comforts with which they were surrounded. They went to American schools and absorbed the ideas established in this nation. Their standards of living rose sharply above those of their parents. As land became harder to acquire, they came to realize that it was impossible both to have large families and to enjoy the comforts and luxuries which they felt were essential. Therefore, these sons and daughters of immigrants had only three to five children.

In the grandchildren of the immigrants, the adjustment of ideals continued. Their families, therefore, ordinarily ran from no children at all to a maximum of three or four.

The net result of this process has been that, in the United States, the number of children per family has fallen from around seven — the number typical when our nation was first established — to below three at the present time. Had the standards of living of our ancestors not risen, had our birth rate not fallen, our people today, instead of being the most prosperous in the world, would be as poverty-stricken as are the Chinese or the Hindus.

Meanwhile, events in America had had repercussions in Europe. The farms of the Mississippi Valley had flooded Europe with cheap food. This gave Europeans more time for thinking. Western Europe began to install schools for the common people. Education gradually raised standards of living there. The birth rate fell — first in France — later in other countries, despite the efforts of militaristic rulers to keep it high. Ordinary Europeans, too, were glimpsing prosperity.

Inventive Genius Versus Population Growth

Since the Renaissance, every Western nation has been the scene of a race between inventive genius and population growth. At any specified time, the degree of prosperity of any given nation has been determined mainly by the status of that race.

During the last two centuries, inventive genius has increased incredibly man's command over nature, and, at first thought, it would be natural to expect that this would have brought prosperity to all nations. However, as we have seen, science has not succeeded in expanding greatly the average production of food per acre. Therefore, wherever the standard of living has been low, the birth rate has always been sufficiently high to win the race, and bring the masses of the people down to the subsistence level. In Malthus' day, population pressure had won out throughout Europe, Asia, and Africa. However, as just pointed out, about the time of his death, a slowly rising standard of living began putting the brakes on the birth rate in France.

Very gradually, the same force manifested itself in other countries, and, little by little, inventive genius gained on population growth. Very, very slowly the common people began to emerge from their enslavement to the hunger wolf. Malthus' vision was gradually transformed into reality.

Basic Force Determining National Prosperity

Casual observation makes evident the fact that, in general, the people of Canada, Australia, New Zealand, and the United States are prosperous, while those of most of Asia and Africa are poverty-stricken, other nations occupying intermediate positions.

It is hardly possible for one really to comprehend the reasons for these striking differences if he does not understand thoroughly the fact that prosperity depends upon the volume of production *per capita*, and that, in turn, production per capita is, as a rule, largely dependent upon the *per capita* supply of available natural resources. This fact is evident enough to the self-sufficient farmer, but, in the case of the city worker, is often obscured by a maze of confusing details concerning such things as money, trade, and contracts. The farmer who produces most of what his family consumes knows full well that a poor crop means hard times. He understands also that it takes much more to feed and clothe six children than to do the same for two children. He is thoroughly aware of the fact that, if he has barely enough land to make a decent living, and if his farm is divided among his three sons, each will, at best, be able to derive from his meager acreage nothing more than a bare subsistence.

After all, in essentials, the nation resembles the self-sufficing farm. The more land and minerals and power available for each inhabitant, the larger is likely to be the output per worker, and the more prosperous will be the people.

It may be asserted that, while the above statement may be true as regards agricultural regions, it certainly does not apply to a great industrial nation like Great Britain. And what about Manhattan, a rocky island which never was very productive agriculturally? Today, nevertheless, its inhabitants nearly top the world in average prosperity!

The answer is that both these instances merely illustrate the existence of "division of labor." The residents of Manhattan are mostly busy in manufacturing and exchanging materials and things produced in all parts of the nation. Were the Southern cotton crop, the Mississippi Valley grain crops, the wool clip from the arid plains, and the monetary transactions necessary for the exchanges of such products to stop, New York's prosperity would melt away like snow before the summer sun. Similarly, Britain, blockaded, quickly finds herself hungry. In truth, therefore, neither Manhattan nor Britain is, by itself, any more a complete entity than is a head without a body. Neither can live without the farms and mines which furnish the fundamentals of existence.

In general, the people of Asia and Africa are at the subsistence level because these continents are grossly overpopulated — in other words, their supply of natural resources *per capita*, and hence their average productivity per man hour is extremely low. All of Europe suffers from the same difficulty, though its different nations are affected in varying degrees. Granted American superiority in organization, initiative, and "know-how," the fundamental, basic reason why, under ordinary conditions, the French, Dutch, Germans, or Scandinavians produce but one-third as much per man hour as do Americans is that they have so much less adequate supplies of natural resources per capita.

The assertion is frequently made that our American industries are so highly productive because we use so much capital per worker. This statement is doubtless correct. But why do we have so much capital? The answer is, because we have saved so much. But why have we saved so much? Clearly, because we have been prosperous, and hence it has been easy for us to save. But why have we been prosperous? We come back to the fact that it is because we have had abundant natural resources *per capita*.

The Standard of Living and Prosperity

Not infrequently we hear the assertion made that the Malthusian principles may operate still in some countries or might even operate in the United States under certain conditions. Such a statement shows a complete lack of understanding of the forces controlling population. The truth is that the Malthusian laws are as omnipresent as is the law of gravity. They have operated everywhere since plant or animal life appeared upon the earth. What is new is the deliberate action of human beings in controlling their birth rate. By this action, they have been able to improve their welfare despite the presence of the immutable law of diminishing returns.

But, in most nations, birth rates are still too high to permit the masses to be prosperous. The people of Europe are still poor mainly because there are too many of them. They have been too slow in raising their standards of living. Aside from France, the countries of western Europe maintained unduly high birth rates up to World War I. The people of eastern and southern Europe still have low standards of living, high birth rates, and the masses in poverty. As yet, they have made but little use of modern methods of birth control.

Had the progressive people of Europe been wise, they would have promptly rid themselves of bandit leaders like Hitler and Mussolini who gave bonuses for large families in order to secure a more ample supply of "cannon fodder" for future campaigns of conquest. They would have realized that, in these days of mechanization, wars are won primarily not by masses of men but rather by aggregations of machinery, and that machinery is acquired only through extensive saving and capital formation, something beyond the reach of overpopulated poverty-stricken nations. Thus, it was the factories and shipyards of America, and not the teeming millions of China, which made it impossible for Japan to win World War II. Today, if the people of Europe knew their true interests, they would build up relations of mutual respect between themselves and neighboring nations. They could then afford to use all feasible means to curtail sharply the birth rates of the less competent classes of their populations. If Western European nations reduced their populations by half and substituted free competition

Adam Smith — The Father of Economics.
{See page 2.}

for regimentation, it is probable that their inhabitants could attain prosperity somewhat equivalent to that existing in the United States today. To secure similar results in Southern Europe would probably require a population reduction of two-thirds, or perhaps even three-fourths.

Thus far, Asia, most of Africa, and parts of Latin America are overwhelmed as completely as ever by "the devastating torrent of children." The standards of living of the masses in those regions are probably no higher than were the standards of their ancestors thousands of years ago. As long as this situation prevails, all attempts to lift these nations out of their poverty are doomed in advance.

Among people with low standards of living, the typical yearly birth rate is probably about 45 per 1,000 inhabitants. Where food is abundant, the typical death rate may be no more than 15 per 1,000. This leaves a net increase of 30 per 1,000 per annum. At this rate, the population would double in about 24 years. When this state of affairs exists, the hopelessness of trying to overcome population pressure by introducing new productive processes is apparent. How futile such an undertaking is likely to prove is well shown by the case of India. In that nation, modern factories have been installed, great irrigation works have been constructed, and the food supply has been markedly increased — net result, a population growth of 50,000,-000 in ten years, and thousands dying of starvation — more people in misery instead of fewer. This is retrogression instead of improvement. Here we have an excellent illustration of the fact that, in any nation having a low standard of living, inventive genius has no chance of winning the race.

American visitors to regions having low standards of living are always shocked by the health conditions prevailing there. Hence our charitably inclined set up in those nations hospitals and clinics. These institutions may relieve pain, but, unless the food supply increases or the birth rate falls, ten thousand hospitals cannot lower the death rate. If China has food for but 400,000,000 and that many people already live there, no more can be fed. For every birth there must be a death. If the birth rate is 50 per 1,000, the death rate must also be 50 per 1,000, instead of the 15 per 1,000 characterizing a well-ordered, prosperous society. Therefore, in each year, 35 out of every 1,000 persons meet an untimely death, and most of the remaining inhabitants drag out a half-starved existence merely because the people of China have not raised their respective standards of living and cut the birth rate.

Most world uplifters who seek to secure the Four Freedoms for all nations apparently have no conception of the magnitude of the problem by which they are confronted. China and India alone probably have not less than 20,000,000 *excess* births per annum. This means that, in each year, 20,000,000 of their inhabitants may die of famine, pestilence, or war, without lessening the total population in the least. Under such circumstances, the futility of depending upon emigration to lessen the population pressure becomes obvious. Within fifteen years, they could send to the United States some 300,000,000 people — enough persons to reduce our nation also to a bare subsistence level resembling their own, and yet this huge outpouring would not have reduced their numbers remaining at home. As soon as the emigration stopped, their excessive numbers of births would again force millions to die of malnutrition or starvation. Their populations would be just as large and just as poverty-stricken as they would have been had no emigration occurred.

Erroneous Views Concerning Poverty's Origin

Though, throughout the world's long history, a bare subsistence has been the lot of most of the earth's inhabitants, it has usually been true that, in each nation, there has flourished a small group of prosperous persons. In some instances, these favored few have been very rich indeed. For example, some of the Indian princes are reputed to be among the wealthiest men in the world. In certain Catholic countries in which the people are very poor, the Church has often built magnificent cathedrals and has decorated them lavishly, the wherewithal for their construction and maintenance being extracted mainly from the pitifully low incomes of the parishioners. In the Orient, wealthy rajahs or mandarins often feast sumptuously while women and children are begging at the palace gates for handfuls of rice to keep themselves alive. The existence of such situations has led to the almost universal belief that grasping landlords and prelates, and despotic rulers have been to no small degree responsible for the dire poverty of the masses under their control.

Before accepting this view as correct, it is well to remember that, where the thermometer reading is very high, it is usually uncomfortable. Could the situation be cured by breaking all thermometers? Perhaps it is worth while to analyze the situation dispassionately.

Let us consider the case of some country having a low standard of living, for example Mexico. Would the Mexican people now be better off economically than would be the case had they and their ancestors contributed nothing to the Church? The answer is that, today, they possess centers of beauty which furnish rare sources of inspiration, and help to lift the people above their otherwise painfully drab surroundings. What culture they have largely radiates from these centers. Moreover, they are just as well fed and clothed and housed as they would have been if the cathedrals had never been built, for their income status is determined by the fact that, as long as their standards of living are low, they multiply up to the food supply, and hence live at a subsistence level.

And is it true that the dire poverty found in various regions is due to the existence of "rack rents" or oppressive taxation? As a rule, investigation will show that the aggregate of rent and taxes is too small to affect greatly the welfare of the people. But let us assume an extreme case in which rent and taxes took half of the total product. The real effect of such levies might be to cut the population in half. Regardless of whether the taxes and rents were or were not levied, as long as the standards of living were low and the birth rates therefore high, the inhabitants would multiply up to the food supply, and the masses would live in poverty. From the humanitarian viewpoint, is it better to have five or to have ten millions of people eking out a miserable existence?

Moreover, it is undoubtedly true that, in poverty-stricken countries, practically all progress in ethics, philosophy, art, and science has come from the little islands of culture protected by the reefs of religion, custom, tradition, or authority. There is always the chance that, from these isles, there may emanate influences which will raise the standards of living of the common people, and, by so doing, enable them to escape from the morass of poverty.

From time to time, throughout history, the common people have revolted, slaughtered the favored few, and seized their wealth, but no instance is recorded in which this process increased the well-being of the masses for any noticeable length of time.

The Sole Method of Uplifting Poor Nations

Experience indicates, therefore, that, as Malthus pointed out, the only possible way of benefiting the common people is to induce them to curtail their birth rate. It follows that we cannot uplift the poverty-stricken areas of the world by aiding their inhabitants to install modern methods of production, by training them in the art of sanitation and the cure of disease, or by lending or giving them equipment, food, or funds. The only possible way of conferring economic benefit upon our less fortunate neighbors is, therefore, by means of precept and example to teach them to raise their respective standards of living, reduce their birth rates, and thus lower their populations, for, as pointed out earlier, the fundamental basis of prosperity is a supply of natural resources large in proportion to population.

Our Present Outlook as Regards Population and Resources

At the beginning of the present century, the advance of our frontier to the Pacific and the rapidity of our population's increase threatened the United States with disaster. Fortunately, however, the first quarter of the century saw a rapid decline in our birth rate, and the virtual barring of immigration. These changes allowed inventive genius to gain a lead in its race with population growth. Present indications are that our population will not rise above 160,000,000 — a number which can apparently be supported in comfort by our existing supply of natural resources.

In so far as we can judge on the basis of our present state of scientific knowledge, petroleum, coal, and soil are our three most important destructible natural resources. Diminution of the supply of these will tend to lessen the productive power of the nation, and, unless our population decreases proportionately, the average scale of living of the people is likely to decline.

If our population shrinks, the chances of our being conquered by some other nation are increased. It therefore behooves us to take all measures necessary to conserve these and any other irreplaceable and essential resources which we are now fortunate enough to possess.

Our Differential Birth Rate

In the United States, as we have seen, the growth of our population has been restrained sufficiently to keep numbers from pressing unduly upon our supply of natural resources. Unfortunately, however, we have as yet failed to protect ourselves adequately against deterioration in the *quality* of our population. At present, the least competent classes of our inhabitants have birth rates far exceeding those applying to the most competent. Thus, in the United States in 1940, native white women 45–49 years of age whose schooling had not gone further than the sixth grade had borne an average of 3.94 children, as compared to an average of only 1.23 children for women who had completed four years of college. Native white women of the same age class living in homes having monthly rental values under $5 had, on the average, given birth to 4.50 children, while those living in homes having rental values of $75 to $99 had averaged but 1.71 children.[2]

This tendency for people possessing the least foresight to have the largest families has prevailed for a long time. Does not the fact that nations have survived this situation for generations prove that the children of the poor and uneducated make just as satisfactory citizens as do the children of the prosperous and the erudite? As a matter of fact, this conclusion is not justified, for, in the past, the high birth rate among the less competent classes was offset by a correspondingly high death rate. In recent years, by contrast, national prosperity and altruism have combined to give to the children of the poor and unlettered medical care of high quality. As a result, most of such children now live to become adults. Since heredity is the most powerful force governing the characteristics of all living creatures, there is no escaping the fact that, at present in the United States, the quality of our race is being bred *down.* This means that, unless and until this differential in the birth rate is remedied, the inevitable result will be an increase in the proportion of our population consisting of imbeciles, morons, epileptics, insane, and other classes of physical and mental weaklings. A high percentage of incompetents means not only an added load to be borne by every producer, but also a lower degree of efficiency in production. It follows that, if the people of the nation really wish to pursue the route leading to sustained prosperity, it behooves them to take such steps as are necessary to reduce greatly the differential existing between the birth rates of the more competent and of the less competent classes.

[2] Population Reference Bureau, *Population Bulletin,* Dec. 1945, pp. 28–29.

Chapter III

FREEDOM AND PROSPERITY

Regimentation Characteristic of Most Economic Life in the Past

In most countries at most times in the past, most economic activities have been carefully regimented. Among primitive peoples, planting and trading were both likely to be governed either by the local chieftain or by a council of the tribe. When society advanced to the feudal stage, it was the function of the lord of the manor to determine what crops and livestock should be grown, what structures should be erected, and what articles should be manufactured. As cities grew up, men engaged in the various fields of business organized themselves into guilds. Each guild controlled its own trade or occupation, and usually laid down minute regulations concerning entrance to the guild and the activities of the members. In general, one could become a member only by serving a long apprenticeship, and non-members could not enter a trade or occupation covered by the guild. The more desirable positions in society were thus effectively monopolized. When the power of the king came to overshadow that of both the nobles and the city guilds, he took over part or all of their functions, in so far as the regulation of trade and manufacturing was concerned. Later, sovereigns discovered that much-needed revenue could be obtained by selling or leasing licenses to trade or manufacture. That, eventually, this source of funds became important is evidenced by Queen Elizabeth's pronouncement that monopoly constituted "the fairest flower in the royal prerogative."

Mercantilism, Cameralism, and Fascism

It was in this stage of British development that officials and others interested in the fiscal problems of the realm developed a general philosophy concerning the correct way of regulating activities. This philosophy came to be known as Mercantilism. The Mercantilists held that the way to make England rich was to buy abroad cheap raw materials, manufacture them in England, and sell to other countries, at high prices, the products manufactured. This system would bring to England large quantities of gold and silver — metals which the British Treasury found it extremely convenient and desirable to amass and hold. According to the Mercantilistic philosophy, the proper policy for England was to establish colonies which would grow raw materials for English factories, and which would accept in payment for the raw materials a fraction of the goods turned out by the factories. The British would also gain revenue from shipping charges made for bringing in raw materials and taking out finished products. It was in an endeavor to carry out this program that the American colonies were established. Essential features of the program were prevention of manufacturing in the colonies and prevention of shipping by the colonies. That anyone would ever seriously object to such "highly reasonable" restrictions presumably seemed improbable to those who planned the colonial ventures.

The Mercantilistic philosophy was by no means confined to Britain. In Germany, practically the same doctrine was called Cameralism. It is not going too far to say that this doctrine has continued to dominate German economic thought and policy down to the present time. In recent years, it has been exemplified by the organization of German industry into cartels, and the regulation of foreign trade through numerous devices such as quotas, tariffs, and exchange controls.

The development of Fascism in Italy was an outgrowth of the same philosophy. Mussolini believed that private industry could be made to function effectively only by aid of governmental direction and regulation. The Nazi philosophy of Hitler was a variant of the same idea. During World War II, a very similar principle was applied to most major activities in the United States and the British Empire.

Socialism and Communism

The process of governmental regulation of private enterprise has always been hampered by the fact that the regulated have persistently originated new and devious ways of evading the regulations. It is, therefore, only natural that many thinkers have been forced to the conclusion that the only way to get real efficiency in production is to have government own and operate all industry. Such a program is called *socialism*.

Altruistic philosophers, shocked by the manifest lack of any close correlation between their conceptions of merit and actual individual rewards for effort, have demanded that government should go further, and should either divide the total product of industry equally among all the inhabitants, or should act as the father of the national family, and distribute available income according to the needs of the respective individuals under its jurisdiction. Such was the philosophy of Lenin. This system, first put into practice on any large scale by Russia, is referred to as *communism*.

To many an idealist, the plan of having every man contribute according to his ability and receive according to his needs seems decidedly superior to any other economic arrangement yet proposed. However, no one has found any method of making it work well in practice. Lenin, discovering no practical way to determine the respective needs of individuals, compromised by requiring uniform pay for all workers. After a few years of experimentation with this system, Russia discarded it entirely. Why?

Apparently, Russia did not throw communism overboard because of any loss of faith in its ethical desirability. It was abandoned solely because experience showed that, with human nature such as it is, communism and efficient production are incompatible. When energetic Paul found that, although he produced three times as much as lackadaisical Ivan, both received identical pay, Paul soon adopted a very leisurely pace, and production stagnated.

Under Stalin, Russia has not only thrown out but reversed the communistic method of distribution, and has made a national hero of Alexei Stakhanov, who introduced into coal mining an efficiency system resembling that which, in the United States, Frederick W. Taylor had long before evolved and applied to a great variety of industrial processes. The thorough-going nature of the rejection of the communistic wage policy by the Russian Government is evidenced by its pronouncement that anyone advocating equal pay was a "counter-revolutionary." Wide differentials in pay have become as common in Russia as in capitalistic nations.

Comparative Merits of Socialism and Competition

State socialism, the system now in vogue in Russia, has some praise-worthy features. For example, when government is responsible for all pro-duction, that part of advertising devoted to the taking of business away from competitors can be dispensed with, and large quantities of labor and mate-rials can therefore be diverted to more constructive uses.

A persistent, unpleasant, and often tragic feature of the competitive system is the heavy volume of losses caused by business failures. Thus, reports of Dun and Bradstreet show that, in 1932, the bottom of the depression in the United States, the current liabilities of firms going to the wall amounted to $928,313,000.

In 1941, out of 3,304,200 concerns in operation at the beginning of the year, 480,100, or 14.5 per cent, closed their doors. Of the 340,200 new concerns starting business in 1944, some 16.1 per cent discontinued operations within twelve months of their respective opening dates.* These failures, of course, represented wrecks of human aspirations, and much waste of effort. Moreover, as long as freedom to start new enterprises exists, the widespread prevalence of such failures is inevitable. Under socialism, on the other hand, failures are relatively few.

However, one must not overlook the fact that, where competition pre-vails, the constant automatic pruning of industry causes merely ripples in the current of production. By contrast, in a socialistic state, any major error on the part of the officials in charge of an industry may affect the welfare of the entire nation. Thus, in Russia, under Lenin, the government seized most surplus crops in the hands of peasants. The next year the peasants reduced their plantings. The summer happened to be dry. As a result, millions died of starvation.

Moreover, the fact that, under competition, the producer who is unable to secure the dollar votes of potential buyers is quickly forced out of business continually adjusts production to demand and insures that consumers will obtain at the lowest possible prices the particular goods which they desire. By contrast, when a self-perpetuating government controls production, the wants of the consumers may be subordinated to matters deemed more im-portant, and the elimination of inefficiency in production may or may not take place. Certainly, such elimination is anything but automatic.

An outstanding merit of the socialistic system is that, in the absence of wars or crop failures, it can prevent business depressions of the type charac-terizing industry in competitive regions. Under free enterprise, the situation is very different. For example, in the United States, at any time from 1930 to 1940, several millions of our potential workers were idling away their time,

* U. S. *Survey of Current Business,* Dec. 1945, pp. 19–20.

and, since they were producing little or nothing and hence were short on spending money, they found their leisure anything but enjoyable. Russia, under socialism, has avoided all such unfortunate situations.

The fact remains, however, that such statistics as are available indicate that, before World War II, physical production per man-hour was but from one-fifth to one-third as great in Russia as in the United States, despite the fact that Russia was operating under an apparently honest and relatively efficient dictatorship. There is nothing to indicate that, at any time, has the typical employed Russian worker ever lived as comfortably as has the American on the relief rolls. Furthermore, the Russian has had little freedom of action, and it is highly doubtful that it is possible for a socialistic state to operate even moderately well except under a dictatorship. It follows that the superiority of state socialism as an economic system remains to be proven. Were the Russian experiment a great success, there would be no need for the "iron curtain."

Weaknesses of Governmental Regulation of Industry

At the present time, few Americans favor either communism or socialism, but many millions lean toward an economic system regulated by government and essentially Mercantilistic or fascistic in nature. However, our wartime experience with such a system is not such as to recommend it for permanent use. Its complete failure during the first year of the war to map out requirements as to strategic materials, and such absurdities as reducing the price on steel scrap when it was urgently needed, rationing sugar while curtailing the production of sugar beets, holding millions of bushels of potatoes off the market until they spoiled, and worst of all, allowing huge strikes to tie up our mines and factories in war time cast doubt upon the ability of government, especially any government having elected officials, ever to control production effectively. This doubt is accentuated by the fact that general observation of the inefficiency of Federal administration in the early part of World War II gave rise to the popular designation of our capital city as "the Washington Madhouse."

Experience indicates that governmental control of industry, regardless of whether the system is socialistic or fascistic in nature, suffers from four inherent defects:

1. Production, being determined by government officials, may not correspond to the wishes of the consuming public. For example, the people may want butter but the officials in control of the dairy industry may devote the resources of the nation to producing cheese.
2. The job of fitting production to the demands of the public is so difficult that it far transcends the ability of even the ablest bureaucrat or commission. Under competition, each one of the millions of entrepreneurs plans how to get and utilize the labor and materials necessary to produce the specific goods demanded by his particular customers. His task is not an easy one, but it is simplicity itself as compared to that of the official who tries to understand all the ever-changing conditions affecting thousands or millions of producers and thousands or millions of customers.

3. The governmentally-fixed price is never such as to make the supply of and the demand for a product exactly balance. Therefore, in some cases, the market is flooded with unsold stocks. In other instances, persons able and willing to buy a good find none of it on the market. This situation gives rise either to distribution on the basis of bribery or favoritism, or to rationing and "black markets."

4. The expense of producing an article does not have to meet the test of the market.

This fourth weakness tends to make governmentally-controlled industry grossly inefficient. Where competition prevails, high-cost producers suffer losses and are forced out of business. Unproductive workers cause their employers to lose money, hence inefficient workers soon lose their jobs. Therefore, both serious errors in judgement and inefficiency are constantly being corrected. Moreover, at any one time, they are likely to be confined to but a small proportion of the concerns operating in any given field.

When government operates a plant, the situation is very different. If production costs are higher than expected, either of two courses may be followed:

1. The good may still be sold at the old price, the loss being shifted to the taxpayers.

2. The price of the product may be raised — a procedure which, of course, lessens the volume of sales.

In neither instance is the manager who is responsible for the loss likely either to be discharged or to suffer a reduction in pay. Therefore, inefficient, extravagant, and wasteful practices may persist for long periods of time, even though they entail heavy losses year after year. Furthermore, these practices are likely to apply to a whole industry, or even to a number of different industries, the result being that the waste may run into millions or even billions of dollars' worth of labor and materials.

Yet, there can be no doubt but that, in "the Thirties," the American people, by and large, favored abandoning free enterprise and competition and turning back to some Mercantilistic, fascistic, or other governmentally regulated system. Why? The answer undoubtedly is that they felt that the competitive system had broken down. They were disgusted with the persistence of unemployment. Furthermore, they had long since forgotten the reasons why our forefathers discarded Mercantilism.

The Eighteenth Century Revolt Against Mercantilism

The early settlers arriving in the American Colonies were, of course, imbued with the spirit of Mercantilism. But they were largely of the adventurous type. They were far away from England. The "Old Country" meant little to their children. Hence, it is not surprising to find that the colonists early began to doubt the wisdom of regimentation. They saw that it was foolish to send to England products for manufacture when they could be manufactured more cheaply in America. The colonists built their own ships and objected to having the carrying trade monopolized by Britain. They could see no point in regulations prescribing the occupations in which they might engage or the enterprises which they might found. It is therefore easy to understand why they sympathized strongly with the new philosophy which, in England, accompanied the Industrial Revolution — namely the philosophy of *laissez faire.*

According to advocates of that doctrine, that government governed best which governed least. Proponents of *laissez faire* held the appropriate functions of government to be protection against foreign enemies, prevention of fraud and crimes of violence, administration of justice, and enforcement of contracts. They believed that the less that government interfered in matters of business, the better for all concerned. This point of view was crystallized by Adam Smith in his epoch-making book — *The Wealth of Nations* — published in 1776 in England. The American Revolution was largely inspired by this doctrine. The Colonies revolted against Mercantilism and espoused the cause of *laissez faire.*

Our Basic Economic Freedoms

The keynote of the American philosophy, expressed first in the Declaration of Independence and later in the Constitution, is freedom — religious, political, and economic freedom. The essential economic freedoms for which our forefathers fought in the American Revolution may be expressed as follows:

1. Freedom to move from place to place.
2. Freedom to acquire, hold, and dispose of private property, either by lease, barter, sale, or bequest. This includes freedom from governmental confiscation of property by taxation or otherwise.
3. Freedom of contract. This concept includes the right to buy labor and other goods at the lowest prices obtainable, and freedom to sell one's services or other goods at the highest prices which can be secured.
4. Freedom to engage in whatever enterprise seems to offer the best opportunity for profit, and to be protected rather than hampered by government in the operation of such enterprise.
5. Freedom from oppression by governmentally-sponsored monopolies.

In England, disciples of Adam Smith, using political methods, were about as successful in gaining these freedoms as were our ancestors in the Colonies who secured liberty by resort to arms. In both nations, the advent of the five freedoms above mentioned resulted in an upsurge of industrial production at a rate never before witnessed in the history of the world. As Adam Smith had pointed out, when every man was left free to pursue his own interests, he was guided as by an invisible hand to do that which was for the advantage of society as a whole. In England, which, unfortunately, still retained its low standard of living, the chief immediate effect of the attainment of these freedoms was to increase the population. In the United States, because of our wide-open spaces and undeveloped resources, these freedoms brought to the people as a whole a rapid advance in their average *scale* of living, and, as previously noted, this advance, in turn, eventually lifted the *standards* of living of our inhabitants, reduced the birth rate, and made our nation the most prosperous on earth.

The Undermining of Our Basic Freedoms

As years passed, these economic freedoms, like the air which we breathe, came to be taken for granted. Most Americans forgot completely that "eternal vigilance is the price of liberty" and did not note the fact that their basic freedoms were being gradually undermined. Foreign trade was strangled by tariffs. Powerful labor monopolies restricted production; used force to prevent men from working; fixed hours and wage rates; and eventually seized and occupied factories and other business property. Government stepped in and fixed wage rates and working time per week. Income and inheritance taxes, initiated at nominal rates, gradually expanded until they practically confiscated large incomes and large estates.

The undermining process was accelerated after the beginning of the great depression of 1929 to 1940. Farmers were told what they could or could not plant. People were forbidden to own gold. Labor union restrictions were given direct support by government. New wage and hour regulations were placed upon the statutes. Social security and unemployment insurance payments were used as bribes to keep people from working. Industries such as coal mining and sugar producing were put under government control. Trading in securities was entangled in an endless mass of red tape.

World War II furnished an excuse for eliminating a large part of such economic freedoms as remained. Rents, wages, and other prices were set by governmental authority. Priorities and quotas were fixed for materials. Tires, gasoline, and foods were rationed. Employees were forbidden to shift from one job to another without governmental permission. Production of automobiles, refrigerators, and other articles was forbidden. Confiscation by taxation was extended. In field after field, freedom gave way to regimentation — and all without much objection on the part of the public, for every encroachment was believed to be justified on the ground that it would help to win the war.

The main reason that the public objected but little was that it had lost its devotion to freedom. A generation had grown up which knew not Moses — which entirely failed to understand the efficiency of competition, the marvels of the free price system, or the wonders which had been wrought by *laissez faire,* in other words, by the competitive capitalistic system. It is therefore worth while to enumerate at this point a few of the unique characteristics of that system.

Unique Advantages of Laissez Faire

Some of the things assured by *laissez faire,* but not possible under any other known system are:

1. Human energy and limited natural resources are directed into the production of the things which human beings most want.
2. At the market price, the supply of any good offered equals the amount demanded, and the necessity of apportioning the supply on the basis of favoritism or bribery is thus obviated.

3. Inefficiency in production is constantly and automatically being eliminated, and efficiency is automatically being rewarded and furthered.

Under *laissez faire,* in the United States, the course of production is governed by the dollar votes of the consumers. At no other election in the nation are the votes so intelligently cast. When a man pays a dollar for a necktie, he votes that more labor and capital be devoted to neckties and less to every one of the millions of other potential products. So silently and smoothly does the system work that its results are almost incredible. Before World War II, when you spent a nickel for a pencil you caused some lumberman in Oregon to cut a trifle more cedar, you determined that a miner in Minnesota would dig a few grams more of iron ore, a second miner in the Malay Peninsula would extract a trifle more tin ore, and a third miner in Siberia would take out a little more graphite; you sent some plantation worker in Sumatra after a fraction of an ounce of rubber; you decreed that ships, railways, factories, wholesalers, and a retailer should cooperate to put another pencil in the place of the one you bought.

Under this system, any producer who fails to comply with the wishes of the consumers is fined, in that he loses either part of his wage or his profit. On the other hand, the Henry Ford who succeeds best in anticipating the wishes of the consumers may reap a hundred-million-dollar reward. When any line of production is short, enlarged profits draw other producers into the field. On the other hand, over-production, by giving rise to losses, drives the highest-cost producers out of the field.

The system operates so effectively that, when Mrs. Jones drops into the grocery store, she finds waiting for her practically all of the items which she wants for dinner, collected from Iowa, California, Florida, and New York. If, in the case of any stray item, the grocer happens to be out, it can readily be obtained next door. No governmental commission or bureau, even if it spends hundreds of millions of dollars in the attempt, can ever hope to approach the marvellous efficiency of this system. Whenever government begins to regulate, the smoothness of operation disappears. Balance gives way to surpluses and shortages. Red tape ties up production. Distribution bogs down. People waste time standing in line to get goods. The whole industrial machine creaks in every joint.

Under *laissez faire,* governmental financial inefficiency is not a matter of very great moment to the citizens, for government is responsible for but few things that affect materially their economic affairs, and the tax burden is light. By contrast, where all industry is controlled by the state, the economic welfare of the nation depends upon how effectively the government can manage the farms, mines, factories, mercantile establishments, and transportation systems under its jurisdiction. Taxes are heavy.

Reasons Why Government Control of Industry Is Inefficient

The difference in the efficiency of industrial management under *laissez faire* and under government control is, to no small extent, due to the difference in the method of choosing the industrial managers. Henry Ford, Walter

Chrysler, and Alfred Sloan were elected by the dollar votes of American automobile buyers to rule the motor car field. They were elected solely because they sold cheaper than anyone else the cars that best suited the fancies of the buyers. By contrast, under governmental management, the head of the automobile industry in a democratic nation would be chosen because he knew how to get out the votes, had a fine radio voice, or was popular in a pivotal State. Knowledge of automobile-making technique would be a purely secondary consideration. His tenure of office would depend, not upon his efficiency in producing motor cars, but upon his efficiency as a politician. On the other hand, the supremacy of Ford, Chrysler, and Sloan in the motor industry could be maintained only as long as they sold cheapest the cars that the buyers liked best.

The difficulty of keeping the control of governmentally-operated industry in the hands of really competent men is so great in the case of a democracy that it seems doubtful that a planned economy can operate successfully under that form of government. To make a socialistic or fascistic state run smoothly, plans should not be disrupted by changes in popular sentiment, as reflected in elections. Officials in charge of industry, if efficient, should be protected against political attacks. Therefore, a planned economy succeeds best if operated by an absolute monarch or by a dictator, unhampered by the necessity of holding elections or catering to the wishes of the people. On the other hand, under a democracy or a republic, *laissez faire* is the logical economic system.

The Folly of Price Fixing

A cardinal principle of *laissez faire* is that government should never interfere with competitive prices, either of labor or of other goods. Prices are the safety valves of our economic system. Whenever they are made rigid, trouble is in the offing. If government fixes prices too high, production in the field becomes excessive. Thus when Brazil raised the price of coffee, such large stocks were accumulated that great quantities were burned. When our government fixed and underwrote the price of cotton, acreage increased to such an extent that the government required the plowing under of part of the crop. When the price of coal was fixed too low, a coal shortage developed throughout the nation. When labor unions elevated wage rates above the competitive level, labor went unsold — in other words, mass unemployment resulted.

Freedom of Profits Under Laissez Faire

According to the philosophy of *laissez faire,* the correct function of government is to maintain free competition, to lay down the rules of the game, and to see that these rules are enforced. When government begins to seize part of the gains of the winners, the players' zest for the game is, of course, much lessened, hence production is curtailed.

As a matter of fact, it is the hope of securing adequate rewards for skill or effort which furnishes the motive power that makes the competitive capitalistic system operate effectively. As long as the investor knows that returns on his capital will not be seized, he searches widely to find promising enterprises in which to invest his funds. When rents are not held down by regulations, landlords seek out the tenants who can utilize their property to best advantage. If superior skill or diligence enables a worker to increase greatly his wage or salary he is likely to use his best endeavors to make himself a more efficient producer.

If the sky is the limit on profits, the businessman can be counted upon to use all his energy and ingenuity to reduce expenses and increase sales. Limit his profits and his enthusiasm disappears, and he goes at his business in a half-hearted way. It follows that, if one desires maximum prosperity, efficiency in production must never be seriously limited by taxation or otherwise. If competition is maintained, large profits can be gained only if the entrepreneur serves the public with unusual skill. Otherwise, competitors will pour into the field and his large profits will disappear. Therefore, as long as competition is active, liberal profits do not mean that the purchaser of the product is paying an unreasonably high price for the product in question. Instead, the largest profits usually accrue to the concerns selling good goods at exceptionally low prices.

Furthermore, large profits in good years are necessary to offset the heavy losses which, in bad years, are likely to be suffered by most producers, whether efficient or inefficient. The frequency and extent of losses in a system of free enterprise is something which many persons do not realize. They may not be surprised to learn that, in a depression year like 1932, of all corporations in the United States actively engaged in business, only one in five showed a profit, but they may find it hard to believe that, in unusually prosperous 1929, two out of five were "in the red." In not a single year from 1930 to 1940 inclusive did half of the active corporations in the United States show a profit. In most of these eleven years, corporations having losses far outnumbered those having gains.[1]

Ample profits enable the efficient concern — the one which serves the public best — to expand, and thus to render ever greater service. Great manufacturing concerns have commonly grown up from small enterprises which have been successful in attracting the dollar votes of the consumers, have therefore made large profits, and have plowed major parts of these profits back into the businesses. This process makes goods cheaper, and thus benefits the consumers. If bureaucracy had limited Henry Ford's profits to some "reasonable" or "liberal" figure such as ten per cent per annum on his few thousands of dollars of investment, the time when Americans generally could ride freely in motor cars might have been delayed for a number of years. What Henry Ford personally gained from his profits was a mere bagatelle as compared to the pleasure received by the millions who were able to own automobiles because Ford's reinvested profits made cars cheap enough to be within the reach of millions of families.

From what has just been said, it is obvious that any tax system which prevents business from securing and retaining large profits hampers production. The policy of taxing larger profits at rates higher than those assessed against lower profits is especially destructive of efficiency.

[1] *Statistical Abstract of the U. S.,* 1942, p. 211.

Monopolies in the United States

Thus far our discussion of the American system has been based upon the assumption that competition, if left undisturbed, can maintain itself indefinitely. But, after all, was not governmental regulation made imperative by the fact that most of our great industries had come to be dominated by huge monopolies? Had not competition broken down? The answer is an emphatic "No"! In the United States, capital has been so abundant and the spirit of competition so intense not only within an industry but also among industries that monopolies have found it practically impossible to keep going without governmental assistance. It has been deemed desirable to protect invention and authorship by granting patents and copyrights. It has been found necessary to give local monopolistic power to concerns such as gas and telephone companies which necessarily utilize the streets, but the rates charged by such concerns are everywhere regulated. Monopolies not sponsored by government, but yet able through monopolistic power to raise prices sufficiently to oppress the public, are and have been extremely rare and short-lived. Newly invented articles protected by patents often sell for a time at high prices, but this is necessary not only to compensate the inventor for his efforts and ingenuity, but also to allow the producer to recover the heavy expense usually required to develop the product and put it on the market. Except for articles of this type, high monopoly prices have been so uncommon that one must rack his brains to think of an example. It is doubtful, indeed, that all such articles combined cost the average American one-tenth of one per cent of his income, hence the existence of occasional instances can scarcely be looked upon as a reason for revamping that economic system which made our nation the envy of all other peoples.

The more one looks into the matter, the more convincing becomes the evidence that, in the United States, at least, all oppressive monopolies are protégés of government. For decades, farm organizations strove to establish monopolistic prices for farm products, but failed miserably until the Federal Government sponsored their activities. Similarly, attempts by labor unions to monopolize the labor market met with only evanescent success until the Government came to their aid. It appears, therefore, that competition is destroyed and monopolistic oppression of the public is initiated mainly through governmental action.

The Major Weakness of Laissez Faire

The fact that, under *laissez faire*, competition is nearly always able to get the best of monopoly, does not prove that *laissez faire* has no weaknesses. As a matter of fact, it has one very serious, but, as we shall see later, remediable weakness — it has been subject to very troublesome fainting spells known as depressions. The fact remains, however, that, even with this unfortunate weakness present, *laissez faire* — in other words economic freedom — has been decidedly more successful than any other system in bringing about prosperity for the people at large. Moreover, *laissez faire* is the only system which enhances prosperity without lessening individual initiative or curtailing personal liberty. Thus far, socialism and fascism have succeeded only where they abolished liberty, and nowhere have they provided abundance.

Legitimate Governmental Limitations on Laissez Faire

Because limitations on *laissez faire* have commonly produced such untoward results, some persons infer that all interference with it is bad. This conclusion is unjustified. In reality, to make *laissez faire* serve the public best, a certain amount of governmental intervention in economic affairs is imperative, but it should be confined to those categories in which compulsion is required if desirable ends are to be attained. They are as follows:

1. City planning — cities allowed to grow like Topsy are ugly and inconvenient.
2. Conservation of natural resources — without governmental interference to prevent waste, much of our priceless heritage of soil, gas, petroleum, coal, and other minerals will be irretrievably lost.
3. Prevention of fraud, theft, and crimes of violence — without such protection, the strong and unscrupulous will take advantage of the weak and the fair-minded.
4. Rendition of certain services which, without compulsion, are likely to be inefficiently performed — examples are adjudication of disputes, education of the masses, and protection against fire and epidemics.
5. Prevention of the oppression of the public by monopolies — the desire to form monopolies is widespread and governmental restraint is sometimes necessary to prevent the development of pernicious monopolies.
6. Requiring all able-bodied individuals to carry disability insurance sufficient in amount to prevent them from casting upon others the duty of caring for them when they become sick or feeble.
7. Control of the supply of money and credit — as we shall see later, such control is essential if depressions are to be prevented.

Application of the seven restraints just enumerated should always be made in a *general* way rather than in a manner particularized to fit the cases of specific individuals or business concerns. In other words, governmental regulations should go no further than to create a favorable atmosphere enabling competition to operate freely. Applied in this way, the seven types of restraints just enumerated would have practically no tendency to lessen either individual liberty or freedom of enterprise. And, from the economic standpoint, this is very important, for *freedom* is one of the keys opening the door to prosperity.

It has just been pointed out that control of money and credit is essential if prosperity is to be maintained. But why is this true? To answer this question, it is necessary to understand something about the nature and uses of money and credit. This subject will be discussed in the next chapter.

Thomas R. Malthus — Messenger of Hope.
{See page 5.}

Chapter IV

MEDIA OF EXCHANGE

Origin of a Medium of Exchange

The primitive clan either subsisted on the gifts of nature or produced from these gifts most of the things which it consumed. However, at a comparatively early stage in human progress, some clans or tribes found that they could gain by exchanging some of the things of which they happened to have a relative surplus for articles which other tribes possessed in comparative abundance. At first, exchanges were made directly. For example, tribes living along the seashore might trade salt for the flint possessed by tribes living in the mountains. Such a system of exchange is known as barter.

This method of trading was fairly satisfactory as long as the types of articles exchanged were few and simple. The Indians, for example, found it possible to trade arrowheads or bows for pipe clay, flint, or salt. Even so, they discovered that it was inconvenient for the man who possessed an extra bow to get in touch with the man who had the coveted salt and wanted a bow. Therefore, the custom grew up of trading other goods for a universally prized ornamental good — wampum — and later exchanging the wampum for the particular articles desired. Thus wampum became a common *medium of exchange.* Later, when white men appeared on the scene, it was found that they prized beaver skins highly, hence beaver skins also became a common medium of exchange.

As long as the parties to the exchange always met face to face, the fact that neither the wampum nor the beaver skins were of uniform quality was unimportant. When, however, a white trader desired to replenish his stock by importing goods from England, he found this lack of standardization to be a great handicap, for he could not tell how many hatchets he could obtain for a hundred beaver skins. This example illustrates the fact that, when trade is to be carried on between widely-separated parties who do not come into direct contact, a thoroughly standardized medium of exchange is a great convenience.

In quite early times in the more advanced countries, gold and silver were used as media of exchange. Their use was, however, inconvenient until governments converted the metals into coins which were guaranteed as to purity of metal and weight, and which, to prevent filing and clipping, were completely covered with stamped designs. Thereafter, coins became the principal media of exchange in all parts of the civilized world. In England, such coins were called *money.* Later this term was applied to any *generally acceptable medium of exchange passing freely from hand to hand without endorsement.*

The Origin of Circulating Credit

Still later, it was discovered that loss from abrasion and danger of theft in transit could be lessened or avoided by *depositing* the precious metal with highly-respected merchants who possessed well-protected storage vaults, and securing from these merchants negotiable receipts; that is, receipts which by endorsement could be transferred to other persons. Soon these receipts were used widely as media of exchange. The storage-vault owners who issued the receipts came to be known as bankers.

The degree to which the receipts were generally acceptable depended, of course, upon the reputation of the banker, in other words, upon his *credit*. What the banker was doing was to exchange his credit for the gold or silver entrusted to him. The receipts were the earliest form of bank credit.

It was not long before certain bankers discovered that, very commonly, the receipts passed through many hands before they were presented for payment, and that, therefore, the interval between the issuance of a receipt and its date of redemption was likely to be long. They noted furthermore that the net result of this state of affairs was that relatively large stocks of gold and silver remained in the vaults. Moreover, they found that the various *deposits* of the same metal were interchangeable. Soon someone developed the bright idea of issuing receipts calling *in toto* for more gold and silver than was actually on hand. The extra receipts thus issued could be used to buy wanted goods or could be lent. To do the latter gradually became customary. The banker who had formerly exchanged his credit for gold or silver only, now exchanged his credit for borrowers' written promises that at later specified dates they would repay the amounts borrowed and in addition would pay *interest* on the loans. Here we have the origin both of the fractional reserve banking system and of bank-credit *inflation*.

Bankers eventually found it convenient to inscribe on intricately-printed papers which could not be readily imitated their promises to pay round sums of gold or silver on demand. These pieces of paper came to be called *bank notes*. Because it was difficult to counterfeit these promises to pay, they could circulate without endorsement.

Use of Circulating Credit by Governments

Fiscal officials of governments soon decided that this bankers' scheme, which had resulted in getting tangible revenue from that intangible thing known as credit, might well be imitated for the benefit of government treasuries; hence they also began to issue elaborately engraved notes promising to pay gold or silver on demand. Gradually these notes came to take the place of coin for monetary uses.

In the United States, gold and silver certificates have been widely used as money. They are backed dollar for dollar by precious metal. Such hundred per cent coverage does not, however, characterize other types of notes issued by our Federal Government. These have frequently been put out in amounts far exceeding the stocks of metal held for their potential redemption. Issuance of notes in excess of reserves means that the Federal Government has traded its credit either for services and material goods or for the promises to pay of various individuals and corporations.

Whenever these Government notes have actually been redeemable on demand in metallic coins, their value has always equaled that of the coins, regardless of the volume of such notes outstanding. However, large issues of notes tend to reduce the purchasing power (that is the goods-buying ability) not only of the notes, but also of the gold and silver backing the notes.

Frequently, governments have issued notes in such quantities that it has proved impossible to redeem them in precious metal. At present, many of the paper bills used as money in the United States do not even promise redemption in any precious metal, to say nothing of being actually redeemable in gold or silver. Thus, United States Federal Reserve notes merely promise to pay "lawful money" — a vague term — for Congress can make any kind of paper "lawful money." Nevertheless, they circulate freely as money.

For this situation there are several reasons, among which are:

1. They are *legal tender* — that is, citizens are compelled to accept them for all debts, both public and private.
2. They can be used to pay taxes or to purchase Government bonds.
3. People generally believe that the amount of paper money which will be issued by the Government will be kept within reasonable bounds.
4. People have confidence in money stamped by the United States Government.

In emergencies, governments frequently issue paper money in vast amounts. At such times the citizens are likely to lose confidence in the buying power of paper money, and a mad rush to exchange it for goods ensues. Such was the case in Germany while the inflation of the early 1920's was in progress, and in China and Hungary after World War II. During an inflation-caused panic, the value of the money unit falls relatively faster than the quantity of money increases. Prices skyrocket at such a rate that it becomes almost physically impossible to carry on business. People waste large fractions of their time trying to spend their money before its value disappears. When this stage arrives, industry collapses, the paper money is repudiated, and the nation's economy is reorganized. All mortgages, bonds, notes, life insurance policies, and bank deposits have had their value destroyed.

Deposit Currency

The evolution of circulating bank credit from simple receipts for gold or silver to carefully-engraved bank notes of various denominations has been described. At present, in the United States, notes of privately-owned banks have almost disappeared from circulation. As time has passed, banks have found that, instead of issuing printed credit money in round denominations, it is really more convenient merely to enter in books of account credits for the respective "depositors." Usually a record is made in the bank's account book and a corresponding record in the "depositor's" account book. The "depositor" can readily shift his account to another person by means of a written order called a check. Since the check must be endorsed each time that it changes hands, it does not correspond to the definition of money. However, the "deposit" recorded on the books of the bank furnishes an admirable substitute for money; in fact, in some ways it is decidedly superior to money. Its greatest advantage lies in the fact that the funds "deposited" cannot readily be lost or stolen. Furthermore, every check can be made to serve as a receipt to show that payment has actually occurred.

Reference has been made above to the terms "deposit" and "depositor." As we have seen, *deposits* originally consisted of gold or silver left with the banker for safekeeping. Nowadays, part of the bank's "deposits" represent credits given to people who bring coin or paper money to the bank, or who, by depositing checks, transfer to the given bank "deposits" in another bank.

Today, however, in very many cases, "deposits" originate through *borrowing*. For example, a customer gives to the banker his note — perhaps secured by collateral — perhaps not. In return, the banker gives to the customer a "deposit" — in other words, an entry in the latter's bank book. What has really happened is that the customer has traded his own credit, which will not circulate freely, for the banker's credit which will circulate freely. For the privilege of exchanging, he pays to the banker a premium known as interest.

During recent years, the Federal Government has come to be the star "depositor" in most commercial banks in the United States. It has attained this position by exchanging its bonds for bank "deposits" — in other words, it has sold bonds to the banks. By this procedure it secured a large part of the funds necessary to conduct World War II, but it has also greatly lessened the commodity value of the dollar.

Since Federal credit in the form of Treasury notes circulates just as freely as does bank credit, the question has been aptly raised as to why the Government should pay to the banks interest for exchanging their deposits for its credit. The only answer seems to be that Government officials feel obliged to cater to the popular belief that bank deposit inflation is less injurious to the public than is paper money inflation. This belief is, of course, entirely fallacious.

The Volume of Circulating Medium

The stock of bank deposits subject to transfer by check is often referred to as *deposit currency*.

All types of coin and of paper receipts or promises to pay which circulate freely from hand to hand without endorsement may be referred to as *pocketbook money*. Pocketbook money and deposit currency combined make up the *circulating medium* used in the nation.

In the United States in April, 1947, the total circulating medium was constituted roughly as follows:[1]

	Millions of Dollars
Gold certificates	$ 51
Silver coins	968
Silver certificates	1,979
Copper and nickel coins	312
Federal Reserve notes	23,685
Other paper money	891
Total pocketbook money	$ 27,885
Total deposit currency	84,200
Total circulating medium	$112,085

[1] For the following data, see the *Federal Reserve Bulletin,* June, 1947, p. 709.

Since, at the date mentioned, gold coin was not allowed to circulate in the United States, since also the possibility of exchanging silver, nickel, and copper coins for gold certificates — a possibility which enhanced the value of such coins — depended upon the willingness of the Federal Government to make the exchange, every dollar of circulating medium outstanding was, to some extent, circulating *credit*. Most of it was typical credit currency, in fact, nearly four-fifths of the total was made up of demand claims against banks — in other words, it consisted of demand deposits or deposit currency. This is one of the reasons for saying that we have a credit economy.

The Exchange of Money for Other Goods

If it were possible for every family to produce all the things it needed for itself, no medium of exchange would be necessary. Furthermore, if families produced different things but exchanged them with other families according to a fixed schedule at dates specified on the schedule, no medium of exchange would be essential, for barter would be reasonably satisfactory. The use of a circulating medium is therefore necessary because "division of labor" exists, and because goods are not exchanged on the basis of any prearranged schedule.

Under conditions actually existing in modern civilized nations, the process of exchanging goods has become so intricate and so essential to the very existence of the people as to make the use of a circulating medium imperative. Imagine, for example, the difficulties which would confront a New York City stenographer if she tried to exchange directly her services for oranges from California, beef from Wyoming, shoes from Massachusetts, cloth from South Carolina, and seats at the local movie theater. It is probably not an exaggeration to say that, were all circulating medium destroyed, millions would die of starvation. The fundamental nature of the function performed by money is further shown by the fact that, even in the worst phases of an inflationary orgy when the value of money is shrinking perhaps fifty per cent daily, people still are unable to dispense with its use and resort wholly to barter, for our economic system has become so complex that barter is entirely inadequate to make the necessary exchanges. Clearly, therefore, the existence of one or more satisfactory media of exchange is a true prerequisite to national prosperity.

Chapter V

FACTS AND FALLACIES CONCERNING
SAVING, SPENDING, AND CONSUMING

Retentive vs. Accumulative Saving

Prosperity depends upon the possession of or acquisition of wealth, but, as Adam Smith pointed out in *The Wealth of Nations,* if there is to be any wealth other than the gifts of nature in their original forms, there must first be saving. But just what is "saving"?

Everyone agrees that it means wealth accumulation. In primitive times, saving referred to the accumulation of material goods such as weapons, skins, food, clothing, ornaments, or shelters. Today, when people speak of saving, they often think of it as a process of accumulating money, bank deposits, or other intangibles.

That the word has highly diverse uses was shown by the present writer in an article published in the *Journal of the American Statistical Association* as long ago as September, 1922. The Committee on Economic Accord distinguishes clearly between "retentive saving" and "accumulative saving." [1] The first is defined as "the process of retaining the wealth or property already accumulated." By contrast, the second — "accumulative saving" — is stated to be "the setting aside for future use of part of current income." [1]

In recent decades, certain writers on economic subjects have given the impression that retentive saving is an almost automatic and painless process. In reality, however, this view is very far from the truth, for on every hand the reader is confronted with cunningly-devised advertisements enticing him to buy luxuries of every imaginable kind. The consuming power of the people of any nation is so great that, if unrestrained, it will quickly use up all the consumable destructible wealth of the nation. Therefore, unless its population contains a considerable proportion of thrifty persons, any nation operating under the competitive capitalistic system will quickly be reduced to extreme poverty. On the other hand, if a nation's population is much given to saving, and if consumption is kept well below production, wealth increases and, other things being equal, the nation grows ever more prosperous.

Much of the huge volume of dissaving which is constantly going on cannot correctly be ascribed to any lack of thrift. From time to time every family is overtaken by serious illness or death, and such events often make it impossible to avoid the dissipation of slowly-accumulated funds. Furthermore, if savings are invested, no matter how carefully, there is always grave danger that the investment will result in a loss. Even if a man keeps his funds in a savings bank, invests solely in bonds of the highest grade, or buys life insurance, the value of his investment may be largely destroyed by an inflation-induced shrinkage in the commodity value of money. If he employs his

[1] Handbook of Accepted Economics, p. 69.

savings as capital in an enterprise, the risk is likely to be accentuated. It follows that it is extremely difficult to find for either an individual or a concern a complete record covering any considerable period of time, which does not show relatively heavy losses of accumulated wealth. Retentive saving is, therefore, a process even more difficult than is accumulative saving.

Gross Versus Net Accumulative Saving

In recent years, most of the voluminous discussion of "saving" has centered about *accumulative* saving. When dealing with this topic, it is imperative to keep in mind the fact that there is a vast difference between *gross* accumulative saving and *net* accumulative saving. Gross saving constitutes a *process*. Net saving is a *result*. *Net* accumulative saving always refers to an increase in *real net worth*.

The total net volume of saving by all the inhabitants of a nation combined is far less than is their gross volume of saving, for while some persons are accumulating vast sums, others are dissipating their wealth rapidly. It follows that there may be no net accumulative saving in a nation as a whole, despite the fact that many of the citizens have saved diligently.

Even in the case of any particular individual, gross saving may far exceed net saving. For example, if each month a man takes one-third of his income and invests it in bonds, he has a relatively large amount of gross accumulative saving to his credit, but if, during the year, the value of all the property which he owns declines more than the total amount of income which he has saved, his *net* accumulative saving for the year is negative — in other words, he experiences *dissaving*.

In so far as the amount of dissaving is concerned, the reason why the net worth of the individual has declined is irrelevant. Whether the loss in value was occasioned by inflation, unwise investment, speculation, gambling, fraud, or robbery, is immaterial. Any decline in net worth, occasioned by any reason whatsoever, constitutes dissaving.

A primary reason why, in any period, the national total of gross saving is far larger than the total of net saving is that both production goods and durable consumption goods are continually wearing out or becoming obsolete. It is therefore possible for a nation to have in a given year a large *positive gross* total of saving and yet have *negative net* saving.

Thrift and Saving

Thrift, though related definitely to *gross* accumulative saving is not necessarily closely correlated with *net* accumulative saving. Because of misfortunes of one kind or another, many extremely thrifty individuals find themselves unable to accumulate a competence. On the other hand, a lucky speculator may gain $10,000 in a single day, and be too busy to think of spending any of his winnings. In such a case, his gain in net worth obviously cannot legitimately be ascribed to thrift, yet his saving is just as real as if he had accumulated the $10,000 by years of diligent toil and skimping. The fact to be noted here is that, while *thrift* is largely subjective in nature, *net accumulative saving* is purely a matter of the balance sheet.

One must not, however, jump to the conclusion that, inasmuch as saving may be due merely to speculative or chance factors, thrift plays but a minor rôle in the process, for this is almost the reverse of the truth. The various accidental forces are just as likely to generate dissaving as saving. It follows that the net total of saving for all individuals combined is mainly the result of keeping consumption below income, and those individuals are rare who can, without practicing thrift, hold consumption below their respective income levels. After all, therefore, thrift underlies most saving and is one of the fundamental prerequisites for national prosperity and progress.

Fictitious Net Savings

Measurements of the net worth of individuals or business concerns are ordinarily stated in monetary terms. In many instances, nominal increases in net worth do not indicate any genuine saving, for the customary method of bookkeeping fails to take cognizance either of changes in the market value of capital assets or of changes in the value of money.

Thus, despite the fact that, during the "Twenties" and "Thirties," American railroads "plowed in" billions of dollars of nominal earnings, the total value of railway securities dropped persistently. The monetary net worth of the railroads was declining; therefore they really had *dissaving*, even though, in many instances, their books of account showed that very considerable sums were being carried to surplus. This was due to the fact that customary accounting methods are not so designed as to record shrinkages in net worth brought about by such indirect influences as governmental regulation of rates, or wage increases forced upon employers by labor unions.

One of the most potent forces giving rise to fictitious saving is inflation. When the latter causes the price level to move upward rapidly, fictitious saving often attains vast proportions. At such times, the respective market prices of land, corporate stocks, and raw materials are all likely to rise sharply, and, when this happens, the owners of these goods commonly believe that they have become much richer. In most cases, however, any attempt to convert their nominally expanded monetary assets into tangible goods reveals the fact that their supposed gains in wealth are illusory, their command over consumers' goods, producers' goods, or both, being no larger than it was before the monetary value of their holdings increased. Therefore, apparent savings resulting from expansion either of the volume of paper money or of the volume of bank deposits are, as a rule, decidedly unreal. If one is to measure the extent of *real* saving, one must either deflate all dollar values by dividing them by appropriate price indexes, or must use only non-monetary data.

Social versus Private Saving

The degree of economic progress of any group of people is best measured by its *net accumulative social saving*. Such saving by the people of a nation may correctly be defined as an increase in the net *real* worth of the nation's total physical and mental assets. It includes net improvements in the stock of consumable goods such as clothing, jewels, automobiles, houses, and house furnishings; net additions to the supply of productive equipment such as factories, railways, canals, ships, power plants, livestock, and raw materials; net increases in the real worth of such public properties as buildings, highways, and naval vessels; and net gains in knowledge of scientific techniques and methods of organization.

Social saving is the process which results in the accumulation of social savings. As an outcome of social saving, three classes of things are accumulated:

1. Knowledge of how to produce efficiently
2. Direct or consumption goods
3. Indirect or production goods

Accumulation of knowledge concerning techniques of organization and production is no less important than is accumulation of material goods. That such is the case is made evident by the fact that, if our heritage of scientific and business information were to be lost, our farms, our mines, our factories, our electric plants, and our transportation systems would become practically useless to us, and most of our population would soon starve to death.

When the people of a nation save large quantities of durable consumption goods, such as clothing, jewelry, furniture, houses, and public buildings, they make life safer and more comfortable for themselves and their children; they assure a larger future flow of services, and hence a larger per capita national *real* income. However, the income from any particular durable good tends to diminish steadily with the passage of time, for even the most enduring of consumption goods gradually wears out or deteriorates, and, therefore, its capacity to render services diminishes. Furthermore, no matter how large the stock of consumption goods may be, it does nothing to increase the future output of material goods; it has no power to make the national income grow larger and larger as the years pass.

By contrast, indirect or production goods — for example, raw materials, farms, factories, and railways — aid in the creation of other goods. Thus seeds grow into crops which supply us with food and fiber. Raw materials are gradually converted into usable products. For instance, cotton becomes cloth which, in turn, appears in the form of clothing. This soon becomes part of a merchant's stock, and later serves the person who wears it. Mines, factories, machines, ships, trucks, and railways all aid in the process of converting the gifts of nature into forms more useful to human beings. In general, therefore, it is true that an abundance of production goods today makes for an abundance of consumption goods at a somewhat later date.

As we have seen, an important part of social saving consists of increased knowledge embedded in the brains of human beings, and in organization of human beings and things. The remainder of social savings is comprised exclusively of *tangible* goods. This part of social savings is equivalent to the social wealth of the community.

However, in the United States, *titles* to the tangible goods in this stock of social wealth are largely held by individuals or corporations, and these titles, or in other words property rights, are evidenced by such instruments as credit, money, deposit accounts, life insurance policies, stocks, bonds, notes, and mortgages, and constitute *private* savings. Such *claim goods* do not form part of *social* savings or of *social* wealth, for their value is nothing more than a reflection of the value of the tangible goods controlled by the property rights.

How Individual Saving Gives Rise to Social Saving

What really makes the nation prosper is an increase in the stock of *material* goods, such as homes, clothing, furniture, automobiles, livestock, soil fertility, factories, transportation facilities, public buildings, and parks. However, a large part of the accumulative saving done by individuals consists in the accumulation of *claim* goods such as money, bank deposits, and insurance policies. Does such accumulation result in any considerable amount of saving of material goods? In other words, does it increase the real wealth of the nation? As a matter of fact, in a complex economy like that of the United States, in which we have extreme "division of labor," such saving is a necessary prelude to any extensive saving of material goods.

There are three important ways in which monetary saving indirectly gives rise to the accumulation of material goods:

1. The saving of "money" makes it possible for the saver to purchase material durable consumption goods which he himself saves. Examples are residential property, automobiles, etc.
2. The saver of "money" may *invest* his savings. For example, he may put them into an enterprise which he owns and controls. Instead, he may participate in a partnership, or he may purchase some stock and thereby become part owner of a corporation. He may directly lend "money" to some business enterprise by purchasing its bonds or notes. He may deposit his "money" in a bank, or use it to purchase life insurance or building and loan stock. In each of these cases, the "money" saved is ordinarily used either to secure raw materials or to facilitate the production of buildings, machines, equipment, or other durable goods.
3. Instead of investing his savings, the saver may hoard cash, and refrain from consuming as large a quantity of goods as he would have consumed had he not saved and hoarded. By such failure to consume, he may increase the inventories on hand at mercantile or manufacturing establishments, thus immediately enlarging the stocks of real social wealth.

It is, however, incorrect to assume, as certain economists have done, that hoarding *necessarily* results in an *equivalent amount* of involuntary saving on the part of others. It is true that, if heretofore the people of the United States have been spending nine billions of dollars per month and now decide to hoard one billion and spend but eight billions each month, the decline in buying will probably cause mercantile inventories to pile up, thus resulting in involuntary goods saving on the part of manufacturers. However, not all of the billion dollar reduction in spending has hitherto gone to buy *tangible* goods. Part has been spent for such things as electric current, house rent, interest, and the services of doctors, lawyers, teachers, cooks, etc. Such services cannot be stored up. While, therefore, hoarding does tend to cause would-be sellers involuntarily to accumulate inventories, the ratio of such accumulation to hoarding is not necessarily on a dollar for dollar basis.

Furthermore, any involuntary social saving resulting from hoarding in time of general pessimism, is likely to be very evanescent, for piling up of inventories quickly results in stoppage of production, and the inventories which have accumulated are soon dissipated.

As stated above, money saved and invested in savings-bank deposits or life insurance is ordinarily employed eventually to increase the nation's stock of buildings, machinery, and equipment. Under such circumstances, private monetary saving normally gives rise to real social saving. During World War II, however, both savings banks and insurance companies used their receipts mainly to purchase Federal bonds. The Government, in turn, employed the proceeds to fight the enemy. Most of the goods purchased had little value after the war. Therefore, in this case, private monetary saving did not result in real social saving.

Part of social saving is almost unrelated to individual monetary saving. Thus, regardless of monetary saving, the growth of forests and the multiplication of livestock may increase the national wealth. Furthermore, individuals may improve their farms or homes without using money in the process. However, as our economic mechanism operates today, it seems safe to say that most saving of material goods is the aftermath of saving money or its equivalent.

Attempts to Use Data on Monetary Saving to Measure Net Social Saving

Since most social saving is an outgrowth of monetary saving by individuals or concerns, it is not at all surprising to find that various economists and statisticians have assumed that statistics of monetary saving may be used to measure the net volume of social saving. In their eagerness to arrive at results promptly, they have therefore pounced upon such readily available data as records of total money in circulation, total deposits in banks, total assets of building and loan companies, total premiums paid to life insurance companies, corporate savings, and new capital issues, and have assumed that these items are satisfactory indicators of the changes which have occurred in the combined net worth of all individuals.

As a matter of fact, it is probably true that the best measure of the monetary value of a railway system is the aggregate market value of its outstanding securities. The same principle holds in the case of other industrial property. Possibly, it is because of this fact that many writers take the position that the aggregate value of claim goods held by all individuals may be used to indicate the approximate volume of saving in the nation. Apparently, it is on the basis of this last assumption that the Keynesians have arrived at their conclusion that our nation has been suffering from "over-saving." They have found, for example, a tremendous increase in the volume of money and demand bank deposits held by private individuals and corporate and noncorporate enterprises, and have jumped to the conclusion that these represent savings uninvested by the public.

Those who assume that an increase in the volume of money and bank deposits can be used to measure national saving ignore the fact that, at present, in this nation, the only way that the money total can increase is for the Government or the Federal Reserve banks to issue new money. Evidently, therefore, measures of saving based upon increases in monetary volume commonly do nothing more than to record the extent of inflation. To call inflation saving is a manifest absurdity.

It is equally absurd to measure saving by the volume of deposits in commercial banks, for an expansion in the total of such deposits ordinarily indicates merely that either individuals or governments are increasing their indebtedness to the banks. To assume that a growth in debt is saving is, of course, highly illogical.

That increases in private holdings of credit instruments give no indication of any saving of tangible goods is perhaps made even more obvious by a consideration of financial happenings since 1930. In the period 1930 to 1938, local, State, and National governments all went into debt to cover relief expenditures. Recently, the Federal Government has borrowed many billions to pay for munitions and the wages and subsistence of our soldiers and sailors. Such expenditures for perishable goods and services certainly give rise to no increase in the real wealth of the nation. Yet the funds of savings banks and life insurance companies have been largely used to buy the bonds issued to cover expenditures for the purposes mentioned. Under such circumstances, the volume of savings-bank deposits and life insurance policies clearly offers no clue whatever to the volume of real net saving taking place in the nation.

Similarly, the fact that demand deposits in all banks in the United States rose from $15 billions in 1933 to $29 billions in 1939 certainly did not indicate that someone had either saved or hoarded $14 billions in the interim. Practically the entire increase was caused by the fact that the banks had given to the United States Government "deposits" in exchange for Federal bonds, the proceeds of which were used by our Government mainly for current expenses. Only in so far as the money went to buy *durable* goods, did the increase in deposits represent social saving. To the extent that the funds borrowed from banks were used to purchase additional *short-lived* goods destined for immediate consumption, the borrowing process certainly did not lead to social saving.

When one considers the facts carefully, it becomes obvious that variations in the total of bank deposits do not necessarily parallel net saving, either in the case of any single individual, or in the case of all individuals considered as a group. Thus, for example, a man may draw money from the savings bank in order to buy a bond. In this case, the decline in his savings-deposit account certainly does not indicate dissaving.

On the other hand, he may be steadily putting money into his savings account even though, at the same time, shrinkage in the value of his other property is several times as great as the amount of his nominal monetary savings, the net result being that, on the whole, his wealth is decreasing.

When an individual pays off his indebtedness to a bank, the payment constitutes neither saving nor dissaving on his part. He has reduced his assets, but he has also reduced his liabilities by an equal amount. His net worth remains unchanged. Moreover, if the time when he pays off his debt to the bank happens to fall in a period of recession, it is unlikely that the payment will result either in an extension of bank credit to some other customer, or in a purchase of goods by the bank itself. Under such circumstances, it is, therefore, improbable that the individual's action will be offset by the actions of others in such a way as to eventuate in net social saving. Only to the extent that the individual, by reducing his consumption, saves new funds to make the payments, does the reduction in his indebtedness ead to social saving.

Those relying upon monetary indicators to measure the extent of net saving in the nation would probably say that the mere fact that the monetary figures do not measure the net saving of any particular individual does not in any way invalidate the use of the monetary data to measure the volume of saving in the nation at large, for an underestimate of the volume of saving in the case of one individual would be offset by an overestimate of the volume of saving in the case of another individual — in other words, the errors would approximately cancel out. What they overlook is that, for the economy as a whole, not only the errors but the data themselves mostly cancel out; hence, figures showing merely increases in the aggregate *assets* of individuals give no clue whatever to the national total of either private or social savings. Net accumulative saving means that the *net worth* of the saver has increased. To arrive at net worth, it is necessary to subtract liabilities from assets, and this the Keynesians have neglected to do. Obviously, if an individual borrows at a bank, his deposit account increases, but his liabilities increase even more, for the bank usually deducts interest in advance. Deposit increases arising in this manner are, therefore, likely to represent a certain amount of *dissaving* on the part of the borrowing individuals. At any rate, they do not represent saving, either private or social.

As previously noted, bank deposit totals have recently expanded tremendously because the Federal Government has sold bonds to the banks and received deposits in exchange. These deposits have largely been paid out to contractors, and have now become private deposits. To no small extent, these deposits are at present owned by men who have exchanged labor for them. In this case, is it not true that the deposits do represent actual savings, for, unlike the case of the deposits created by borrowing, the present owners did not give in exchange for them notes, and therefore these owners have no such liabilities to counterbalance their newly-acquired assets?

As a matter of fact, even in this instance, the offsetting liability exists. To obtain these deposits in the first place, the Federal Government gave to the banks notes or bonds — namely its promise to pay. It thus created liabilities equal to the newly-created assets. Unfortunately, the Government has no tangible assets which it can use to cover these liabilities. Hence, to secure funds to pay its debts, the Government must tax the citizens. For all practical purposes, therefore, the liabilities rest on the shoulders of the citizens. For every dollar of deposits, there is a dollar of tax liability. If the debt is to be retired, it is the citizens themselves who must pay it off.

Since the goods bought with the proceeds of the borrowing have been used up in the war, they obviously have not increased the real wealth of the nation. Therefore, this vast aggregation of war-created deposits cannot legitimately be counted as either private saving or social saving.

But, to many, it may still seem obvious that since, between 1939 and 1945, the national total of money and bank deposits on hand grew from $72 to $179 billions, *someone* must have saved $107 billions. Let us see whether or not this assumption has any foundation in fact. When the Federal Reserve Banks created notes, their liabilities increased to the same extent as did their assets. The same was true when the member banks created deposits. Therefore, the banks accumulated no net savings by expanding the currency. The Government gained assets in the form of deposits but incurred equal indebtedness to the banks. Therefore, monetary expansion gave it no net saving. Those who sold material goods to the Government gave up assets equal in value to the cash acquired. Clearly, then, the issuance of money and deposits gave them no savings. Soldiers, sailors, and other Government employees who sold their services to the Government spent most of their pay; hence any savings which they made were certainly in no sense equivalent to the new circulating medium created. It appears, then, that the belief that expansion in the nation's total amount of cash holdings must mean an equal number of dollars of saving by someone has no foundation in fact.

But what about the war bonds paid for out of the savings of individuals and corporations? Do not these represent savings by the public as a whole? Unfortunately, they do not, for every war bond, nominally a liability of the Government, is in reality a liability of the taxpayers. But since, for specific individuals, bond holdings and tax liabilities do not match, it follows that some bond holders really do have positive savings, while others have negative savings. On the whole, both bonds and savings cancel out.

The fact that the billions of war-created bank deposits and bonds held by individuals represent no social saving does not, however, mean that their possession may not, in the post-War period, stimulate greatly the buying of goods by those who acquired such deposits and cashable bonds by refraining from consumption. Many of these owners, overlooking or ignoring such increases in their tax liabilities as have resulted from the bond issues, will use their purchasing power to buy the homes, automobiles, refrigerators, and numerous other things which they need and want, and such buying will tend to increase industrial activity and employment.

However, the notion that, in the years 1941 to 1945 inclusive, individuals in the United States accumulated some $150 billions of savings,* and that these savings were waiting to be spent when goods became available after the war, must, for two reasons, be taken with many grains of salt.

1. It seems probable that those who estimated expenditures by consumers did not allow sufficiently for black-market profit margins, and hence that the $150 billion net saving estimate is much too high.
2. Many of those who actually accumulated war bonds, savings deposits, and the like, counted them as capital reserves, and hence had

* U. S. *Survey of Current Business,* Jan. 1946, p. 4.

no thought of using these savings to buy perishable or semi-durable consumption goods.

As a matter of fact, most of the strong post-war demand for automobiles, refrigerators, and other semi-durable goods was presumably due to the fact that Governmentally-depressed prices, rationing, and the scarcity of necessities (brought about by price control by Government) enabled consumers to utilize abnormally large fractions of their respective incomes for the purchase of luxuries and semi-luxuries. The notion that it was the result of a great unspent accumulation of savings was largely an illusion.

That growth in the volume of money and deposits in the nation gives no indication of the extent of any saving which may have occurred becomes obvious if one considers what would have been the situation if, between 1939 and 1945, every individual in the United States had spent for perishable goods all his income on the day he received it — never saving a penny. Would the spending have reduced the supply of cash in the banks and in the hands of the public? Clearly, the answer is "No." The volume of deposits and pocketbook money would not have changed.

One may go further and inquire what would have been the effect upon the "backlog of demand" supposed to exist at the end of World War II, if every individual had been compelled to spend at once every dollar of his money and his checking account. A moment's thought will make it evident that, like the widow's cruse of oil, the apparent "backlog of demand" would not have diminished in the slightest.

These examples prove conclusively that information concerning the amount of cash on hand tells nothing about either the volume of saving or the extent of any unsatisfied demand for goods.

The Magnitude of Our Savings

It is presumably true that a summation of accurate figures showing, for any period, the increase in the respective individual net worths of all the inhabitants of the nation would equal the net increase in the value of all the wealth owned by all of the inhabitants. However, in so far as is known, no one has ever attempted to make such a compilation. One reason why they have not is that figures on the net worths of individuals are notable by their absence. Furthermore, just how to account correctly for the potential tax liabilities of individuals would puzzle even the most venturesome statistician. At present, therefore, measuring the nation's volume of accumulative saving by utilizing data pertaining to individual wealth and income appears to be non-feasible. Certainly those statisticians who have pretended to measure the total volume of saving by using data covering selected types of *assets*, while ignoring *liabilities* almost completely, have not even made a beginning on the problem, and their published results, instead of enlightening the public, have served to deceive, not only the lay readers, but many professional economists as well.

As just pointed out, if one could ascertain the increases in the respective net worths of all individuals in the nation, each net worth first being corrected for changes in the value of the money unit, the result would approximate the net accumulative private social saving in the nation, for all credits of one individual would be offset by the debits of another individual, hence the net remainder would correspond to the value of the physical assets possessed by all individuals combined. However, since no accounts are available which show the true net worths of the various individuals in any nation at any specified date, it is not feasible to use this method for calculating the total volume of savings in any nation.

To attack the problem by adding up the changes which have occurred in the worths of the various categories of tangible goods existing in the given nation seems at first to be a much more feasible method of arriving at the desired result. Experiment shows, however, that this procedure also is fraught with difficulties, some of which are as follows:

1. To a large extent, material goods are not standardized, hence there are no well-defined units to be used in the measuring process.
2. The prices of such goods are changing at a great variety of rates, and records of such changes are largely non-existent.
3. Diminution in the stocks of very important natural resources such as petroleum, gas, coal, forests, and soil fertility cannot be evaluated with any approach to accuracy. Furthermore, exhaustion of such assets may be partially or entirely offset by increases in the stocks of goods which man has helped to create.
4. Plant and equipment used in transportation, communication, or manufacturing often become obsolete long before they are physically worn out. It is very difficult to measure loss of value caused by obsolescence.

Even though, as indicated above, all purported statistical measurements of the extent of net material saving in a nation must be considered materially inaccurate, we can, nevertheless, be sure that, in the United States during the last century, the total volume of net saving has been enormous. Our great cities with their palatial skyscrapers and their vast network of gas mains, water mains, electric wires, steam pipes, sewers, and subways; our intricate transportation and communication system; our huge factories; our thirty millions of automobiles — all bear witness to that fact.

The increase of our nation's population has been so great that a very large amount of accumulative saving has been necessary, merely to keep the per capita wealth constant — in other words, to provide the expanding generations with equipment and comforts equivalent to those possessed by their forebears. But saving in the United States has gone far beyond this point, for the average American is now equipped with facilities for production such as his ancestors never even dreamed of. Furthermore, in his home, he is surrounded by comforts and luxuries far outclassing anything possessed by his grandparents. As a matter of fact, as regards solid comfort, as regards luxurious entertainment, as regards facilities for travel, the typical American workingman today is far better off than was Louis XIV, the most magnificent monarch that the world had seen up to his time. All of this advancement in material wealth is ascribable mainly to the fact that some of our inhabitants have been thrifty, have limited consumption, and have succeeded in accumulating large amounts of net savings.

Starvation — result of "a devastating torrent of children."

[See page 13.]

Was the Depression Characterized by Over-saving?

In recent years, as earlier noted, numerous writers on economics have expressed great concern about the existence in the United States of a large volume of "over-saving." Has there actually been any such "over-saving?" As previously brought out, to measure accurately the net volume of saving in the nation seems to be an impossible task. The best that one can possibly do is to amass certain figures which enable one roughly to approximate the truth. The data here presented serve to throw light on the question of whether net accumulative saving in the depression decade, that is between January 1, 1930, and January 1, 1940, was larger than the saving in the decade January 1, 1920, to January 1, 1930. Unless the saving for the depression decade was the larger, the belief that "over-saving" is a characteristic of depression would seem to lack any foundation in fact.

Since the typical new building constructed in the United States has a low depreciation rate — in other words, since it tends to last for many years — the volume of new construction occurring in a given period indicates in a very rough way the amount of national saving made up of new structures. A comparison of figures based upon the United States *Survey of Current Business* for August, 1930, Page 64, and the *Statistical Abstract of the United States* for 1942, Page 984, indicates that the number of square feet of floor space constructed in the years 1930 to 1939 inclusive, was only 3,380,973,-000 as compared to an area in the vicinity of 6,180,000,000 built in the preceding decade. It seems probable that the existence of a larger supply of buildings made total depreciation greater in the later than in the earlier decade. Certainly, therefore, the building figures indicate that, as regards structures, the depression decade was marked by under — rather than over-saving. That this situation was not confined to those savings taking the form of buildings is indicated by the data appearing in Table I. These figures, gleaned from the *Statistical Abstract*, cover, for a variety of important items, inventories at the beginning of and at the end of each of the decades mentioned. Since only three of the thirteen items are expressed in terms of money, the majority are not directly affected by any changes which may have occurred in the purchasing power of the dollar, and, even in those three instances, it seems unlikely that changes in the value of the monetary unit invalidate the comparisons.

Reference to the last two columns of Table I reveals the fact that only four of the thirteen items recorded showed gains larger in the depression decade than in the ten years preceding. The median of the percentages of increase was smaller for the later of the two decades. The best evidence available therefore indicates strongly that, as compared to the preceding ten years, the depression decade was decidedly not a period in which "over-saving" was the rule, but that, in reality, the reverse was true. As might be expected, when production was low, savings were meager.

How Much Saving Do We Need?

Those who worry about "over-saving" would do well to consider carefully the fact that, without monetary saving, there would be relatively little accumulation of social capital. Without such capital, modern methods of

Table I

INDICATORS OF COMPARATIVE VOLUMES OF NET ACCUMULATIVE SAVING
IN THE DECADES 1920–1929 AND 1930–1939

	Quantity at Beginning of			Per Cent Increase	
	1920	1930	1940	1920 to 1929	1930 to 1939
Millions of acres in farms[a].................	956	987	1,061	3	8
Millions of acres available for crops[a]......	503	522	530	4	1
Value of farm buildings (billions) [a].........	$ 11.5	$ 12.9	$ 10.4	13	− 19
Cattle on farms (millions) [b]...............	70.4	61.0	68.2	− 13	11
Sheep and swine on farms (millions) [b]......	97.5	101.3	107.7	4	6
Passenger automobiles (millions) [c].........	6.8	23.1	26.2	241	13
Motor trucks (thousands) [c]...............	794	3,380	4,414	325	30
Gross tonnage of merchant marine (millions) [d].............................	16.3	16.1	14.0	− 1	− 13
Steam railways, investment (billions) [e]......	19.3	25.5	25.5	32	0
Tractive effort of steam locomotives (billions of lbs.) [f].......................	2.31	2.55	2.07	10	− 19
Electric generating plants, installed capacity (millions of kws.) [g]....................	13.1	31.6	40.3	140	27
Prime movers in factories; horsepower (millions) [h].............................	19.4	19.3	21.2	− 1	10
Value of corp. inventory plus capital assets, less deprec. (billions) [i]..................	118	138	118	17	− 14
Median percentage of increase.........				10	6

A. = *Statistical Abstract* of the U. S.
[a] = A. 1942, p. 694
[b] = A. 1942, p. 746
[c] = A. 1942, p. 470; includes road tractors.
[d] = A. 1942, p. 516; figures are for June 30.
[e] = A. 1942, p. 485
[f] = A. 1923, p. 387; 1942, p. 481. Class I R.R.'s only.
[g] = A. 1934, p. 325; 1942, p. 453
[h] = A. 1942, p. 888
[i] = A. 1934, p. 183; 1942, p. 233; the figure in the first column is for the beginning of 1927, data for earlier years being unavailable. The indications are that the value in 1920 was much smaller than in 1926. (see A. 1923, p. 724).

production could not exist, for there would be no way to get together the materials and equipment needed for present-day farming, mining, manufacturing, transportation, or merchandizing. In a typical modern factory, each employee utilizes from $3,000 to $10,000 worth of equipment. It is largely because he is thus equipped that the physical product per man-hour in American factories is from two to four times as great as the physical product per man-hour in European countries. It is primarily this superiority of equipment that enables the American factory worker to draw two to four times as much real pay per hour as does the typical European factory worker.

Experience gained during World War II shows clearly that maximum production is obtained only by having machines which embody the latest improvements. However, within a surprisingly short time, the most up-to-date equipment wears out or becomes obsolete. The result is that a large fraction of the gross receipts of industry are required to cover depreciation and obsolescence. Furthermore, our working population is increasing at the rate of some 400,000 per year. To provide each of these workers with

$5,000 worth of equipment requires annual saving of $2,000,000,000 in excess of the amount necessary to cover depreciation and obsolescence.

But this is not all. As Carl Snyder has so well shown in *Capitalism the Creator,* the nation has progressed only as it has accumulated additional social capital per worker. To provide only $200 *additional* equipment annually for each of the 55,000,000 men and women in the nation's working force would call for $11,000,000,000 of net accumulative saving each year, and, even at this rate, it would take a generation to double our supply of social capital. In reality, the supply of production goods increases very slowly. For example, the reported "capital assets" of all corporations in the United States amounted to $97,523,000,000 in 1926, and, in 1939, the corresponding total was only $100,226,000,000. Thus, in thirteen years, the gain was only $2,703,000,000 or less than 3 per cent, although population had increased 11 per cent. Therefore, capital supply per worker had shrunk noticeably. While we have no corresponding figures for non-corporate enterprises, it is doubtful that their record is better than that of the corporations. Apparently, then, during this period, we were suffering from an entirely inadequate rate of saving rather than from "over-saving." All in all, it appears that, before a nation could really suffer from "over-saving" of productive equipment, this type of saving would have to occur at a rate far transcending any ever observed in this or any other nation.

Can Over-Saving Be a Menace?

As we have seen, the myth of "over-saving" has originated with those who have attempted to measure saving by adding up individuals' assets while ignoring their liabilities, and have therefore arrived at figures entirely unrelated to the actual changes in the stocks of material goods and mental assets on hand. But even if national saving were on as magnificent a scale as some of these people allege to be the case, what reason would there be for assuming that it would injure us? How can we be harmed by having a great abundance of labor-saving devices, commodious homes, luxurious house furnishings, attractive clothing, or fine automobiles? Everyone knows that, whenever such articles become superabundant, they become cheap, and that such cheapness stimulates their consumption, hence any excess supply tends to disappear. Surely, we cannot have too much technical skill or organizing ability. Clearly, therefore, the presence of large quantities of such goods cannot threaten the nation's welfare.

But what about such things as factories and machines? Does not overcapacity cause trouble? Why should it? If a manufacturer has too many buildings or machines, all that happens is that he uses the most efficient ones and holds the rest in reserve to take care of some unusual volume of orders. No damage is done.

If we think of saving solely in terms of the accumulation by an individual of money or bank deposits, we know that "over-saving" always has two automatic brakes: —

1. The more dollars that a person accumulates, the less utility does each dollar have to its owner, hence he tends to spend more freely

than formerly for consumption goods, and this process quickly eliminates any "surplus" savings.

2. The more loanable funds accumulated by all individuals and business concerns combined, the lower will profit and interest rates tend
to be. But low profit and interest rates discourage saving, and therefore tend to end promptly any possible "over-saving."

The Over-Saving Under-Spending Fallacy

Such being the case, how can one explain the fact that many thinking
people have come to believe that "over-saving" may be a real menace to society? The answer is that they have observed that, when people stop spending, business declines. They have assumed further that saving is the opposite of spending, and that "under-spending" must be due to "over-saving."
They have been led astray by the erroneous assertion that an increase in
bank-deposit volume represents an increase in the amount of saving. Furthermore, they have noted the fact that, as the national income increases, a larger
proportion of it tends to be saved. From this springboard, they have jumped
to the conclusion that, as per capita income grows, a smaller proportion of
the national income tends to be spent to purchase the products of industry,
and that the shortage of buying thus brought about causes unsold products
to accumulate, production to slow down, idleness to multiply, and poverty
to sweep the nation.

The validity of this line of argument seems to be belied by the economic
history of the United States, for, as all economists are aware, our per capita
national income has been rising ever since the nation was founded, and
presumably, therefore, the percentage of the national income saved has been
increasing for a century and a half. Therefore, to prove their case, the Keynesians must show why we have not, during all these years, been experiencing
a perpetually deepening depression.

As a matter of fact, the whole theory of "over-saving" and resulting depression is based upon a false assumption concerning the relationship existing between saving and the volume of buying. This fallacious assumption is
that saving is the antithesis of buying — that money saved is money unspent.

Saving Does Not Lessen the Volume of Spending

In reality, there is no necessary inverse correlation between the volume
of saving and the volume of spending, for, on the average, over a period of
months, practically all money saved is used to buy goods. The truth is that
most newly-saved "cash" funds are spent rather promptly. For example, if
saved "money" is deposited in a commercial bank, it increases the lending
power of the bank. The result may be to make possible a loan to some merchant who immediately spends the proceeds for merchandise. If a workingman deposits his money in a savings bank, the savings bank is likely to lend
the money promptly — perhaps to a contractor who spends it to buy labor
and materials to build a house. Saved money paid as premiums to life insurance companies is spent in about the same way as is the money deposited in
savings banks, or is lent to large corporations which spend the money to
buy new plant or equipment. The wealthy man saves a million dollars and

invests it in the stock of a new corporation. That corporation spends the money for wages, salaries, and materials. The books of a corporation show large savings — amounts carried to surplus — but those amounts do not represent hoardings of money or deposits. As a rule, the money has been spent for labor and materials to improve the plant or enlarge the scale of operations. Both individuals and enterprises lend to government huge sums, but the amounts lent seldom reduce the total volume of spending, for most of the borrowed money is promptly spent for labor and factory products. In general, therefore, over a period of months, the total of savings *spent* probably equals approximately the amount of money *saved* during the same period. Hence the notion that increased monetary saving necessarily means a reduction in the total value of goods bought is completely erroneous. What is really true is that an increase in savings generally means a *restriction of consumption,* and an *increase in* the output and sales of goods used for *production.* To assume that spending is the opposite of saving is, therefore, highly fallacious.

Spending Does Not Lessen the Volume of Savings

Furthermore, it is just as erroneous to assume that the mere act of spending diminishes in the slightest degree the savings of the spender. That spending does not lessen saving is equally true whether the goods bought consist of fresh fruit, houses, or government bonds, for presumably the goods are worth as much as the money paid for them. Thus the purchase of a share of stock does not lessen the net worth of the buyer. All that has occurred is that he has exchanged cash for an equally valuable asset — namely part ownership of a corporation. His net worth, and therefore the volume of his savings, has not been affected. Exactly the same principle holds when a man buys an automobile, a suit of clothes, or even an ice cream cone.

Consumption the Opposite of Saving

The thing which really tends to deplete savings is not *spending* but *consumption.* As the automobile deteriorates or goes out of style, as the suit becomes frayed, as the ice cream cone is eaten, the total net worth of the owner shrinks, unless the loss in the value of wealth caused by consumption has, in the meantime, been offset by additions to the value of other wealth. The more perishable the goods bought, the more likely is it that they will be consumed or quickly destroyed, and that the wealth of the nation will therefore be promptly diminished. Other things being equal, *consumption lessens* the wealth of the nation; *saving increases* the wealth of the nation.

Under-investment

It is difficult to find any tenet of economic theory upon which Keynesians, orthodox economists, and businessmen agree. However, it is safe to say that, in recent years, many in each of these three groups have expressed the view that, during the depression, "saving" outran "investment." As evidence supporting this view they point to the fact that the volume of new securities floated was extremely low, while, at the same time, the banks were overflowing with deposits. They also note the fact that the ratio of bank deposits to the national income increased, and that the velocity of circulation of deposits decreased. They, therefore, conclude that some untoward force caused "underinvesting."

As a rule, the three groups mentioned also agree on another point — namely, that a larger volume of "investing" would have increased the volume of employment, strengthened private enterprise, and benefited the nation as a whole. But, when it comes to defining *investing*, they are likely to be as far apart as the poles. What does the word really mean. Are *investing* and *spending* different concepts?

Chapter VI

INVESTING

Investing Defined

That an adequate amount of "investment" is one of the keys to prosperity is the central theme in hundreds of articles published in recent years, but, unfortunately, most of the writers have failed to state exactly what they mean by "investment." Some apparently have had in mind the purchase of any durable goods. Others have assumed that investing consists primarily of the purchase of securities. Still others have employed usages lying somewhere within the range of these extremes.

Since the Keynesians are always advocating the idea of having the government "take up the slack" when private investment proves "inadequate," and since governments usually purchase mainly consumption goods, rather than production goods, it appears that the disciples of Keynes identify investing with the purchase of durable goods of any kind.

Keynes *himself* asserted that "saving" always equals "investment," but he failed to define either term. As we have seen, *net saving* always equals increase in *net worth*. Perhaps this is what Keynes had in mind.

Since writers are so hazy as to what they mean by "investment" and "investing," it appears that a necessary preliminary to any discussion in this field is a clarification of the terms and concepts used.

It will be remembered that, in the case of savings, it is necessary to distinguish between accumulative saving and retentive saving. Similarly it is necessary to differentiate new investment during a specified period of time from the total investment existing at a given instant of time. The latter represents the residuum remaining out of funds invested in the past. In this chapter, attention will first be directed primarily to the act of investing rather than to the results of past investing.

"To invest" according |to Webster, is "to lay out (money or capital) in business with the view of obtaining an income or profit." Webster's definition reflects ordinary business usage, and also conforms to the customary teachings of orthodox economists.

Investing Relates to Private Property and Capital

From this point of view, investing is a process which deals primarily with wealth considered from the private rather than from the social standpoint. It will be remembered that the social wealth of a nation consists of its accumulated stock of production goods and consumption goods. On the other hand, the private wealth of the inhabitants of a country is made up of the *property rights* which they possess.

Property rights consist of legal titles to privileges or things. Such titles are sometimes recorded or set forth in documents such as notes, mortgages, bonds, stocks, charters, franchises, leases, patents, or copyrights. Property rights may conveniently be classified into two broad categories:

1. Property rights in consumption goods. Included under this head are titles to food, clothing, residences, passenger automobiles, etc.
2. Property rights held in the hope of gaining further wealth. Prominent among these are titles to such things as real estate held for lease or speculation, farms, business establishments owned by individuals or partnerships, life insurance, bank deposits, stocks, bonds, and mortgages. This class of property rights makes up the *capital* supply of the nation. Capital may be briefly defined as *acquisitive wealth* — that is, wealth used to acquire other wealth.

A point which is commonly overlooked is that a given thing may be capital to one person and not to another. Thus a bond is part of the capital of its owner, but is a liability of the issuing corporation. A landlord's equity in an apartment house is part of his capital, but, from the standpoint of the tenants, the apartment house is a direct or consumption good, for they are consuming its services. The mortgage on the apartment house is capital to the mortgage holder, though it is a debt of the landlord.

Frequently, it is difficult to draw the line which separates that part of private wealth which is capital from that which is not capital. Thus the buyer of a home may purchase it primarily because he hopes to sell it later at a profit. However, while waiting for the opportunity to sell at an advantage, he lives in it. Nevertheless, he thinks of it primarily as a speculation or investment. Similarly, in dull times, Oriental merchants often trade their stocks of merchandise for diamonds or other precious stones, and their wives wear the jewels, yet the merchant still considers them as part of his capital. Clearly, such border-line cases partake of the characteristics both of consumption goods and capital.

The fact has been previously noted that *private* saving consists of an increase in the net amount of property rights held by an individual or business concern. Additions to property rights are commonly called income. While titles to home-produced goods such as poultry, dairy products, fruits, vegetables, meat, and wood make up a sizable fraction of the property acquired by farmers, most of the income of the people of the United States is received originally in the form of money or bank deposits. As long as the newly-acquired property is held in this form, it brings in no revenue to its owners. Therefore, the general tendency is to apportion such income rather promptly into two shares. One is to be spent to buy consumption goods, and the other is to be put into capital — in other words, is to be *invested. Investing generally means, therefore, the exchange of money or bank deposits for property which it is hoped will produce revenue or gain, in the form of interest, rent, or profit.*

Buying of Consumption Goods Not Investing

On the basis of this definition, when durable goods such as residences, automobiles, refrigerators, radios, and clothing are purchased for direct use, the act is not classed as investing, for the returns from such articles are expected to be in the form of direct services rather than in the form of monetary rewards.

Similarly, when government constructs a mammoth navy, or builds a huge pyramid or a great highway system, it is not investing, for these additions to national wealth do not promise to bring in any net monetary revenue. Even though a governmentally-owned power plant or water system may realize revenues through the sale of goods, there is usually no attempt to secure maximum profits. Ordinarily, the chief goal is, instead, to favor the consumers of the products. All in all, therefore, it seems logical to assume that, in the United States, true investments are made almost exclusively by individuals or business concerns — in other words that investing is primarily a private rather than a public function.

It is perhaps worth while to note at this point that if Keynes' statement that investment always equals saving has any significance, it certainly has little or no relation to "investing" as the business man thinks of the term, and as it is used here. A large part of individual saving consists of the accumulation of direct goods such as clothing, jewelry, house furnishings, books, automobiles, and residences. Yet the purchase of such goods for direct use does not constitute investing. Furthermore, individuals may add to their holdings of money or of demand bank deposits. Since these forms of property bring in no revenue, they are not investments.

It follows that gross accumulative saving in any year may differ widely indeed from the amount of investing taking place in the same year.

Investing in Immaterial Things

One of the most important types of investing done by the progressive American family is investing in education. Experience shows that, from the purely financial standpoint, a dollar spent on technical training is likely, in the long run, to yield a higher net rate of return than is a dollar put into tangible enterprises, and our citizens have not been slow to take advantage of this fact.

Another form of investing which business enterprises have often found profitable is the putting of money into research. Some such research deals with pure science, more with techniques of production or methods of organization.

Investing a Term Without Ethical Significance

From the individual's standpoint, any exchange of money or deposits for something promising profit may legitimately be classed as investing, regardless of the ethical or unethical nature of the project. Thus, if experience gives weight to the idea that the venture is likely to prove profitable, funds put into the promotion of a prize-fight or the purchase of a set of burglar tools may correctly be included in the investment category.

How Investing Gives Rise to New Production Goods

When the average American proceeds to invest part of his money income, he ordinarily does not use his funds to purchase directly the physical equipment which industry needs to make it productive. Instead, his saved pocket book money, or part of his checking account, is first converted into an *intermediate* investment such as a savings-bank deposit, life insurance, or building and loan stock. The recipients of such investments are likely to use the funds thus obtained to buy securities issued by corporations or governments. Therefore, a dollar of the original investor's funds may be turned over a number of times before it is finally used to aid in purchasing a building, machine, or other production good, or to buy labor. Hence, in calculating *net* total investing for the nation, it is obviously not permissible to add together the money invested by individuals in the stock of a corporation and the money invested by the corporation in plant, equipment, or materials. It follows that *gross* investing must be distinguished from *net* investing.

Gross Investing Versus Net Investing.

The distinction between gross investing and net investing is much like that between gross saving and net saving. A large part of the money put into industry goes merely to replace old plant and equipment which has worn out or become obsolete. The result is that the *net* addition to the value of all productive property may, in any interim, constitute but a small fraction of the gross amount invested during that period. In some cases, the net may even be negative.

The approximate extent of gross investment in business plant and equipment is shown in Table II. The figures in the last column of this table indicate that, according to George Terborgh's estimates, some 8 to 11 per cent of the national income is customarily used to buy new business plant and equipment. During the years 1932, 1933, and 1934, when orders for goods were very scarce, the proportion of the national income invested in new plant and equipment fell off sharply, but, thereafter, the percentage advanced nearly to the normal level.

The idea that, once an investment has been made, it can be counted upon to reproduce itself automatically, and that, as a result, *gross* investing virtually equals *net* investing is, therefore, far from the truth. In reality, the two quantities are decidedly different. A very large proportion of all new concerns fail, and a sizable fraction of the total investment in them disappears. Old concerns not infrequently become bankrupt. More commonly, their assets shrink in value. Such was decidedly the case with American steam and street railways in the period 1920 to 1940. Most of the early canal companies disappeared from the picture. Many other businesses have become outmoded and dwindled away. Losses therefore tend to cause a shrinkage in the net capital invested in business enterprise.

On the other hand, concerns plow into their businesses very sizable proportions of their net incomes. Part of such savings appear on their income statements. Part are buried in reserve accounts of one kind or another.

Inflation's Effects upon Investors

Changes in net worth, as shown on the balance sheets of corporations, do not necessarily give a true picture of the net volume of investment, for the figures reported are, of course, all in terms of dollars, and, unfortunately, the value of our dollars has had the bad habit of varying from month to month and from year to year. This variability may be very costly to investors. For example, if prices double, the average dollar deposited in a bank or invested in notes, bonds, mortgages, or life insurance loses half of its real value — it's command over goods.

It follows that inflation is a device for surreptitiously taxing such investments. In the pre-war period, 1933 to 1941, (see Table III), the na-

Table II

GROSS ANNUAL INVESTMENT IN BUSINESS PLANT AND EQUIPMENT
compared with the
TOTAL NATIONAL INCOME
FOR THE PERIOD BETWEEN THE WORLD WARS

Year	Total Value of New Business Plant & Equipment Bought[a] (Billions)	Total National Income (Billions)	Per Cent of National Income Invested in New Plant & Equipment
1919	$ 7.09	$65.90[b]	10.8
1920	8.33	76.38[b]	10.9
1921	5.23	60.30[b]	8.7
1922	5.78	61.51[b]	9.4
1923	7.90	72.91[b]	10.8
1924	7.65	73.38[b]	10.4
1925	8.19	77.84[b]	10.5
1926	9.13	82.80[b]	11.0
1927	8.78	81.40[b]	10.8
1928	8.85	83.40[b]	10.6
1929	10.16	87.79[b]	11.6
1930	8.34	77.60[b]	10.7
1931	5.12	60.31[b]	8.5
1932	2.80	42.58[b]	6.6
1933	2.37	41.82[b]	5.7
1934	3.44	49.55[b]	6.9
1935	4.35	54.41[b]	8.0
1936	5.78	62.75[b]	9.2
1937	7.57	70.12[b]	10.8
1938	5.39	64.87[b]	8.3
1939	6.11	70.8[c]	8.6
1940	7.71	77.3[c]	10.0
1941	8.47	94.7[c]	8.9

[a] George Terborgh, Federal Reserve Bulletin, Sept. 1939, p. 731; Feb. 1940, p. 116; Feb. 1941, p. 103; April 1942, p. 318. (Frederick C. Dirks)

[b] See Simon Kuznets, National Income and Its Composition 1919–1938, pp. 310–311. Figures represent "Net Income Originating, Adjusted." Gains from sales of capital assets or changes in values of inventories are excluded.

[c] Estimates by the U. S. Dept. of Commerce. See the Survey of Current Business, April 1942, p. 17.

tion's currency supply was inflated to the extent of nearly twenty-eight billions of dollars. After 1941, the speed of inflation greatly increased. This meant that the thrifty classes of the population, in addition to paying high taxes on incomes, were being subjected to heavy capital levies — in other words, many billions of dollars worth of their slowly accumulated savings were being filched from them without most of them being aware of what was going on. To the politician and the fiscal bureaucrat, inflation is, therefore, a heaven-sent boon; to the devotee of thrift it is a devastating calamity.

Mature Economy Fallacies

In recent years, a number of American economists have advanced the theory that our economy has become mature, and hence that the opportunity for investing has shrivelled away. They assert, furthermore, that our economic difficulties have, in part, been due to the vanishing of our frontier, and in part to the dearth of new industries. These explanations are supposed to account for the small volume of investing during the "Thirties."

In a nation as prolific of ideas as the United States — a nation filled with inhabitants having a multitude of active unsatisfied wants, such explanations seems too absurd to be taken seriously. The fact, is, however, that many people have accepted them as correct. Very effective answers to their lines of argument have been given by George Terborgh in his address before the National Industrial Conference Board on November 23, 1943. He said in part:

"Great emphasis is laid on the investment opportunities opened up by the development of new territories such as our own West. No one will deny that a considerable part of the new capital formation in this country during the nineteenth century was incident to the conquest of the frontier. So what? Are we to infer, with the mature economy theorists, that because the geographical frontier has disappeared we confront a dearth of investment opportunity? The western frontier vanished fifty years ago. If its passing created a dearth of investment, surely we would have heard about it long since. We are fortunate in having reliable estimates of private capital formation in this country since 1879. The record shows no evidence that the passing of the frontier reduced investment even relatively. The first three decades of this century showed about the same ratio of private capital formation to national income as the last two decades of the preceding one, and if anything a higher rate of growth in the real national product. To invoke the vanishing frontier a half century after the event to support a gloomy view of the future of private investment is to rattle dry bones.

". . . There is no real historical evidence that the tapering of population growth brings economic stagnation. The relative increase in population in this country began to fall off shortly after the middle of the last century, and had been reduced by more than half before 1929. Do we find evidence of increasing economic stagnation as this decline proceeded? On the contrary, the first three decades of the twentieth century showed a more dynamic and sustained prosperity than the last three decades of the nineteenth. Moreover, if we look outside the United States we find no credible evidence that countries near their population peak have been in general less prosperous than others with high rates of increase, or even than they themselves were in earlier stages of their development.

". . . Declining population growth? Changes in population growth rates are glacial in movement, a statistician's dream of orderly gradualism. Why should a trend that had proceeded harmlessly for three quarters of a century suddenly turn malignant in 1929?

". . . The 'mature economy' theory explains neither the great depression nor the prosperity that preceded it, a fact that has been tacitly admitted by its proponents as to the prosperity but not as to the depression. The vigorous activity of the twenties has always been something of an embarrassment to them, and they have been impelled to find special reasons why the economy, in the face of the unfavorable trends which they assume, enjoyed one of the best decades in its history. Why did it defy the slow doom inherent in its maturity?

". . . Until they can supply some real substantiation of their lamentations, the 'maturity' economists would do well to give us a rest on this theme.

". . . One melancholy refrain in the writings of the 'mature economy' school is what they conceive to be a present dearth of new industries of major importance from an investment standpoint. It is the practice of these writers to explain the vitality of private investment in the past by reference to some so-called 'new' industry then in a phase of rapid growth. For the early decades of the nineteenth century they cite turnpikes and canals; for the remainder of the century, railroads. For the early years of this century it was the electrical industries; for the postwar period, the automobile.

"This interpretation of economic history reminds me of one of Nietzsche's aphorisms: 'The man is a thinker; that is to say, he makes things simpler than they are.' No one will deny that these industries stimulated investment in the periods with which they are so glibly identified, but it is easy to exaggerate their importance. Capital formation is a tree with a thousand roots. The great bulk of its nourishment comes always from long-established industries, not from new ones. Even in the periods of their greatest relative contribution, the railroads, the electricals, or the automobile composed only a minor fraction of the total current investment, and were dwarfed by the single industry of building construction, one of the most ancient of all outlets for capital.

"The railroads expanded their investment after 1900, when they were supposed to have yielded leadership to the electrical industries, more than they had done prior to that date. The electrical industries in turn increased their investment more during the alleged leadership of the automobile than during their entire previous history. But this is not all. More money was invested in railroads during the era tagged 'electrical' than in the electrical industries themselves, while more was invested in electrical lines during the era tagged 'automotive' than in the automobile industry. Moreover, the investment in railroads and electricals together during the 'automotive' era (the decade of the twenties) exceeded by a wide margin the investment in the automobile and satellite industries, plus the investment in highways and in petroleum production and distribution which can reasonably be credited to the influence of the automobile. For this same period the investment in all these current and former leading industries was less than 20 per cent of the total capital formation of the country. This illustrates the gross oversimplification and exaggeration inherent in the bellwether industry theory.

"The necessity for a spectacular 'new' industry for the support of private investment, if it ever existed, is definitely past. In a primitive economy a single invention like the steam engine can have a revolutionary impact, but the chance for such sensational effects diminishes as the technology becomes more highly elaborated and complex. Progress becomes diffused in thousands of innovations of less consequence individually but with cumulative effects just as dynamic, and just as stimulative of investment, as the single revolutionary invention in a simple society. The important thing is the total flow of technological development, not its concentration.

"With the expansion of industrial research technical progress is not only accelerated but made more even in flow, thus eliminating the gaps between major inventions which affected the continuity of investment opportunity in earlier days.

". . . The dearth of new industries? Why was the supposed dearth suddenly manifest in 1929, without warning, on the heels of a vigorous investment boom? Surely the rich and varied technological progress of the twenties did not abruptly reach a stalemate at that point."

In a competitive society, there can, of course, be no such thing as any absolute amount of opportunity for investment. In so far as evidence is available, there seems to be no definite limit to the extent to which per capita production can be expanded by increasing investment per inhabitant. However, because of the existence of the law of diminishing productivity, it is true that, other things being equal, the larger the number of dollars invested, the lower will tend to be the return on the average dollar. Thus doubling the investment per worker cannot be expected to double the output per man-hour. The result is that, as investment increases, the investor gets a smaller rate of return per dollar invested. This shrinkage in returns causes the potential investor to consume more and save less. The supply of funds available for investment is, therefore, always limited by the "propensity to consume."

Profit Rates and Interest Rates

In our economic system, the investor has a choice between two different ways of investing his funds: —

1. He can participate in enterprise as an entrepreneur either by engaging in business directly or by purchasing stock in a corporation. In this case, any return which he may receive is referred to as a profit or a dividend. The ratio of the annual net return to the investment may be called the profit rate.
2. He can lend his money to another individual, to a government, or to an enterprise. The current return on such an investment is called interest. The ratio of the current return to the principal is referred to as the interest rate.

Interest rates and profit rates are undoubtedly related, for whenever (after allowing for any difference in risk which may exist) interest rates are higher than profit rates, some entrepreneurs will tend to curtail their business activities and lend their funds to borrowers. On the other hand, whenever the net profit rates are the higher, some lenders will be tempted to start new enterprises, and many persons will stop buying bonds and will use their money to buy stocks. Unless, however, the differential is very large, it is not likely to cause more than a small minority of individuals to change their investing habits. Therefore, it is erroneous to assume that every change in profit rates is likely to give rise promptly to a corresponding change in interest rates, or *vice versa*.

The Keynesians have emphasized greatly the idea that increasing the volume of investment lowers interest rates. As a trend factor, this is probably true, for since, at any given time, the volumes of natural resources and labor are relatively fixed, any addition to the capital supply commonly results in the use of a larger number of units of equipment per unit of resources and labor. According to the generally accepted principle of diminishing productivity, an increase in equipment volume will tend to lessen the average physical return per unit, and such shrinkage may well lessen the return per dollar's worth of investment.

As it happens, however, interest and profit rates are often influenced greatly by short-term forces which are related to demand, rather than to the productivity generated by the investment of additional units of capital. Thus, existing statistical records show that a period of optimism is usually characterized both by rising interest rates and a rapidly increasing volume of investing. Though it is true that, very commonly, entrepreneurs borrowing funds at such times discover eventually that they have paid too much for the loans, and have therefore lost money by going into debt, that discovery is not likely to be made until several months or years later. It is, therefore, decidedly erroneous to assume that, at a particular time, there exists any close degree of inverse correlation between the volume of investing and the interest rate.

What the Keynesians apparently overlook is that interest rates are determined by the law of supply and demand, and that, therefore, they are influenced as much by the demand for as by the supply of loanable funds. In times of optimism, interest rates rise, not because the supply of loanable funds is short, but because the demand for loanable funds is strong.

Since the followers of Keynes are always worrying about "over-saving" and "under-investment," one would suppose that they would favor very high interest rates in order to entice more persons to invest. Strangely enough, however, they usually advocate measures designed to keep interest rates low. Apparently they are willing to sacrifice logic to expediency, for they know that low interest rates will enable the government to borrow inexpensively to finance the public works programs which they so strongly advocate.

As a matter of fact, the previously-noted shortage of social saving during the depression decade was greatly accentuated by the "easy money" (in other words, the low-interest-rate) policy of the Federal Government — a policy made possible by the willingness to inflate persistently our stock of circulating medium. When interest rates are as low as they have been in the United States during the last decade, none but the most thrifty are induced to save by the lure of the income obtainable from the saved funds. The slowing down in the rate of capital accumulation was, therefore, a result naturally to be expected.

Investing and the Volume of Employment

As noted earlier, both conservative business men and the Keynesians usually agree that the only way to increase the volume of employment in the nation is to have a large volume of investing. As a matter of fact, one is not justified in drawing any such conclusion unless one appends to the original proposition the corollary that wage rates must not be allowed to fall below the existing levels. It is undoubtedly true that high wages are possible only where abundant capital has provided the workers with up-to-date tools and equipment. Paradoxically enough, however, the lower the wage level in a nation, the *lower* tends to be the percentage of workers unemployed, for, unless charity is available, poverty-stricken persons are obliged to accept employment on any terms offered.

Therefore, the statement that the amount of employment in a nation is dependent upon the amount of saving and investment is based upon the assumption that wage rates are not to fall. Were wage rates completely flexible, everyone desiring a job could find it, regardless of the abundance or scarcity of invested funds. In fact, it is exactly in those countries having the *smallest* per capita volume of investment that unemployment is never a serious problem. However, it is those same countries that have the largest proportions of wage earners compelled to exist in poverty.

The Belief that Investing Can Cure Depression

Depressions are characterized by great shrinkages in the outputs of such goods as machine tools and railway rolling stock. This fact has led many writers on economics to conclude that the way to get out of depression and assure prosperity is to stimulate investing, their theory being that money invested in enterprise would be used to build and equip new railways, factories, and power plants.

Unfortunately, this line of argument puts the cart before the horse. Factories are not built merely because someone has invested money, or wants to invest money. Instead, they are built because some one believes that the demand for goods of a given type is strong enough to justify the construction of a factory to make such goods. Unless profits are in sight, it is impossible to induce entrepreneurs to do much in the way of factory building and machine production. The hypothesis that business revival can be brought out by encouraging investment or by subsidizing the equipment-producing industries is, therefore, no more logical than is the notion that the way to warm a room is to hold a lighted match under the thermometer.

Basis of Under-Investing Hypothesis

As previously noted, the Keynesians make no real distinction between spending for consumption goods and investing. However, to support their thesis that hoarding was the prime cause of the 1930–1940 depression, the figures showing for each year the volume of new securities floated seem to serve them admirably, for, as Table III indicates, during the entire period 1931 to 1941, security investing remained at a low level, while the volume of currency in circulation was increasing.

The figures in the table show that investing was active during the late 1920's, reaching a peak of ten billions of dollars in 1929. Then it dropped abruptly, and, in no year from 1931 to 1941, did the volume reach a level as high as that attained during the lowest year in the preceding decade. Yet, between 1933 and 1941, the volume of money and demand deposits in the hands of the public rose from $21 billions to nearly $49 billions, an increase

Capital eliminates drudgery.
{See pages 34 to 88.}

Table III

COMPARATIVE MOVEMENTS OF THE
TOTAL VOLUME OF NEW SECURITY FLOTATIONS
AND THE
VOLUME OF CIRCULATING MEDIUM
(Billions of Dollars)

Year	Security Flotations (excluding short-term notes and refunding issues)[a]	Circulating Medium, June 30		
		Total	Demand Deposits [b]	Money [c]
1919	3.26	27.22	22.34	4.88
1920	3.09	28.80	23.33	5.47
1921	3.41	26.06	21.15	4.91
1922	4.20	25.61	21.15	4.46
1923	4.16	26.88	22.06	4.82
1924	5.32	27.88	23.03	4.85
1925	6.00	29.63	24.81	4.82
1926	6.09	30.15	25.26	4.89
1927	7.57	30.03	25.18	4.85
1928	7.90	30.35	25.55	4.80
1929	10.00	29.00	24.25	4.75
1930	6.50	28.61	24.09	4.52
1931	2.83	26.15	21.33	4.82
1932	1.16	22.09	16.40	5.69
1933	.69	20.96	15.24	5.72
1934	1.35	22.89	17.52	5.37
1935	1.40	27.12	21.55	5.57
1936	1.95	31.64	25.40	6.24
1937	2.05	33.38	26.93	6.45
1938	2.35	33.31	25.85	6.46
1939	2.29	35.95	28.90	7.05
1940	1.94	41.01	33.16	7.85
1941	2.81	48.81	39.20	9.61

[a] Various issues of the *Statistical Abstract of the U. S.*
[b] Data here shown exclude interbank and Federal deposits. Estimates are based upon data found in the *Statistical Abstract of the U. S.,* for 1928, p. 259, 1929, pp. 267–9, and for 1942, p. 291–3. In making these estimates, the ratio of *demand* to *total* individual deposits in the years preceding 1929 is assumed to have been 0.02 smaller for non-national banks than the corresponding ratio for national banks at the same date. This assumption is based upon the ratio in 1929–1931, the first years for which actual data illustrating the relationship are available.
[c] See the *Statistical Abstracts of the U. S.,* for 1929, p. 245 and 1942, p. 275.

of $28 billions. In fact, the volume of circulating medium outstanding in 1941 was $18 billions above the 1929 peak. The ratio of cash on hand to total national money income climbed rapidly between 1933 and 1940. On its face, this increasing ratio seems to give indubitable evidence that, during the depression, Americans in general accumulated great quantities of purchasing power, and that they failed to invest, or indeed to spend for anything, a large fraction of their aggregate income. In other words, the facts appear to prove the existence of unused purchasing power, and of "under-investing," "under-spending," or "hoarding."

However, before we draw definite conclusions, it may be desirable to look into the meaning and significance of these terms, for those using them rarely, if ever, take the trouble to define them carefully. "Under-investing" or "under-spending" are under what? How does hoarding differ from ordinary saving? Is there something unethical or anti-social in hoarding? How significant is it as a factor determining prosperity?

Chapter VII

"UNDER-INVESTING"

Supposed Reasons for "Under-Investing"

It would be highly erroneous to infer that the Keynesians are the only ones who believe that the late period of depression was characterized by a marked degree of "under-investing" which resulted in the amassing of a vast stock of idle money. This view is, indeed, shared by many able business men and numerous conservative economists. They cite evidence such as that presented in Table III — evidence showing clearly that, although, in those years, both money and demand deposits were piling up steadily, new-security flotations remained at very low levels. The conservatives say that the "under-investing" was due to lack of confidence in the future outlook for business; the Keynesians explain it on the grounds of liquidity preference. Both conservatives and radicals commonly cite as evidence the existence of a stock of "idle money" so large as to be out of keeping with the meager volume of business characterizing the depression years. Both have favored the adoption of measures which would force this "idle money" to go to work.

Liquidity Preference

Disciples of Keynes sometimes explain that the smallness of the volume of new-security investing during the depression was due to the high degree of "liquidity preference" existing at that time among possessors of wealth. "Liquidity preference" means the desire of an individual to keep his assets in liquid form — that is to keep them readily exchangeable. Since money and demand deposits are the most "liquid" of all assets, a high degree of "liquidity preference" means a strong desire to keep one's wealth in the form of money or its equivalent.

The term "liquidity preference" is so unfamiliar to the ordinary reader as to lead him to assume that he is now coming into contact with a new concept. In reality, it is a very old idea masquerading under a new name. At all times, every merchant has "liquidity preference" in regard to the stocks of goods on his shelves — that is he would like to sell them all if he could get enough cash for them. Always, however, the crucial issue is what prices can be obtained for the various articles. When, to the owner, the price offered for any good seems unreasonably high, he wishes to sell it, that is, he has a high "liquidity preference" in the case of that particular article. On the other hand, when the price offered for a good seems to be unreasonably low, the owner is disinclined to sell it; in other words, he has a preference for non-liquidity. The sale of a good means that the liquidity preference of the seller is greater than that of the buyer — that is, the seller prefers cash to the good in question, while the buyer prefers the good to the money which he must pay for it. All of this is obvious and commonplace.

The Keynesians, however, connect liquidity preference, not with the desires of various individuals to buy or sell, but, instead, with conditions accompanying depression. They imply that, at such times, a general desire for liquidity preference prevents the investment of savings, and causes an increase in the volume of bank deposits — an increase brought about by the piling up of uninvested funds.

They are doubtless correct in their assumption that, in time of recession, very many people are likely to have high liquidity preferences — in other words, they probably prefer holding cash to holding securities, land, or commodities. At such times, this preference is natural enough, for, if the prices of securities, land, and commodities are expected to fall, it is usually better to own money than to own other goods, since, later, the same goods will command less money or can be bought for less money. Another way of putting it is to say that, in terms of other goods, the value of money is rising. The stronger liquidity preference becomes, the faster will prices fall, for many will be trying to exchange other goods for money, and relatively few will desire to exchange money for other goods.

While liquidity preference may lead to a small degree of hoarding of actual money, its effect in this respect is likely to be negligible, for those most likely to have high liquidity preference — namely those seeking to sell securities and commodities — use relatively little money in their transactions. They deal mostly with deposits. When they sell, it is their deposit accounts which are increased.

At this point of the argument, one must not overlook the fact, that, for every sale, there must be an equivalent purchase. Clearly, if John Jones, by selling securities, *increases* his deposit balance by $5,000, others must have *diminished* the total of their balances by $5,000. It follows that sales brought about by the high liquidity preference of sellers have no tendency whatever to increase the national total of deposits.

As it happens, however, the general rise in liquidity preference characterizing a period of recession commonly produces an effect quite the opposite of that visualized by the Keynesians, for, in times of pessimism, bank deposits, instead of increasing in volume, usually shrink rapidly, largely because, at such times, bankers "call" loans right and left, and lend only to the "best risks." Strong preference for liquidity is, therefore, likely to be paralleled by a rapid shrinkage in the total volume of circulating medium. Ironically enough, therefore, *the more that liquidity is demanded, the less is liquidity possible.*

Idle Money as an Indication of Under-Investing

As noted above, during the depression, both the Keynesians and numerous conservative business men accepted the great growth of bank deposits coupled with a small volume of new security flotations as proof that uninvested funds were piling up. Unfortunately, many orthodox economists also accepted this line of reasoning as valid. Strangely enough, all parties seem to have overlooked the fact that the amount of circulating medium cannot be affected by the act of investing either money or demand deposits. The truth of this statement is easily demonstrated by an example: —

Let us suppose that a law were passed requiring every non-bank private holder of money and demand deposits to invest next week in corporate securities every dollar of cash now held. Would this law, if enforced, necessarily increase materially the flotation of new securities? Would it lessen the volume of circulating medium remaining in possession of the public?

It is clear that, if this hypothetical mandate were enforced, sales of securities during the coming week would approximate the total volume of money and deposits in circulation — in other words sales would be enormous, but how would the volume of circulating medium in the hands of private parties have been affected? The answer is: "Not at all!" Some of the dollars formerly owned by John Smith would now be in the hands of Richard Roe — but the total number held by all the people of the nation would not have changed. It could not change, for the total number of such dollars is fixed by the Federal Government and the banks. The only way to reduce the total is through withdrawal by the Government of money from circulation, through the paying off of loans made by banks, or through the sale of securities or other assets held by banks.

Furthermore, it would not necessarily follow that this security-buying orgy would greatly increase the flotation of new stocks and bonds, for, if the public did not consider new securities good risks, nearly all of the money and deposits might be spent for securities already outstanding.

Problem Still to Be Solved

From what has just been said, it is evident that, while changes in the total volume of circulating medium throw much light upon governmental and banking financial policies, they tell nothing whatsoever about the existence or non-existence of "over-saving," "under-investment," or "hoarding." It also becomes clear that, if we are to discover why investing in newly issued securities declined so much in popularity after 1929, we must look elsewhere for our explanation.

Supposed Reasons for Shortage of Investment During the Depression

Since, as we have just seen, the increase in the volume of bank deposits occurring during the depression was not caused by under-investing, we have as yet gained no light on the problem of why the volume of new security flotations was abnormally low during the period 1931 to 1944. What was responsible for this situation? Why, in any year in the period just mentioned, did the total volume of investment in new common stock issues never rise above $285 millions, although, in the entire period 1922 to 1929 inclusive, it never fell below $277 millions, and, in 1929, reached a peak of $4,407 millions, or more than fifteen times the 1937 minor crest? Why, in a relatively prosperous year like 1941, was the total only $110 millions — materially less than the $194 millions floated in the depression year 1921? [1] What was the real reason that people ceased to buy new securities? Was it because corporate earnings were unsatisfactory? Was it because investors feared New Deal policies? Was it because Federal restrictions made it impossible to market new securities?

Table IV brings out the fact that the volume of common stocks issued, on the one hand, and stock prices, stock market activity, and corporate

[1] See Table IV, Column A.

earnings, on the other hand, have marked tendencies to move upward and downward synchronously. Nevertheless, the highly unstable and erratic behavior of the ratios in Columns C, E, and G shows conclusively that the short-time movements of the volume of common stocks issued is not correlated closely with any one of the other three variables under consideration. The indications are, therefore, that, to discover the forces responsible for the surprising slump occurring since 1921 in the volume of new stock issues marketed, it is necessary to look outside of the market itself.

Table IV

RELATIONSHIP BETWEEN THE
TOTAL VALUE OF ALL NEW ISSUES OF COMMON STOCK
AND
CORPORATE EARNINGS, SHARES SOLD, AND COMMON STOCK PRICES

	A	B	C	D	E	F	G
Year	Value of New Common Stock Issued[a] (Millions)	Corporate Net Income		Common Stock Prices		No. of Shares Sold on N. Y. Exchange	
		Millions of Dollars[c]	B — A	Index[b] (Base 1926)	D — A	Millions[b]	F — A
1919	710	8,416	11.8	70.7	0.10	317	0.45
1920	555	5,873	10.6	64.2	0.12	227	0.41
1921	194	458	2.4	55.2	0.28	173	0.89
1922	277	4,770	17.2	67.7	0.24	259	0.94
1923	324	6,308	19.5	69.0	0.21	236	0.73
1924	511	5,363	10.5	72.8	0.14	282	0.55
1925	558	7,621	13.6	89.7	0.16	454	0.81
1926	578	7,505	13.0	100.0	0.17	451	0.78
1927	600	6,510	10.9	118.3	0.20	577	0.96
1928	1,812	8,227	4.5	149.9	0.08	920	0.51
1929	4,407	8,740	2.0	190.3	0.04	1,125	0.26
1930	1,091	1,551	1.4	149.4	0.14	810	0.74
1931	195	−3,288	—	94.7	0.49	577	2.96
1932	10	−5,644	—	48.6	4.86	425	42.50
1933	105	−2,547	—	63.0	0.60	655	6.24
1934	31	94	3.0	72.4	2.34	324	10.45
1935	15	1,696	113.0	78.3	5.22	382	25.48
1936	262	7,326	27.9	111.0	0.42	496	1.89
1937	285	7,354	25.8	111.8	0.39	409	1.43
1938	25	3,673	146.9	83.3	3.33	297	11.88
1939	87	6,735	77.4	89.2	1.03	262	3.01
1940	108	8,919	82.6	83.6	0.77	208	1.92
1941	110	16,333	148.5	75.9	0.69	171	1.56
1942	34	23,052	678.0	65.7	1.93	126	3.71
1943	56	27,819	496.8	87.0	1.55	279	4.98
1944	163	26,299	161.3	94.6	0.58	263	1.61

[a] *Statistical Abstract of the U. S.* 129, p. 315; 1934, p. 278; 1938, p. 297; and 1946, p. 452.
[b] *Statistical Abstract of the U. S.*, 1941, pp. 204; 336; and 338; 1946, pp. 444 and 446.
[c] U. S. *Statistics of Income*, 1944, Part 2, prel. report, p. 21.

For the reader's information it may be stated that, while it is difficult to measure "lack of confidence" and the effect of governmental policies, careful investigation fails to support the contention that they were the forces primarily responsible for the paucity of investing in the depression years. What force did, then, actually account for this decline? The clue to the solution of the problem is really to be found in Table V, the table showing the typical relationship existing between the income of an individual and the extent of his savings.

Relationship of Accumulative Saving to Size of Family Income

In all parts of the world, the bulk of net private accumulative saving is done by families constituting only a small minority of the total population. The lowest income classes contribute little or nothing to net saving. For example, in our own nation, the typical poverty-stricken family consumes each year goods worth somewhat more than its income, the excess consumption being at the expense of merchants who have extended credit, of friends from whom the family has borrowed money, or of charity. The thrifty, unskilled laborer's family saves regularly part of its current realized income, but ordinarily is soon compelled to use its meager savings to meet an emergency of one kind or another. Therefore, on the average, consumption by such families approximately equals their income. Families of prosperous mechanics gradually accumulate insurance and often pay for homes; hence, on the average, their spendings for consumption are somewhat less than their incomes. The total consumption of a middle-class family is often well below its income, hence it may build up a substantial volume of savings. The very wealthy find it easy to save; hence, they lay aside large fractions of their respective current incomes.

Very enlightening information concerning the quantitative relationships existing between individual incomes and the tendency to save is furnished by the 1935–36 study made by the National Resources Committee. It covered a sample of families large enough to be thoroughly representative of all low and medium-sized incomes. Data extracted from the findings of this committee appear in Table V and are illustrated in Chart 1.

The Committee's study indicates that, on the average, families having incomes under $1,250 per year consume more than their incomes. As previously stated, this is made possible by the fact that they go ever deeper into debt, or subsist partly upon gifts from relatives or friends, or upon charity. The same study indicates that, in 1935–6, the total positive saving of families having incomes from $1,250 to $5,000 inclusive was but $2,781 millions as compared to the $4,730 millions saved by the relatively small number of families having incomes of $5,000 or more each. Nearly half of the accumulative saving of the nation is done by families having annual incomes of $15,000 or over. It therefore appears to be true that concentration of income in the hands of the wealthier classes leads to far more saving than would occur if income were equally distributed.

Obviously, in times of prosperity, the proportion of the population included in the upper income brackets increases. The evidence presented in Table V therefore clearly points to the conclusion that the fraction of the

Table V

COMPARATIVE SAVINGS OF VARIOUS INCOME CLASSES RESIDING IN
THE UNITED STATES IN 1935 — 36 *

Family Annual Income	Per Cent of Family Income Saved	Aggregate Annual Savings of Class	
		Millions of Dollars	Per Cent of Savings for All Classes
All income classes.................	10.1	$5,978	100.0
Under $500........................	− 38.8	− 800	− 13.4
$500–$750........................	− 10.5	− 382	− 6.4
$750–$1,000......................	− 4.9	− 254	− 4.3
$1,000–$1,250....................	− 1.7	− 97	− 1.6
$1,250–$1,500....................	1.9	95	1.6
$1,500–$1,750....................	4.2	196	3.3
$1,750–$2,000....................	5.8	245	4.1
$2,000–$2,500...........'........	8.9	587	9.8
$2,500–$3,000....................	12.0	482	8.1
$3,000–$4,000....................	16.1	742	12.4
$4,000–$5,000....................	21.2	434	7.2
$5,000–$10,000...................	29.8	1,218	20.4
$10,000–$15,000.................	38.9	679	11.4
$15,000–$20,000.................	40.2	473	7.9
$20,000 and over.................	50.8	2,360	39.5

* For data, see the *Statistical Abstract of the U. S.* for 1941, p. 349.

national income going into gross savings is likely to be materially larger in prosperous years than in times of depression.

After-Tax Incomes

It is quite clear that the same dollar of income cannot be spent for two different things. Therefore, money paid out for taxes cannot be used to buy new securities. Hence one would naturally expect to find the total volume of sales of new securities to be correlated less closely with the total income of any class of the population than with the income which the given class has available after paying the tax bills. Unfortunately, figures showing for the various classes of the population incomes after *all* taxes have been paid are not readily available. However, data can be obtained showing, for the higher brackets, the approximate amounts of income remaining for the recipients after they have paid their *Federal income* taxes. Such figures are presented in Table VII and will hereafter be referred to as the "after-tax incomes" of the individuals in question.

Correlation of After-Tax Income and Investing

Since, as previously pointed out, investing is done primarily out of savings, and since most of the saving is done by people having large incomes, one would expect to find investing and income related to one another. The data presented in Table VI and Charts 2, 3, and 4 prove that this hypothesis accords with the facts.

As might be expected, part of the income accruing within any calendar year is not likely to be spent until the next calendar year. Therefore, it is not surprising to learn that the highest degree of correlation between after-tax income and security purchases is obtained when, for each year, income for

CHART 1

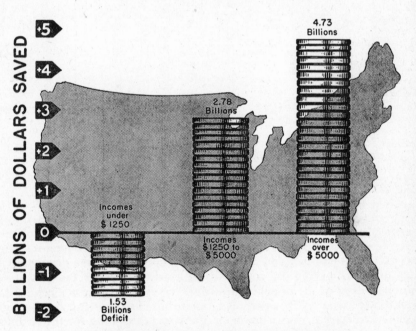

TOTAL FAMILY SAVINGS IN THE UNITED STATES

classified according to

THE RESPECTIVE INCOMES OF THE FAMILIES*. . . . .

BILLIONS OF DOLLARS SAVED

+5
+4
+3
+2
+1
0
-1
-2

4.73 Billions

2.78 Billions

Incomes under $1250

Incomes $1250 to $5000

Incomes over $5000

1.53 Billions Deficit

This chart shows that current expenses absorb most of the income of families in the lower brackets. Savings in the $1250 to $5000 class go to purchase homes, meet emergencies, etc. Thus the burden of accumulating that vast supply of new capital which is primarily responsible for the nation's economic progress rests upon high earners or those with incomes from past labor.

* Data taken from the *Statistical Abstract of the U. S.*, 1941, p. 349 and compiled by the National Resources' Committee's report on *Consumer Expenditures* in 1935-36.

the preceding year and income for the current year are both considered. Experimentation shows that the correlation is highest when the income for the preceding year is given half the weight of that for the current year. The figures on after-tax income appearing in Table VI have all been computed on that basis.

The data entered in the sixth column of Table VI show the amounts of new stocks and bonds, excluding direct issues of the Federal Government, floated in the United States in each of the years 1919 to 1939 inclusive. These figures have been compiled by *The Commercial and Financial Chronicle*. They cover issues put out by State, local, and foreign governments, and by

Table VI

THE TOTAL VALUE OF NEW ISSUES OF STOCKS AND BONDS
(EXCLUDING BONDS ISSUED DIRECTLY BY THE FEDERAL GOVERNMENT)
COMPARED ANNUALLY WITH THE
AGGREGATES OF AFTER-TAX INCOMES
RECEIVED RESPECTIVELY BY TWO CLASSES OF INCOME RECIPIENTS

Calendar Year	Weighted Average for Given and Preceding Year[a] of Total After-Tax Income of All Individuals in the Given Class (Millions of Dollars)			Value of Flotations of All New Stocks and Bonds Not Issued Directly by the Federal Government (Millions of Dollars)		
	Receiving Less than $5000 in Given Year[b]	Receiving $5000 or More in Given Year[b]	Preceding Column Minus $3000[c]	Expected (74%[c] of Preceding Column)	Actual[d]	Percentage Error of Estimate
1919	$52,832	$ 6,894	$3,894	$2,883	$3,264	−11.7
1920	57,908	7,556	4,556	3,371	3,095	+ 8.9
1921	53,426	6,341	3,341	2,473	3,415	−27.5
1922	49,592	6,603	3,603	2,666	4,199	−36.5
1923	54,618	7,485	4,485	3,319	4,160	−20.2
1924	57,234	8,632	5,632	4,168	5,316	−21.6
1925	57,242	11,069	8,069	5,971	5,999	− 0.4
1926	59,275	12,024	9,024	6,678	6,095	+ 9.6
1927	60,021	12,999	9,999	7,399	7,570	− 2.3
1928	59,253	14,953	11,953	8,845	7,904	+11.9
1929	61,511	15,733	12,733	9,423	9,997	− 5.7
1930	62,176	11,936	8,936	6,613	6,503	+ 1.7
1931	56,124	7,821	4,821	3,568	2,827	+26.2
1932	46,032	4,872	1,872	1,385	1,158	+19.6
1933	41,159	3,860	860	636	693	− 8.2
1934	44,525	4,287	1,287	952	1,354	−29.6
1935	49,077	5,160	2,160	1,598	1,400	+14.1
1936	54,597	6,988	3,988	2,951	1,950	+51.4
1937	59,145	7,745	4,745	3,512	2,052	+71.2
1938	57,572	6,745	3,745	2,772	2,352	+17.9
1939	59,037	6,789	3,789	2,804	2,293	+22.2
				Av. of percentages		19.9

[a] Preceding year weighted 1, current year 2.
[b] Computed from the data in the last two columns of Table VII.
[c] When the data in Columns 4 and 6 of this table are plotted against one another, the resulting points are found to arrange themselves near a straight line having a 74% slope and cutting the income scale at approximately $3,000 (see Chart 3).
[d] These figures are taken from various issues of the U. S. *Statistical Abstract.* They have been compiled by the *Commercial and Financial Chronicle.* Refunding issues are not included here.

various Federal agencies such as the Farm Loan Board. However, the totals for prosperous years are made up largely of corporate issues. Refunding issues and short-term notes are excluded. The reason for eliminating the latter is that most such notes are sold not to individuals but to banks.

The figures in Table VI are confined to the interval between the two World Wars, the intent being to exclude from the inquiry periods affected by war financing operations. A detailed analysis (not here presented) of the after-tax income figures from 1918 to 1938 inclusive for the various higher income brackets shows that marked correlation exists between after-tax income totals in the various income brackets above $100,000 and the total volume of *stocks* sold. By contrast, correlation between after-tax income totals and the volume of corporate and municipal bonds sold is higher in the

CHART 2

THE TOTAL VALUE OF NEW ISSUES OF STOCKS AND BONDS
(EXCLUDING ALL DIRECT FEDERAL BOND ISSUES)
COMPARED WITH THE
AGGREGATE OF AFTER-TAX INCOME
RECEIVED BY ALL INDIVIDUALS HAVING INCOMES OF
UNDER $5,000▼

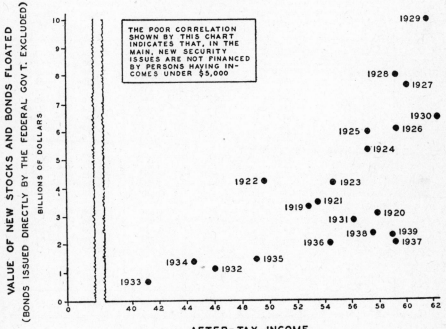

VALUE OF NEW STOCKS AND BONDS FLOATED
(BONDS ISSUED DIRECTLY BY THE FEDERAL GOV'T. EXCLUDED)
BILLIONS OF DOLLARS

THE POOR CORRELATION SHOWN BY THIS CHART INDICATES THAT, IN THE MAIN, NEW SECURITY ISSUES ARE NOT FINANCED BY PERSONS HAVING INCOMES UNDER $5,000

AFTER-TAX INCOME
BILLIONS OF DOLLARS

(PREVIOUS YEAR'S INCOME WEIGHTED 1,
CURRENT YEAR'S INCOME WEIGHTED 2)

▼FOR DATA, SEE TABLE VI, COLUMN 2

$10,000 to $100,000 brackets than it is in the brackets representing still higher incomes.

In Chart 2, total flotations of new securities are compared for the various years with the total income of that part of the population made up of persons

CHART 3

THE TOTAL VALUE OF NEW ISSUES OF STOCKS AND BONDS
(EXCLUDING ALL DIRECT FEDERAL BOND ISSUES)
COMPARED WITH THE
AGGREGATE OF AFTER-TAX INCOME
RECEIVED BY ALL INDIVIDUALS HAVING INCOMES OF
$5,000 OR OVER▼

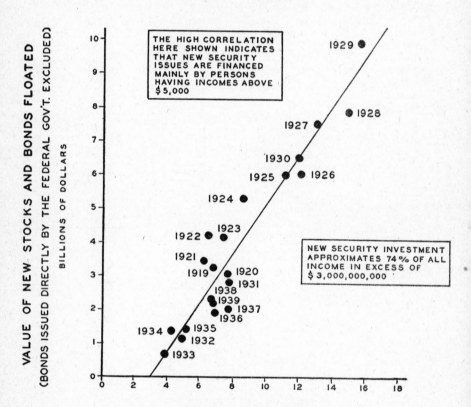

VALUE OF NEW STOCKS AND BONDS FLOATED
(BONDS ISSUED DIRECTLY BY THE FEDERAL GOV'T. EXCLUDED)
BILLIONS OF DOLLARS

THE HIGH CORRELATION HERE SHOWN INDICATES THAT NEW SECURITY ISSUES ARE FINANCED MAINLY BY PERSONS HAVING INCOMES ABOVE $5,000

NEW SECURITY INVESTMENT APPROXIMATES 74% OF ALL INCOME IN EXCESS OF $3,000,000,000

AFTER-TAX INCOME
BILLIONS OF DOLLARS

(PREVIOUS YEAR'S INCOME WEIGHTED I,
CURRENT YEAR'S INCOME WEIGHTED 2)

▼FOR DATA, SEE TABLE VI, COLUMN 3

having incomes below $5,000. In Chart 3, a similar comparison is made with those having incomes over $5,000. Both of these charts are scatter diagrams. The degree of correlation existing is shown by the closeness of the points to a straight line. In Chart 4, the same data appearing in Chart 3 have been plotted as two historigrams.

Chart 2 shows that the correlation between incomes under $5,000 and the total volume of new securities floated is very slight. This chart therefore indicates that people in the lower income brackets do not buy any consid-

CHART 4

COMPARISON OF THE
ACTUAL VOLUME OF NEW SECURITIES ISSUED
WITH THE
VOLUME TO BE EXPECTED ON THE BASIS OF
AFTER-TAX INCOMES IN BRACKETS ABOVE $5,000▾

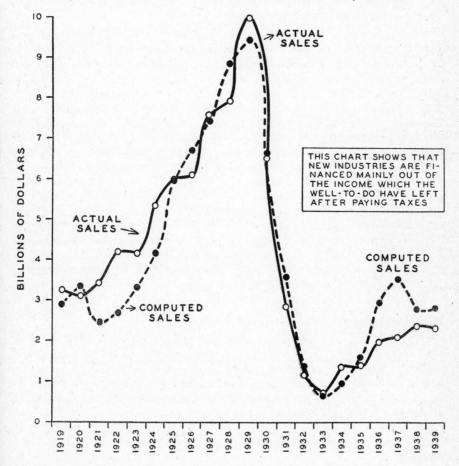

THIS CHART SHOWS THAT NEW INDUSTRIES ARE FINANCED MAINLY OUT OF THE INCOME WHICH THE WELL-TO-DO HAVE LEFT AFTER PAYING TAXES

▾FOR DATA, SEE TABLE VI, COLUMNS 5 AND 6.

erable share of the new securities issued. By contrast, Charts 3 and 4 both show the existence of a surprisingly high degree of direct correlation. Although it is true that, in some individual years, the two variables diverge rather widely, there does not appear to have been any considerable segment of the period 1919 to 1939 in which the volume of new security flotation was not dominated by the aggregate income, after Federal income tax payments, remaining to individuals having incomes of $5,000 or larger.

Degree of Correlation Existing

The fact that, in some years, the percentages of error recorded in the last column of Table VI are large, shows, of course, that investment is not purely an automatic process. For example, from 1921 to 1924, the potential buyers evidently anticipated recovery, and bought more heavily than their immediate incomes justified. On the other hand, in 1932, 1933, 1935, and 1937, they were pessimistic, and bought materially less than their customary quotas. These sizable deviations prove that aggregate after-tax income of the prosperous classes is only the dominant, and not the sole, force determining the volume of security flotations.

The closeness of the relationships indicated by Table VI stands, however, in marked contrast to the sketchy relationships shown by Table IV to exist between new security flotation and other supposedly influential causal forces. The average error of the estimates in Table VI is only 20 per cent. This indicates that, in most years, all other forces combined had but little influence on the volume of new security flotation. That volume was dominated by the after-tax incomes of the well-to-do. Theories that the scantiness of new security sales during the depression was mainly caused by liquidity preference, by unfavorable conditions in the security markets, by burdensome regulations promulgated by the Securities and Exchange Commission, by low corporate earnings, or by fear of oppressive action by government receive but little support from the statistical evidence at hand. At most, these forces seem to have played minor rather than major rôles. True, securities can be marketed only when market conditions are favorable, but they are favorable only when potential buyers have surplus income to invest. If this analysis is correct, it shows that the ability of private corporations, States, and municipalities to float their securities is dependent primarily upon the volume of after-tax income remaining to individuals having, before taxes, incomes of $5,000 or more each.

Apportionment of After-Tax Income of the Prosperous

Chart 3 indicates, that, on the whole, during the period 1919 to 1939, this prosperous part of the population customarily spent each year about $3 billions for expenses of a more or less fixed nature. In 1939, this amounted to about $4,400 per income-tax payer. In other years, this sum would be somewhat different, for the number of persons reporting incomes of $5,000 or over varies materially from year to year. The same chart shows that, after meeting these minimum expenses, the general tendency was to invest in newly-issued securities 74 per cent, or nearly three-fourth of all remaining income. [2]

[2] Preliminary Treasury Department estimates of income and taxes in 1947 indicate that the relationships indicated in Table VI, after adjustment for price level changes, still held good in 1947

A glance at Table VI now makes perfectly clear the reason why, in 1929, it was possible to float nearly $10 billions of new securities. In that year, individuals had nearly $13 billions of income left over after paying out the $3 billions which they deemed it necessary to spend for living expenses. We also see why, in 1933, new security flotation fell far below the billion mark. In that year, the income of the prosperous classes over their customary bill for living expenses was less than a billion dollars. Again we have verification of the old saying — "You can't get blood out of a turnip."

Investing and Free Enterprise

Unfortunately, it is not feasible to follow up the study of capital invest-

Table VII

THE TOTAL BURDEN OF THE FEDERAL INCOME TAX
COMPARED FOR
ALL INDIVIDUALS HAVING INCOMES UNDER $5000
AND
ALL INDIVIDUALS HAVING INCOMES OF $5000 AND OVER
(All amounts represent millions of dollars)

| Calendar Year | Total Realized Income of Individuals Having Incomes of | | | Federal Income Taxes | | | | Total Realized Income After Federal Income Taxes Going to Individuals Having Incomes of | | |
| | | | | Paid by Individuals Having Incomes of | | | % of Income Paid by $5000 and Over Class[e] | | | |
	Any Size[a]	Under $5000[c]	$5000 and Over[d]	Any Size[d]	Under $5000[d]	$5000 and Over[d]		Any Size[c]	Under $5000[c]	$5000 and Over[c]
1918	56,956	50,425	6,531	1,128	145	983	15	55,828	50,280	5,548
1919	62,945	54,237	8,708	1,270	129	1,141	13	61,675	54,108	7,567
1920	68,434	59,974	8,460	1,075	166	909	11	67,359	59,808	7,551
1921	56,689	50,327	6,362	719	93	626	10	55,970	50,234	5,736
1922	57,171	49,368	7,803	861	96	765	10	56,310	49,272	7,038
1923	65,662	57,372	8,290	662	81	581	7	65,000	57,291	7,709
1924	67,003	57,252	9,751	704	47	657	7	66,299	57,205	9,094
1925	70,051	57,273	12,778	735	13	722	6	69,316	57,260	12,056
1926	73,523	60,296	13,227	732	13	719	5	72,791	60,283	12,508
1927	73,966	59,902	14,064	831	12	819	6	73,135	59,890	13,245
1928	75,904	58,947	16,957	1,164	13	1,151	7	74,740	58,934	15,806
1929	79,498	62,803	16,695	1,002	4	998	6	78,496	62,799	15,697
1930	72,398	61,875	10,523	477	10	467	4	71,921	61,865	10,056
1931	60,203	53,260	6,943	246	7	239	3	59,957	53,253	6,704
1932	46,708	42,465	4,243	330	43	287	7	46,378	42,422	3,956
1933	44,713	40,563	4,150	374	36	338	8	44,339	40,527	3,812
1934	51,560	46,559	5,001	511	35	476	10	51,049	46,524	4,525
1935	56,488[b]	50,393	6,095	657	40	617	10	55,831	50,353	5,478
1936	65,677[b]	56,780	8,897	1,214	61	1,153	13	64,463	56,719	7,744
1937	69,246[b]	60,430	8,816	1,142	72	1,070	12	68,104	60,358	7,746
1938	63,041[b]	56,244	6,797	766	64	702	10	62,275	56,180	6,095
1939	68,532[b]	60,557	7,975	929	91	838	11	67,603	60,466	7,137
1940	75,000[b]	64,897	10,103	1,496	189	1,307	13	73,504	64,708	8,796
1941	89,500[b]	77,900	11,600	3,896	1,245	2,651	23	85,604	76,655	8,949

[a] The National Industrial Conference Board, *National Income in the U. S., 1799–1938*, p. 7.
[b] Obtained by telephone from the National Industrial Conference Board.
[c] Obtained by subtraction.
[d] Preliminary Report on *Statistics of Income for 1941, Part 1*, Table 4, U. S. Bureau of Internal Revenue.
[e] Calculated by division.

ment by individuals in corporate securities by a corresponding study of similar investment in enterprises operated by individuals. Data adequate for the last-mentioned purpose have not been discovered, and probably do not exist. However, it seems reasonable to suppose that, to obtain new capital, small enterprises must also depend largely upon the savings of the prosperous sections of the population. It appears, therefore, that, if private enterprise is to continue to grow, there must be a reservoir of "surplus income" for it to tap.

Killing the Goose

One must not make the error of assuming that practically all of the saving in the nation is the work of individuals. As a matter of fact, in normal times, business enterprises tend to "plow in" large percentages of their earnings; that is, they spend on current operations far less than the aggregate of their incomes. Thus, in the period 1909 to 1926 inclusive, reports of the corporations of the United States indicated that, on the average, they saved no less than 45 per cent of their entire net earnings.[3]

Taxes on net corporate earnings tend to take away funds which would normally be set aside for plant expansion, and hence tend to slow down the growth of industry. In recent years, corporation incomes have been taxed at high rates. Since the wealthy invest heavily in corporate stocks, dividends are important constituents of their incomes. Taxes on corporate earnings therefore hit the wealthy hard.

Table VII shows that, before World War II, direct Federal taxes on individual incomes above $5,000 were gradually stepped up from an average rate of 3 per cent in 1931, until, a decade later, they reached 23 per cent, and, in 1942, under the stress of war, rose to 31 per cent. In the highest income brackets, State and Federal income taxes combined came to confiscate most of the income. Industrial expansion to meet the needs of the nation for World War II was largely financed by the Federal Government. If the policy of taxing away large incomes is continued, dependence upon government for capital may become chronic, and, if this occurs, free enterprise will gradually give way to fascism or socialism.

It appears, then, that such questions as who is to do the necessary saving, and how an adequate volume of capital accumulation and investment can be assured, are problems of great concern to all persons interested in establishing continuing prosperity. Some of the issues involved will be discussed in the next chapter.

[3]See the report of the National Bureau of Economic Research, entitled *The National Income and Its Purchasing Power,* pp. 278–280.

Chapter VIII

CAPITAL AND THE SOCIAL WELFARE

Capital and Productivity

In an earlier chapter, it was pointed out that the United States is so much more prosperous than China mainly because our per capita supply of national resources is far larger than China's. However, one cannot explain our own country's amazing *progress* since 1789 on the basis of its rich endowment by nature. When the Constitution went into operation, the new nation had a plethora of natural resources of all kinds — virgin forests, untouched mines, unharnessed water power, and vast areas of rich potential farm land. Nevertheless, average incomes were low. Why?

The answer is that the country was ill-supplied with indirect or production goods — that is with such things as raw materials, livestock, tools, machines, equipment, factories, and good roads. The scantiness of such things was due mainly to the fact that, as yet, most people were poor, and hence their net savings were too small to enable them to provide themselves with an adequate supply of production goods.

As time passed, however, through accumulative and retentive saving, capital was gradually amassed and invested both in education and in productive equipment. As this process continued, our industries turned out a larger and larger average output per worker. Eventually, average productivity per man-hour far outstripped that existing in any other nation.

Logic would lead one to expect that per capita production would vary somewhat in proportion to the value of the equipment and resources utilized per worker. Available statistics indicate that this assumption roughly accords with the facts, at least in so far as the American manufacturing industry is concerned. For many years, the United States Census Bureau collected from factory owners statistics showing for their respective enterprises the gross values of the products turned out and the amounts of capital invested. The figures on capital are, of course, only approximations, but their behavior over a long period of years indicates that the estimates for different dates are reasonably comparable. The data as reported appear in Table VIII, and are illustrated in Chart 5.

The fact that the two graphs in Chart 5 are so nearly parallel seems to show rather conclusively that output is dominated by capital supply. However, Table VIII brings out the fact that the value added by manufacture does not increase as rapidly as does the capital supply. In 1849, the gross value of output was nearly double the capital value. In 1939, the capital supply was only 42 per cent larger than the gross value of products. This difference in growth illustrates the fact that, as capital supply increases, the added productivity resulting from each dollar added diminishes — in other words, the law of diminishing productivity is, as might be expected, applicable to this case.

What effect has this capital investment and resulting increase in output per worker had upon the factory operative's pay? From the standpoint of abstract justice, it would seem that the typical worker's pay should not have advanced noticeably, for he has been responsible for but a very small part of the saving required to accumulate the capital. Moreover, owing to the widespread use of mechanical devices and electric power, a factory job is much less tiresome today than was the case a century ago.

However, the forces of competition take no cognizance of any such principle of justice. They work in such a manner that the added returns arising from the productivity of tools and machines do not go, in the main, to the savers who furnished the capital to buy the machines. Instead, they go to the workers who operate the machines. Hence, returns per dollar of invested capital are lower than they were a century ago, while returns per hour of labor have been multiplied.

Since it is impossible to measure accurately changes in the average price of the goods making up a workingman's budget, and since the contents of that budget have changed with the passage of time, it is not feasible to compute the exact relative increase during the last century in the average *hourly real* wage of the factory worker. The best available evidence indicates, however, that, in 1947, it was at least *five* times as high as in 1847. This means that, in 1947, the typical factory worker received for *one* hour of labor as much in the way of services and material goods as his 1847 predecessor

Table VIII

MANUFACTURING CAPITAL INVESTMENT PER WAGE WORKER
COMPARED WITH
GROSS ANNUAL VALUE OF PRODUCT PER FACTORY WAGE WORKER

Year	Value Per Wage Earner	
	Capital Actual	Gross Annual Value of Product
1849	$557	$1,065†
1859	769	1,436†
1869	825	1,646†
1879	1,021	1,970†
1889	1,532	2,200†
1899	1,850	2,435†
1904	2,319	2,700‡
1909	2,790	3,130‡
1914	3,240	3,450‡
1919	4,885	6,850‡
1929	6,152*	8,120‡
1939	5,080*	7,210‡

Source of Data: U. S. *Censuses of Manufactures* and U. S. *Statistics of Incomes of Corporations.*

* Equals net capital assets plus inventories plus cash plus miscellaneous assets.
† Includes hand trades.
‡ Excludes hand trades. For 1899, both figures are available. They do not differ widely.

could earn in five hours. This gain was certainly not due to the fact that he worked harder. Indeed, the reverse was true, for, at the later date, most of the heavy lifting was done by machines. True, the worker in 1947 was better educated than was his counterpart of 1847. However, one reason that he was better educated was that accumulated capital had endowed great libraries, research laboratories, universities, and public schools, and had provided them with their multitudinous facilities.

Since, in the aggregate, wage workers are the chief beneficiaries of capital accumulation and investment, it follows that the intelligent workingman

CHART 5

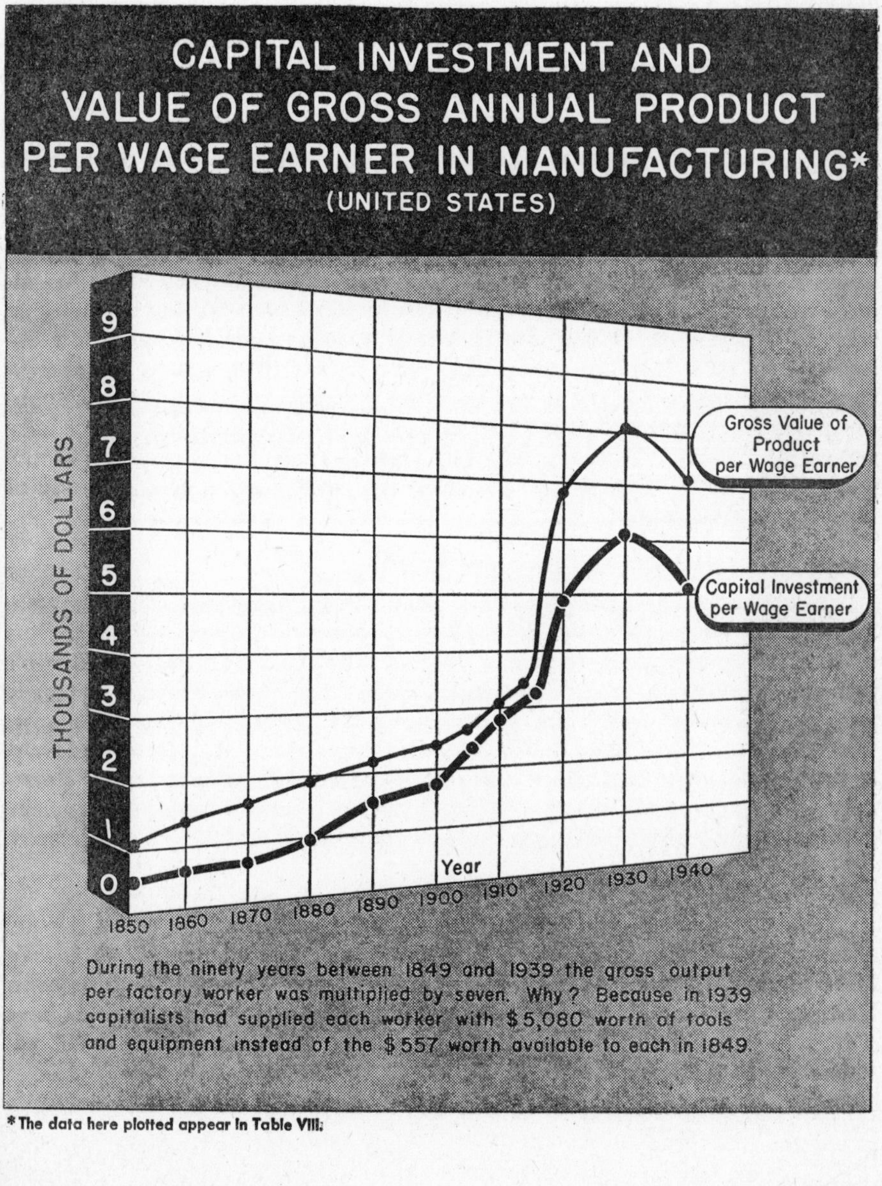
CAPITAL INVESTMENT AND
VALUE OF GROSS ANNUAL PRODUCT
PER WAGE EARNER IN MANUFACTURING*
(UNITED STATES)
THOUSANDS OF DOLLARS
0
1
2
3
4
5
6
7
8
9
Year
1850
1860
1870
1880
1890
1900
1910
1920
1930
1940
Gross Value of
Product
per Wage Earner
Capital Investment
per Wage Earner
During the ninety years between 1849 and 1939 the gross output
per factory worker was multiplied by seven. Why? Because in 1939
capitalists had supplied each worker with $5,080 worth of tools
and equipment instead of the $557 worth available to each in 1849.

* The data here plotted appear in Table VIII.

who acts in his own interest will persistently oppose any measures which tend to lessen the total volume of saving in the nation. Unfortunately, however, many members of the working class fail to understand on which side their bread is buttered.

In 1850, the average factory worker put in 69 hours a week at his job. In 1947, he objected to working more than 40 hours. What caused the change? The answer is very simple. In 1850, his hourly production was so small and hence his hourly earnings were so meager that he could not obtain for himself and family even the bare necessities of life unless he worked many hours each week. Later, as accumulated capital made production and wage rates expand, he could secure the required necessities by working perhaps three hours per day. Having satisfied elemental wants, he decided to devote about four hours per day to getting money to buy conveniences or luxuries, and to substitute leisure for the four additional hours formerly worked. If production per man hour again declined to the levels of a century ago, today's workers would again insist on working as many hours weekly as did their great-grandfathers, and no union which tried to enforce a short working week could retain its members.

During the last hundred years, despite the reduction in weekly working hours from 69 to 40, the average factory worker's *real weekly* wage has almost trebled. This change has revolutionized his way of life and given him a scale of living equal to that which, formerly, none but the favored few enjoyed. And this amazing attainment must be ascribed almost entirely to capital accumulation. Had it not been for persistent abstinence from consumption by millions of savers and investors, this advance could never have occurred. Clearly, therefore, whether viewed from the standpoint of the public at large or from that of the ordinary workingman, saving is one of the keys to prosperity.

Saving Necessary Under All Economic Systems

The importance of saving is not dependent upon the economic system existing in a nation. Without it, economic progress is impossible, regardless of whether communism, socialism, fascism, or *laissez faire* prevails. Lenin's communistic Russia, Stalin's socialistic Russia, and Hitler's fascist Germany all have saved vigorously, but, in each case, the government has done most of the saving by setting aside for future use part of the produce of industry. In each of the cases mentioned, the amount of saving has been largely determined by government officials. By contrast, in a nation where *laissez faire* dominates, most of the saving is done by individuals and business concerns.

The Effect of Cutting Down Individual Saving

The fact was pointed out in the preceding chapter that, of all the net accumulative saving done by individuals in the United States, more than three-fourths is done by persons having annual incomes of $5,000 or over. Here we have the major source of the new capital which industry must have if it is to expand and increase its total output. If this source is dried up, industry will languish.

An excellent illustration of this fact is furnished by the experience of

Great Britain during the last three decades. In order to secure funds to subsidize unemployment and support various social "reforms," the British Government levied sharply progressive-income and inheritance taxes, and these absorbed a large proportion of the savings which would normally have gone into capital formation. The natural result was that British industry was overtaken by a creeping paralysis. Then the very "reformers" responsible for the nation's plight declared that the failure of the English manufacturers and mine owners to modernize their plants proved conclusively that capitalism had broken down. They convinced the voters that this was true; hence a socialistic government was elected, and given a mandate to take over and operate the leading industries of the nation.

As shown by Table VII, the United States has, since 1932, been proceeding along the same path which led to the downfall of capitalism in England. Very heavy taxes have been laid upon those individual incomes located in the higher brackets, and such levies have diverted into the Federal Treasury funds formerly largely devoted to financing new business ventures. Taxes on corporate incomes have taken away a sizable fraction of the revenues which, under previous conditions, were used for plant expansion. Heavy inheritance taxes have discouraged the accumulation of wealth.

Responsibility for those confiscatory taxes which, in both England and the United States, have been interfering so seriously with the accumulation of capital rests, of course, upon the extravagant spending programs of the two governments mentioned. Boondoggling, public works, housing projects, a varied array of expensive subsidies, bonuses, pensions, and loans, both domestic and foreign, have all combined to add billions annually to the budgets and pile up huge public debts.

The Philosophy of Deficit Financing

True, followers of John Maynard Keynes often assert that, since we owe the national debt to ourselves, there is no reason to worry about it or to restrict its size. They point out that, since interest charges equal interest receipts, they cost the nation nothing. The Keynesians contend, furthermore, that lavish governmental spending is justifiable not only in war time but also in time of depression. They assert that, in times of unemployment, large scale public spending is imperative, for if distress is not alleviated, the result may well be bloody revolution.

The fact which they overlook is that public spending to relieve distress nearly always perpetuates and accentuates that distress. In countries not rich enough to afford any considerable volume of charity, depressions are short-lived, for hunger soon compels able-bodied persons to accept jobs at the best wages obtainable. When the idle go to work, production increases, and the depression inevitably fades away.

In prosperous nations, by contrast, doles may keep millions idle for years, and their idleness brings about general depression, lessens the national output, and keeps the nation poor. This, in turn, reduces governmental revenues, and leads both to the imposition of heavy taxes upon the more thrifty and industrious sections of the population and to deficit financing and currency inflation.

How deficit financing to relieve distress works out in practice is well illustrated by the experience of our own country between 1930 and World War II.

Deficit Financing in the United States.

In the fiscal year ending in 1929, the ordinary expenditures of the Federal Government were only $3.3 billions; yet this figure was higher than that for any other year since 1922. With the advent of depression, the Government, instead of curtailing expenditures, entered upon a spending program designed to relieve distress and incidentally to hold for the party in power the votes of the less affluent sections of the population. By 1935, this policy had more than doubled Federal expenditures. Tax receipts meanwhile declined. The result was a persistent deficit, increasing from $0.5 billion in the fiscal year 1931 to $3.2 billions in 1935.

The program of those who favored Governmental spending to bring about recovery called for a "cyclically balanced budget," any deficits in bad years being offset by surpluses in good years. In 1936 and early 1937, business improved greatly. According to the previously announced program of the spenders, the time had therefore arrived in which to make a beginning on paying off the debt accumulated during the depression. What really happened, however, was that expenditures rose instead of falling, and the deficit expanded instead of shrinking. By 1936, it had run up to $4.5 billions. The Federal debt, which had been reduced to $16.2 billions in 1930, advanced to $28.7 billions in 1935, to $36.4 billions in 1937, and to $43.0 billions in 1940.

The conclusion to be drawn from these figures is that it is not politically feasible to balance a budget on a cyclical basis, for, as soon as it is conceded that it is permissible for a government to spend more than its income, there is no logical place to stop, hence the deficit climbs year after year. Under the cyclical-balancing plan, spending begets spending, and the auspicious time actually to balance the budget is a will-o'-the-wisp which ever recedes as it is approached. It follows that the only way to keep government on a sound financial basis is to balance the budget *every* year, regardless of whether times are good or bad.

The Correct Financial Policy for War Time

However, most authorities on public finance hold that this policy must go by the board in case of a major war. Are they, however, justified in making this exception to the general rule? Since a war cannot be fought with future men, future food, future ships, or future arms or munitions, it is obvious that no part of the war's real cost can be postponed to the future. By no hook or crook can the present generation avoid bearing the entire cost of the war while the war is going on. Is it not, therefore, evident that the only thing postponed to the future is settlement of the question as to whether, in later years, the children of Richard Roe shall pay money to, or extract money from, the children of John Doe? Would it not be more manly and businesslike for John Doe and Richard Roe to settle the question of payment between themselves instead of "passing the buck" to their children?

If we had raised by taxation every dollar of the nation's expense in fighting World War II, the immediate financial burden would not have been increased by one iota. The average scale of living of our people would certainly not have been lowered more than was the case under deficit financing. There would have been no excuse for price regulation. Moreover, at the end of the war, there would have been no annoying aftermath of inflation and debt.

World War II has left us with a debt amounting to almost $300 billions. If it is ever put on a sound financial basis, the interest charges will probably total $8 billions to $10 billions per annum, or nearly three times the entire cost of operating the Government in an active year like 1929. Even though the Keynesians are correct in stating that the interest charge does not lessen the national income, its very size constitutes a continuous menace to our welfare, for lavish governmental spending for *any* purpose endangers the existence of our competitive capitalistic system.

While expenditures for unemployment insurance and for some types of boondoggling are inherently pernicious, the objects of most governmental spending are, in themselves, highly laudable. As a rule, however, private enterprise could attain more satisfactory results at far less cost.

But whether the ends sought are desirable or otherwise, every proposal to appropriate large sums of money for pensions, relief, social security, medical care, public works, housing projects, foreign loans or other purposes, worthy or unworthy, ought to be viewed with alarm, for *all* heavy spending programs tend to destroy the system of private enterprise — the system which has worked more effectively than any other plan of production yet devised.

Why Lavish Governmental Spending Is a Menace

There are two reasons why this is true.

The *first* is that legislators and other officials of government, being elected by popular vote, dare not offend the masses. Persons having large incomes have few votes; those having small incomes have many votes. Therefore, politicians tend to confiscate almost the entire incomes of the few persons in the upper brackets before they levy any considerable taxes upon the millions in the lower brackets.

Here we have the real menace arising from a huge public debt. The threat to national progress lies in the fact that the low-income masses usually succeed in concentrating the tax burden upon the small percentage of families having large incomes, the group responsible for much of the nation's capital accumulation. Let us see how this works out.

At a 3 per cent rate, the interest on a $300 billion debt comes to $9 billions per year. However, in 1942, this amount, while constituting less than 8 per cent of the national income, equalled the *entire* income of the 380,550 persons in the United States having incomes of $10,000 or over, and would have absorbed 60 per cent of the total income of the 1,297,522 individuals receiving more than $5,000 each.[1]

[1] Prel. *Statistics of Income* for 1942, Part 1, p. 18.

The thing to be especially noted is that members of this last-mentioned class, while possessing less than 3 per cent of the voting power of the nation, are responsible for more than 79 per cent of the nation's net individual saving.[2] The customary procedure is for the 97 per cent of the voters (who, as it happens, possess some 87 per cent of the national income) to shift to the shoulders of the more well-to-do 3 per cent a tax burden sufficiently heavy to absorb a large share of the income of the latter class. Such a procedure tends to destroy most of the incentives which lead the technician or industrial organizer to use his best efforts to increase production. Progressive taxation may, therefore, be used by the majority in such a way as to destroy free enterprise and national prosperity; and all this may be accomplished without one voter in a hundred being aware that he helped to kill the goose that laid the golden eggs.

Furthermore, after the victims have had large fractions of their incomes taken by government, they are in no position to furnish that great quantity of capital which must be provided if our industries are to expand sufficiently to keep our economy progressing at its customary rate. Therefore, unless government takes over the capital-accumulation job, business will stagnate. But, when government furnishes the capital, it soon controls the industries of the nation — in other words, private enterprise is supplanted by socialism.

As stated previously, the way that confiscatory taxation works out in practice is well illustrated by England's experience. The crushing taxes levied during the last three decades upon the incomes of the wealthy have dried up the sources of the capital needed to keep their industries up-to-date, hence British producers have found it more and more difficult to compete in the world markets. If experience elsewhere is any criterion, the new socialistic regime will prove even more inefficient than those which preceded it. The lesson to be learned from England's experience is that spending by government to promote social reforms is likely to prove a roundabout but effective way of destroying the competitive capitalistic free-enterprise system and the prosperity that is its offspring.

A *second* reason why lavish public spending tends to block economic progress and lower the average family's scale of living is that governments which attempt to carry out a great variety of expensive reforms usually find that legitimate financial procedures fail to raise the required funds, hence they either print paper money or borrow from the banks, thus increasing the currency supply. This inflationary process slowly but surely lessens the real worth of money, bank deposits, notes, mortgages, bonds, life insurance policies, annuities, and all other instruments payable in a fixed number of given monetary units. As people gradually come to realize that their accumulated savings are being filched away and may eventually disappear, thrift disintegrates and capital formation dwindles.

The decline in saving is accentuated by the fact that governments engaged in deficit spending ordinarily keep their interest payments down by lending at very low rates funds obtained by means of inflation. As previously pointed out, by reducing returns on investments, this policy tends to eliminate that part of saving induced by the prospect of being paid adequately

[2] See Table V.

for abstinence and waiting — and this type of saving is a very important source of new capital.

The destructive influence which an inflationary low interest rate policy can exercise upon saving is shown by its effect upon life insurance. Since, obviously, inflation lessens the commodity value of the dollar, it increases the size of the policy needed to afford to the beneficiary a given degree of protection. Moreover, the extent of the increase needed is usually accentuated by the fact that inflation is likely to continue for a considerable time. The fear that this will happen lessens still further the present purchasing power of the dollar. Therefore, inflation penalizes the man seeking protection for his family not only by forcing him to buy more dollars' worth of insurance but also by raising the cost per $1,000 purchased. The cost goes up because the low rates of return obtainable on their investments compel insurance companies to raise their premium charges. If they fail so to do they will be unable to meet their obligations. This three-fold penalty on the purchaser of life insurance can scarcely be considered conducive to thrift.

Another malign effect of governmentally-maintained low interest rates is that they play havoc with every institution largely dependent upon the income from its investments. Many colleges, churches, libraries, museums, and research organizations, Foundations, and other endowed institutions which were formerly considered to have assured incomes adequate for their needs, have had their revenues grievously curtailed. Thus the intents of the altruistic persons who granted the endowments have been thwarted.

Social Security

In most progressive nations, the function of assuring individuals that, when old age or sickness arrives, the hunger wolf will not appear at the door has been largely taken over by government. As a rule, with the passage of time, the expenses connected with such social security programs have expanded steadily, and more and more of the burden has been thrown upon the shoulders of the well-to-do, thus drying up the sources of new capital. There is, then, a distinct tendency for social welfare programs to bring about the downfall of capitalism and the advent of stateism.

It seems evident, however, that, unless government intervenes, many of the sick and aged will suffer from lack of the necessities or conveniences of life. If it is a legitimate function of government to prevent such distress, it certainly seems better to take care of the incapacitated in a systematic orderly way than to distribute relief in a haphazard manner. But British and German experience indicates that following such a systematic orderly procedure tends to destroy capitalism and substitute for it either socialism or fascism. Here we have an apparent dilemma. Must we choose between social insecurity and stateism?

Fortunately, it is entirely unnecessary to make such a choice, provided we are willing to attack the problem scientifically. What is the logical solution?

It is, of course, obviously true that large numbers of people, when overtaken by sickness or old age, find themselves without any adequate sources of support. In some cases, the persons in need have never enjoyed incomes sufficiently large to make it possible for them to save enough to provide for old age or misfortune. Fortunately, in the United States, this class of citizens constitutes but a minor fraction of the gainfully occupied.

More numerous, perhaps, are persons who have been thrifty and have saved considerable sums, but who have lost their savings in whole or in part by selecting poor investment media, or have had the value of their savings undermined by currency inflation resulting from unsound governmental financial policies.

However, those who find themselves in want when they are overtaken by old age or misfortune consist, in large part, of those who have for years enjoyed incomes large enough to enable them to save consistently for the rainy day, but who have spent their incomes as received, their philosophy being "never trouble trouble till trouble troubles you." These thriftless people have taken it for granted that, should hard times come, the thrifty would take care of them, and, because of the charitable nature of our people, their prognostications have usually proved correct.

Clearly, this arrangement is grossly unjust, for, in very many cases, the thrifty upon whom the burden is cast have, in the past, enjoyed incomes materially smaller than those of the persons who later call upon them for assistance. This situation is one which cannot be remedied without compulsion, and no one but government is in a position to supply this compulsion. Our existing social security legislation has been enacted in an endeavor to remedy the obvious injustice inherent in this situation by compelling all employed persons to provide for the future vicissitudes of life. However, the present social security program has four glaring weaknesses:

1. It does not apply to all classes of the population. This omission disregards the fact that almost everyone, no matter how affluent he now is, may need financial assistance in his old age.
2. The benefits provided for are not computed on a sound actuarial basis, but, instead, mix charity with insurance.
3. Persons cannot receive old age pensions as long as they continue regular employment. This provision of the law was evidently inserted by economic illiterates who believed that the number of jobs in the nation was fixed, and that it was unfair for a man having a pension to take away another man's job. They did not realize that their action not only condemned the aged to poverty but also reduced the national income by cutting off the goods which the elderly could and should produce.
4. The amounts which individuals must contribute are controlled by legislation, and hence must inevitably be determined on a political rather than an economic basis.

It seems clear that, if we are to succeed in our quest for sustained prosperity for the nation as a whole, our social security system must be completely overhauled and be made to fit into the framework of the competitive capitalistic system rather than into that of a socialistic "welfare state." Is this feasible?

As a matter of fact, it is not particularly difficult to devise a plan which is both workable and economically sound. The automobile insurance laws already operating in some of our States might well be used as models upon which to base the needed legislation. These statutes require owners to take out insurance, but do not set up a State insurance fund. They allow the automobile owner to insure with any reliable company.

Since the cost of adequate protection against disability necessarily absorbs a noticeable fraction of the average man's income, it follows that government must exercise considerable compulsion or else the thriftless will fail to pay their premiums when due. Therefore the present procedure of requiring employers to deduct premiums from wages and salaries ought to be continued, but the deductions should cover the *entire* premiums. The employee should be required to take out with some insurance company, approved as to soundness by government, a policy guaranteeing that, in case the insured is disabled, he will receive an income sufficient to prevent him from becoming either a public charge or a burden to the charitably inclined. Benefits should be paid *only to the disabled,* payments being in proportion to the degree of disability. This limitation would keep insurance premiums down. Moreover, elderly persons would thereby be encouraged to continue their employment as long as their health permits. Regular employment would make them much happier than if they were idle, and their productivity would add to the nation's prosperity. Premium rates should be arrived at by competition — not fixed by government.

No private company would be able to compete successfully for this type of insurance unless it devised effective ways of reducing malingering to a minimum. Fortunately, in the United States, there almost certainly are many well-managed insurance companies which are both able and willing to write insurance of the type just described.

Every married employee should be required to carry a policy for his wife as well as for himself. The *initial* monthly premium on every policy paid for by an employee should be perhaps fifty per cent higher than the standard rates on the policies in question. Premiums at this advanced level should be continued until the employee accumulated an unemployment reserve equal to the basic premium for a year. This reserve should then be kept intact unless the worker in question loses his job. In that case, the reserve would be used during his period of idleness to keep his premiums paid in full. When the worker again found employment, he would be required to build the reserve up again until it once more equalled a year's premiums. When the insured person was no longer able to work, any surplus remaining would become his property.

Every employee should be required by law to file with his employer the name of the company carrying his compulsory disability insurance, and the employer should remit directly to that company the amounts necessary to cover the premiums. In the case of indigent unemployables, the insurance premiums should be paid by the governments of the localities in which the persons reside. Self-employed persons should be required to submit annually with their income-tax reports receipts for their disability insurance premiums. Penalties for delinquency should be about the same as those for failure to pay Federal taxes.

The system just outlined would gradually eliminate the opportunity for the thriftless to sponge upon the thrifty. Every tub would be compelled to stand upon its own bottom. Every person would be assured of regular care in case of either temporary or permanent disability, and, except in the case of the indigents whose premiums were paid by the local governments, any benefits received would have no taint of charity. Moreover, since the insurance would be handled by private enterprise, each insurance company, in order to avoid the risk of failure, would be compelled to keep all transactions on a business basis.

Putting disability insurance on such a basis would eliminate the existing grave danger that the growing cost of the public social security program will gradually make it impossible to maintain a capitalistic competitive system in the United States. The establishment of a sound compulsory disability insurance program operated by private companies would give to the average man and woman a feeling of security hitherto unknown, and would also go far toward maintaining continuous prosperity in the nation.

But Why the Depression?

As we have now learned, the foundation stones upon which our national prosperity rests are abundant resources per capita, free competition, and ample saving, capital formation, and investment. Critics of *laissez faire,* however, delight in pointing out that we had all of these things in 1929, but that, suddenly, we found ourselves tumbling into the depression crevasse. It is impossible to deny that their statement of the situation is approximately correct. Evidently "something was rotten in Denmark." What was it?

Some of the critics say that the trouble was a shortage of "purchasing power." Does this analysis of the problem have any validity? Before we can answer this question, we must delve into the nature of "purchasing power." This will be done in the next chapter.

Chapter IX

OUR STOCK OF SPENDABLE FUNDS

"Purchasing Power," Circulating Medium and Spendable Funds

In recent years, various writers on economics have laid great stress upon the relationship between "purchasing power" and prosperity. Often, however, these writers have failed to define "purchasing power" precisely. Just what does the term mean? Apparently, it refers to something that can be used to purchase something else. If this concept is correct, it appears that any good may constitute "purchasing power," for the possessor may trade it for some other good which he desires. Furthermore, if a man's credit is acceptable, he may use his note to pay for goods bought. In this case, his personal credit constitutes part of his "purchasing power." However, as pointed out in an earlier chapter, circulating medium, whether it consists of pocketbook money or bank deposits, has one special characteristic which differentiates it from other goods — it is readily and often immediately exchangeable for a vast variety of things. The holder of circulating medium therefore has *ready* purchasing power. As a matter of fact, in advanced nations, most purchases are paid for with money or bank deposits. Since, in the United States, nearly all purchases are made with money or money equivalents, we might say that, in this country at present, total ready purchasing power is equivalent to the total stock of circulating medium.

However, the value of our money has exhibited an unfortunate tendency to fluctuate widely from time to time, our dollar in some years purchasing a volume of goods only half as great as it would buy in other years. The term "purchasing power" is widely used to cover this relationship between money and the things which it will buy. This use of the phrase evidently is very different from the one discussed above. Hence, it appears desirable to invent a term referring to values as measured in money, and which will cover solely the ready buying power of one or more individuals. The term chosen is *spendable funds*. It will be defined for any group as the stock of both pocketbook money and demand deposits available at the time for the purchase of goods. It therefore refers solely to circulating medium.

At this point, it seems worth while to note the extent and nature of the changes occurring in the United States during the last quarter century in the total volume of circulating medium.

Changes in the Volume of Circulating Medium

Data on reported changes in the amount of money in circulation and also figures showing the volume of the demand deposits of individuals, enterprises, and government in the commercial banks of the United States appear in Table IX. Table X shows factors affecting the total volume of demand deposits in all reporting banks which were members of the Federal Reserve System. Table XI gives the composition of the stock of actual money as it existed in the United States at the recorded dates.

89

Table IX

CHANGES IN THE AMOUNT OF CIRCULATING MEDIUM
in the United States
(Billions of Dollars)

Year	Demand Deposits, June 30					Money in Circulation[h]		Total Circulating Medium[i]	
	Excluding Federal and Inter-bank		Est. U. S. Deposits	Total	Change in Past Year	June 30	Change in Past Year	June 30	Change in Past Year
	National Banks	Other Commercial Banks							
1918	8.40[ab]	10.61[cd]	0.66[ae]	19.67		4.48		24.15	
1919	9.64[ab]	12.70[cd]	0.66[ae]	23.00	+ 3.33	4.88	+ .40	27.88	+ 3.73
1920	9.90[ab]	13.43[cd]	0.58[ae]	23.91	+ .91	5.47	+ .59	29.38	+ 1.50
1921	9.03[ab]	12.12[cd]	0.41[ae]	21.56	− 2.35	4.91	− .56	26.47	− 2.91
1922	9.05[ab]	12.10[cd]	0.48[ae]	21.63	+ .07	4.46	− .45	26.09	− .38
1923	9.54[ab]	12.52[cd]	0.45[ae]	22.51	+ .88	4.82	+ .36	27.33	+ 1.24
1924	9.94[ab]	13.09[cd]	0.34[ae]	23.37	+ .86	4.85	+ .03	28.22	+. 89
1925	10.72[ab]	14.09[cd]	0.37[ae]	25.18	+ 1.81	4.82	− .03	30.00	+ 1.78
1926	10.92[ab]	14.34[cd]	0.37[ae]	25.63	+ .45	4.89	+ .07	30.52	+ .52
1927	10.98[ab]	14.20[cd]	0.35[ae]	25.53	− .10	4.85	− .04	30.38	−. 14
1928	11.51[ab]	14.04[cd]	0.36[ae]	25.91	+ .38	4.80	− .05	30.71	+ .33
1929	10.50[b]	13.75[d]	0.30[ae]	24.55	− 1.26	4.75	− .05	29.30	− 1.31
1930	10.93[b]	13.16[d]	0.31[ae]	24.40	− .25	4.52	− .23	28.92	− .48
1931	10.11[b]	11.22[d]	0.44[ae]	21.77	− 2.63	4.82	+ .30	26.59	− 2.33
1932	7.94[b]	8.46[d]	0.54[ae]	16.95	− 4.82	5.69	+ .87	22.64	− 3.95
1933	7.88[b]	7.36[d]	0.82[ae]	16.07	− .88	5.72	+ .03	21.79	− .85
1934	9.27[b]	8.25[d]	1.74[f]	19.26	+ 3.19	5.37	− .35	24.63	+ 2.84
1935	11.27[b]	10.28[d]	0.82[f]	22.38	+ 3.12	5.57	+ .20	27.95	+ 3.32
1936	13.45[b]	11.95[d]	1.14[f]	26.55	+ 4.17	6.24	+ .67	32.79	+ 4.84
1937	14.40[b]	12.53[d]	0.67[f]	27.60	+ 1.05	6.45	+ .21	34.05	+ 1.26
1938	13.89[b]	11.96[d]	0.60[f]	26.45	− 1.15	6.46	+ .01	32.91	− 1.14
1939	15.58[b]	13.32[d]	0.78[f]	29.69	+ 3.24	7.05	+ .59	36.74	+ 3.83
1940	17.91[b]	15.25[d]	0.81[f]	33.97	+ 4.28	7.85	+ .80	41.82	+ 5.08
1941	21.39[b]	17.81[d]	0.73[f]	39.94	+ 5.97	9.61	+1.76	49.55	+ 7.73
1942	24.69[j]	19.75[j]	1.90[j]	46.34	+ 6.40	12.38	+2.77	55.26	+ 5.71
1943	33.41[j]	26.44[g]	7.70[k]	67.55[k]	+21.21	17.42[k]	+5.04	84.97	+29.71
1944	35.74[j]	29.09[g]	18.76[k]	83.59[k]	+16.04	22.50[k]	+5.08	106.09	+21.12
1945	40.28[j]	32.96[g]	23.48[k]	96.72[k]	+13.13	26.75[k]	+4.25	123.47	+17.38
1946			12.94[k]	98.04[k]	+ 1.32	28.24[k]	+1.49	126.28	+ 2.81

a Average of figures for both ends of given year.
b Data taken from *Statistical Abstracts of the U. S.* for 1928, p. 259; 1929, p. 269; and 1941, pp. 282-4.
c Estimated by multiplying total individual deposits in other commercial banks by the estimated ratio of demand to total individual deposits. This ratio was assumed to be 0.02 smaller than the ratio for national banks at the same date. This assumption was based upon the comparison observed to exist in 1929-31 — years for which suitable data for both national banks and other commercial banks are available.
d For data, see the *Statistical Abstract of the U. S.,* for 1929, p. 267-9; and 1942, pp. 291-3.
e Reported total for member banks with $100,000,000 added to cover estimated U. S. deposits in non-member banks. For data see the *Statistical Abstract of the U. S.* 1929, p. 262; 1934, p. 230; for 1941, p. 278.
f See the *Statistical Abstract of the U. S.* for 1938, pp. 249-51; 1941, pp. 285-7; and 1943, p. 316.
g Obtained by subtraction.
h See the *Statistical Abstract of the U. S.* for 1929, p. 245; and 1942, p. 275.
i Equals "Demand Deposits" plus "Money in Circulation."
j Reports of U. S. Comptroller of the Currency 1941, p. 29; 1942, p. 9; 1943, p. 4; 1944, p. 6; 1945, p. 6.
k *Federal Reserve Bulletin* 1944, pp. 783; 789; and 899; 1945, pp. 242-, 245-; 797; 1946, pp. 889-, 892-, 895; 1947, pp. 712 and 715.

The Origin of New Demand Deposits

It will perhaps help us to understand exactly why the volume of spendable funds has been increasing so rapidly since 1933 if we examine in some detail the process by which new demand deposits and new money come into being.

There are three procedures which may cause an increase in the demand bank-deposit total for the nation: —

1. Individuals, enterprises, or governmental units may increase bank deposits by depositing pocketbook money in the banks.
2. Individuals, enterprises, or governmental units may increase "de-

Table X

FORCES AFFECTING THE VOLUME OF DEMAND DEPOSITS
(Balance Sheet Items for Members of Federal Reserve System in 101 Cities)
(Billions of Dollars)

Year	Net Demand Deposits[a]		Loans		Federal Obligations Held (Direct & Guaranteed)		Other Securities	
	June	Change in Past Year	June	Change in Past Year	June	Change in Past Year	June	Change in Past Year
1919	10.29[b]		12.60[eg]		2.19[b]		1.98[eg]	
1920	11.35[b]	+ 1.06	13.48[eg]	+0.88	1.56[b]	− 0.63	1.89[eg]	−0.09
1921	10.05[b]	− 1.30	11.88[b]	−1.60	1.37[b]	− 0.19	2.07[b]	+ .18
1922	11.12[b]	+ 1.07	10.78[b]	−1.10	2.10[b]	+ 0.73	2.30[b]	+ .23
1923	11.10[b]	− .02	11.85[b]	+1.07	2.53[b]	+ .43	2.16[b]	− .14
1924	11.84[b]	+ .74	12.14[b]	+ .29	2.31[b]	− .22	2.51[b]	+ .35
1925	12.72[b]	+ .88	13.20[b]	+1.06	2.55[b]	+ .24	2.95[b]	+ .44
1926	13.25[b]	+ .53	14.13[b]	+ .93	2.51[b]	− .04	3.17[b]	+ .22
1927	13.40[b]	+ .15	14.76[b]	+ .63	2.57[b]	+ .06	3.52[b]	+ .35
1928	13.24[b]	− .16	15.75[b]	+ .99	3.02[b]	+ .45	3.66[b]	+ .14
1929	13.00[c]	− .24	16.48[c]	+ .73	2.91[c]	− .11	2.84[c]	− .82
1930	13.63[c]	+ .63	17.05[c]	+ .57	2.82[c]	− .09	3.15[c]	+ .31
1931	13.42[c]	− .21	14.62[c]	−2.43	4.05[c]	+ 1.23	3.77[c]	+ .62
1932	11.01[c]	− 2.41	11.42[c]	−3.20	4.20[c]	+ .15	3.26[c]	− .51
1933	11.31[c]	+ .30	8.99[c]	−2.43	5.36[c]	+ 1.16	3.07[c]	− .19
1934	13.15[c]	+ 1.84	8.55[c]	− .44	7.46[c]	+ 2.10	2.62[c]	− .45
1935	13.62[f]	+ .47	8.03[c]	− .52	8.85[c]	+ 1.39	3.01[c]	+ .39
1936	14.67[c]	+ 1.05	8.53[c]	+ .50	10.50[c]	+ 1.65	3.33[c]	+ .32
1937	15.19[c]	+ .52	9.70[c]	+1.17	9.51[c]	− .99	3.12[c]	− .21
1938	15.04[c]	− .15	8.38[d]	−1.32	9.32[d]	− .19	2.99[d]	− .13
1939	18.68[c]	+ 3.64	8.09[d]	− .29	10.50[d]	+ 1.18	3.29[d]	+ .30
1940	22.12[c]	+ 3.44	8.45[d]	+ .36	11.60[d]	+ 1.10	3.54[d]	+ .25
1941	25.73[c]	+ 3.61	10.25[d]	+1.80	14.25[d]	+ 2.65	3.65[d]	+ .11
1942	28.59[c]	+ 2.86	10.81[d]	+ .56	17.32[d]	+ 3.07	3.53[d]	− .12
1943	40.04[c]	+11.45	9.59[d]	−1.22	33.93[d]	+16.61	3.07[d]	− .46
1944	47.52[c]	+ 7.48	12.16[c]	+2.57	39.92[c]	+ 5.99	2.95[c]	− .12
1945	53.41[c]	+ 5.89	13.83[c]	+1.67	46.54[c]	+ 6.62	3.16[c]	+ .21
1946	50.39[c]	− 3.02	14.92[c]	+1.09	43.44[c]	− 3.10	3.39[c]	+ .23

[a] Excludes inter-bank deposits but includes government deposits.
[b] *Statistical Abstract of the U. S.*, 1929, p. 261; figures for end of June.
[c] *Statistical Abstract of the U. S.*, 1938, p. 244; averages for the month.
[d] *Statistical Abstract of the U. S.*, 1943, p. 326; averages for the month.
[e] *U. S. Survey of Current Business*, various issues; figures for end of June.
[f] *U. S. Survey of Current Business*, 1936, Supp. p. 46 — govt. deposits estimated.
[g] Average for 12 months.

Table XI

CHANGES IN THE AMOUNT OF MONEY REPORTED AS BEING IN CIRCULATION
IN THE CONTINENTAL UNITED STATES
(Millions of Dollars)

Year	Total		Gold and Gold Certificates		Silver and Silver Certificates		Minor Coins		National Bank Notes		Federal Reserve Notes		Other U. S. Notes	
	June 30[a]	Change in Past Year	June 30	Change in Past Year	June 30	Change in Past Year	June 30	Change in Past Year	June 30	Change in Past Year	June 30	Change in Past Year	June 30[c]	Change in Past Year
1918	4,482		1,048		664		75		691		1,698		305	
1919	4,877	+ 395	803	− 245	472	− 192	82	+ 7	639	− 52	2,450	+ 752	431	+ 126
1920	5,468	+ 591	734	− 69	423	− 49	91	+ 9	690	+ 51	3,065	+ 615	465	+ 34
1921	4,911	− 557	648	− 86	460	+ 37	91	0	721	+ 31	2,600	− 465	391	− 74
1922	4,463	− 448	589	− 59	553	+ 93	89	− 2	728	+ 7	2,139	− 461	366	− 25
1923	4,823	+ 360	791	+ 202	669	+ 116	94	+ 5	711	− 17	2,235	+ 96	324	− 42
1924	4,849	+ 26	1,194	+ 403	671	+ 2	97	+ 3	734	+ 23	1,843	− 392	309	− 15
1925	4,815	− 34	1,407	+ 213	699	+ 28	100	+ 3	682	− 52	1,636	− 207	291	− 18
1926	4,885	+ 70	1,449	+ 42	699	0	104	+ 4	652	− 30	1,679	+ 43	302	+ 11
1927	4,851	− 34	1,392	− 57	700	+ 1	108	+ 4	650	− 2	1,703	+ 24	298	− 4
1928	4,797	− 54	1,396	+ 4	709	+ 9	111	+ 3	650	0	1,626	− 77	304	+ 6
1929	4,746	− 51	1,303	− 93	715	+ 6	115	+ 4	653	+ 3	1,693	+ 67	267	− 37
1930	4,522	− 224	1,352	+ 49	707	− 8	117	+ 2	651	− 2	1,402	− 291	293	+ 26
1931	4,821	+ 299	1,359	+ 7	685	− 22	117	0	648	− 3	1,708	+ 306	304	+ 11
1932	5,695	+ 874	1,168	− 191	639	− 46	114	− 3	701	+ 53	2,780	+ 1,072	293	− 11
1933	5,721	+ 26	585	− 583	646	+ 7	113	− 1	920	+ 219	3,061	+ 281	396	+ 103
1934	5,373	− 348	150	− 435	712	+ 66	119	+ 6	902	− 18	3,068	+ 7	422	+ 26
1935	5,567	+ 194	117	− 33	1,030	+ 318	125	+ 6	704	− 198	3,223	+ 155	368	− 54
1936	6,241	+ 674	101	− 16	1,306	+ 276	135	+ 10	366	− 338	4,002	+ 779	331	− 37
1937	6,447	+ 206	88	− 13	1,457	+ 151	144	+ 9	269	− 97	4,169	+ 167	320	− 11
1938	6,461	+ 14	79	− 9	1,611	+ 154	146	+ 2	217	− 52	4,114	− 55	294	− 26
1939	7,047	+ 586	72	− 7	1,857	+ 246	155	+ 9	186	− 31	4,484	+ 370	293	− 1
1940	7,847	+ 800	67	− 5	2,012	+ 155	169	+ 14	165	− 21	5,163	+ 679	271	− 22
1941	9,612	+ 1,765	63	− 4	2,200	+ 188	194	+ 25	150	− 15	6,684	+ 1,521	321	+ 50
1942	12,383	+ 2,771	59	− 4	2,324	+ 124	213	+ 19	139	− 11	9,310	+ 2,626	337	+ 16
1943	17,421[b]	+ 5,038	57[b]	− 2	2,344[b]	+ 20	236[b]	+ 23	132[b]	− 7	13,747[b]	+ 4,437	906[b]	+ 569
1944	22,504[b]	+ 5,083	54[b]	− 3	2,392[b]	+ 50	263[b]	+ 27	126[b]	− 6	18,750[b]	+ 5,003	919[b]	+ 13
1945	26,746[b]	+ 4,242	52[b]	− 2	2,566[b]	+ 174	292[b]	+ 29	120[b]	− 6	22,867[b]	+ 4,117	850[b]	− 69
1946	28,245[b]	+ 1,499	50[b]	− 2	3,009[b]	+ 443	317[b]	+ 25	114[b]	− 6	23,973[b]	+ 1,106	781[b]	− 69

[a] Statistical Abstract of the U. S., 1929, p.245 and 1942, p.275.
[b] Federal Reserve Bulletin, Aug. 1944, p. 783, Aug. 1945, p. 793; Aug. 1946, p. 889.
[c] Includes Federal Reserve Bank Notes.

posits" by borrowing from the banks. The amounts borrowed are usually evidenced by notes or bonds.

3. Banks may increase "deposits" by exchanging "deposits" for stocks, gold, or other property.

In practice, demand deposits are created mainly by borrowing. The borrower exchanges his credit, which is not freely spendable, for the bank's credit which is generally acceptable. As a rule, those deposits which originate in loans, are eliminated only as the debts are paid off.

Relative Stability of Different Types of Bank Assets Supporting Deposits

Assets supporting the deposit liabilities of all banks considered as a system may conveniently be divided into four categories, namely:

1. Money.
2. Notes of corporations, partnerships, or individuals.
3. Securities of private corporations.
4. Securities of governmental bodies.

These types of assets differ in their respective tendencies toward variability in volume. A study of the year to year changes in the different items enables us to understand the natures of the forces which have caused the volume of deposit currency to expand or contract.

The aggregate of bank holdings of notes of private individuals and concerns fluctuates greatly, for it is influenced both by the existing volume of business in the nation and by the willingness of bankers to lend money. When prices are rising and business is active, many customers wish to borrow, and bankers are generally optimistic concerning the financial standing of these would-be borrowers. Therefore, lending proceeds apace. By contrast, when pessimism appears, and business is dull, businessmen have less need to borrow, and bankers are reluctant to lend to most would-be borrowers, hence the volume of loans shrinks.

The volume of bank investments in securities also fluctuates materially. For this there are three reasons: —

1. Bankers are anxious to buy securities when they expect price advances, and are anxious to sell them when they expect price declines.
2. If a "run" on banks starts, they may be forced to sell securities in order to obtain money to pay frightened depositors.
3. When it is difficult to find satisfactory borrowers, bankers invest their surplus funds in securities in order to obtain at least minimum revenues.

Variations in the Volume of Deposit Currency

Table IX shows that the volume of deposit currency fluctuated widely during the period covered, rising more than 4 billions of dollars between 1918 and 1920, dropping nearly 10 billions between 1928 and 1933, rising 11 billions between 1933 and 1937, and more than 70 billions in addition between 1937 and 1946, the 1946 volume being more than six times that of 1933. From 1933 to 1946, the volume of pocketbook money and deposit currency combined increased nearly five fold. What were the forces responsible for these huge variations? To answer this question, Table X has been prepared. This table is based upon data from the member banks in 101 large cities, suitable statistics from other localities not being available. Table X indicates that the increase between 1918 and 1928 in the volume of bank deposits was due to an expansion in the volume of loans, reinforced by a growth in security investments — an increase in the bank holdings of both "Federal Obligations" and "Other Securities" having occurred. The shrinkage in the volume of deposit currency occurring between 1930 and 1932 was caused partly by bank failures and partly by a reduction in the volume of loans — the total of securities held having actually increased during that period. The growth in demand deposits between 1933 and 1935 was due wholly to purchases of Federal securities, for both loans and other investments declined in volume. Between 1935 and 1936, all of the three factors mentioned united to increase the total of demand deposits. On the other hand, between 1936 and 1938, investments in Federal securities diminished noticeably, while other loans and investments remained fairly stationary. The great expansion occurring between 1938 and 1943 in the volume of deposit currency was occasioned by a moderate increase in the aggregate of loans, and a huge increase in the holdings of direct and indirect obligations of the Federal Government. The latter reached a peak in 1945, but loans kept on growing.

The Volume of Pocketbook Money

Table IX shows that deposits are not alone in their great expansion in volume during recent years. There has also been a huge increase in the volume of pocketbook money reported by the United States Comptroller of the Currency as being "in circulation." All money outside of the Treasury and the Federal Reserve Banks is so classed. Part of this money is, of course, held by the various banks and other enterprises in the United States. More is in possession of individuals. An unknown amount is stored away in safe deposit boxes or hiding places. Changes in the past in the volume of pocketbook money have been caused by:

1. Coinage of gold or silver brought to the mint.
2. Coinage of silver, nickel, or copper bought in the open market.
3. The issuance of silver or gold certificates against precious metals deposited in the United States Treasury.
4. The printing by the United States Government of "greenbacks" or Treasury notes.
5. Note issuance by National Banks.
6. Note issuance by Federal Reserve Banks.[1]

Monetary Elasticity

The first five of the types of money issuance just listed have usually been governed by legislation or by forces almost unrelated to the volume of trade; hence, before the Federal Reserve System came into existence, our money supply showed little responsiveness to the needs of business, and therefore

[1] Since these Federal Reserve notes may be issued in exchange for deposits of member banks, increases in their volume may result in equal increases in the volume of member bank credit.

was said to be *inelastic*. Inasmuch as, at that time, the law required banks to keep their reserves in the form of specified types of pocketbook money, the inelasticity just mentioned was likely to cause serious difficulty whenever the public became pessimistic, for, at such times, there was a strong tendency to hoard money, and money for hoarding was drawn from the banks. Such withdrawals often brought the reserves of some of the banks below the amounts required by law, and hence the banks were forced to call loans and resort to various devices to secure the needed money. Here we have the origin of serious "money panics" like the one of 1907. The Federal Reserve Act overcame this difficulty by changing the nature of the reserves required of member banks. This Act provided that these reserves should not be kept in the form of pocket-book money, but, instead, should consist merely of "deposits" in the Federal Reserve Banks.

Under this new system, any bank possessing legally acceptable assets can replenish its reserves by sending some of these assets to the local Federal Reserve Bank and exchanging them for a "deposit" in the Federal Reserve Bank. This possibility enables all sound member banks not only to meet runs successfully, but also to accommodate any increase in the demands of business concerns, either for loans or for pocket-book money. Ever since the member banks have been permitted to use "deposits" in Federal Reserve Banks as their legal reserves, no further "money panics" have occurred.

Variations in Kinds of Money

Between 1919 and 1935, fluctuations in our supply of pocketbook money were only moderate in size. By contrast, between 1935 and 1946; this supply quintupled. Table XI shows that this growth was almost entirely due to a great expansion in the volume of silver certificates and Federal Reserve notes, the quantity of the latter having been multiplied by seven. The amount of silver and silver certificates has more than quadrupled since 1933. This remarkable increase has been due, in the main, to the Government's silver-buying campaign.

Correlation Between Money and Deposit Volumes

Reference to Table IX shows the existence of considerable correlation between *changes* in the volumes of demand deposits and *changes* in the volume of pocketbook money. Thus, in 20 out of the 28 years covered, the two quantities moved in the same direction.

The existence of this direct correlation is explained by the fact that banks respond to the demands of their customers for actual money. Whenever a customer needs such currency to make small purchases or to pay wages, or whenever a merchant requires till money, a check is cashed at the depositor's bank, and money is taken away. Ordinarily, the Federal Reserve Bank supplies promptly any amount of notes requested by a member bank, printing new notes if necessary. The chief limitation on its power to issue notes is the legal requirement that it must maintain a gold-certificate reserve amounting to a specified percentage of the value of its notes outstanding. If it happens that a member bank, by drawing Federal Reserve notes from the Federal Reserve Bank, depletes unduly its required reserve at the Federal

Reserve Bank, it sends to the latter drafts or collateral to replenish its reserve.

One might expect that the correlation between the respective movements of demand deposits and Federal Reserve notes would be even closer than it is, for business, when active, calls for both additional check payments and additional money payments; and when the commercial banks find that their supply of pocketbook money is scarcely adequate to meet the calls of their customers, they are able to buy or borrow Federal Reserve notes from the Federal Reserve Banks. On the other hand, when their supply of pocketbook money becomes redundant, they can send Federal Reserve notes to the Federal Reserve Banks and use the proceeds to increase their reserves. By making such adjustments possible, the Federal Reserve System has made our money supply genuinely elastic.

However, surprisingly enough, we find that, in reality, the correlation between the respective changes in supplies of demand deposits and Federal Reserve notes is far from perfect, their movements being in opposite directions in 9 of the 28 years covered by Tables IX and XI. Reasons for this divergence of movements are various. For example, in 1924-5 there was an expansion of demand deposits, although the volume of Federal Reserve notes shrank sharply, the cause for the difference in behavior apparently being that a great influx of gold made any other form of monetary expansion superfluous — the supply of new gold certificates being ample to meet all needs for additional money. In 1931 to 1933, by contrast, although the volume of bank deposits was contracting sharply, the volume of Federal Reserve notes was expanding rapidly, the expansion presumably being brought about by two forces: first, the need of replacing gold certificates, which were disappearing from circulation as gold went abroad; and second, the accumulation by individuals of large money reserves. Such accumulation was probably due both to the actual failure of some banks and to the fear that other banks would fail.

Whenever depositors begin to fear that the banks in which they have deposits are likely to fail, they, of course, try to exchange their "deposits" for pocketbook money. If they succeed, some of the money secured will not be deposited in any bank. It is, therefore, possible that, at times, an increase in the amount of Federal Reserve notes outstanding may actually indicate a growing tendency to hoard cash.

One result of a "run" on the banks is to cause payments made in pocketbook money to supersede payments by check. In so far as this is the case, payments in actual money will, of course, constitute an increasing proportion of the total value of business transactions.

Money in Circulation and Hoarding

In the *Federal Reserve Bulletin* for April, 1942 (pp. 312-316), evidence was presented showing that the volume of bills in $50 or larger denominations had been increasing rapidly. It was suggested that this fact might indicate a growth in the hoarding of money. However, it is well to remember that, to a large extent, members of the laboring class are their own bankers, and many of them prefer to keep their emergency reserves in notes of large rather than small denominations. It is necessary also to note that, in 1942, the volume of payments to employees was increasing very rapidly. As a matter of fact, ratios in the last column of Table XII are about the same for 1942 as for 1918, and show little change between 1934 and 1942.

Table XII

RATIO OF THE SUPPLY OF POCKET-BOOK MONEY TO THE TOTAL COMPENSATION OF EMPLOYEES IN THE UNITED STATES

Year	Total Pocket-Book Money in Circulation[a] June 30 (Millions)	Total Compensation of Employees (Billions)	Ratio of Money in Circulation to Total Compensation of Employees
1918	$4,482	$32.32[b]	0.14
1919	4,877	35.40[b]	0.14
1920	5,468	42.28[b]	.13
1921	4,911	36.21[b]	.14
1922	4,463	37.70[b]	.12
1923	4,823	42.89[b]	.11
1924	4,849	44.49[b]	.11
1925	4,815	46.85[b]	.10
1926	4,885	48.50[c]	.10
1927	4,851	48.20[c]	.10
1928	4,797	49.00[c]	.10
1929	4,746	50.73[c]	.09
1930	4,522	46.39[d]	.10
1931	4,821	39.32[d]	.12
1932	5,695	30.90[d]	.18
1933	5,721	29.24[d]	.20
1934	5,373	33.92[d]	.16
1935	5,567	36.90[d]	.15
1936	6,241	42.39[d]	.16
1937	6,447	47.42[d]	.14
1938	6,461	44.48[d]	.15
1939	7,047	47.60[d]	.15
1940	7,847	51.57[d]	.15
1941	9,612	64.5[d]	.15
1942	12,260	84.1[d]	.15
1943	17,421	106.3[d]	.16
1944	22,504	116.0[d]	.19
1945	26,746	114.5[d]	.23
1946	28,245	109.8[d]	.26

[a] See Table XI, second column.

[b] See *The National Income and Its Purchasing Power* (a report of the National Bureau of Economic Research) p. 122.

[c] Approximated on the basis of estimates made by the National Bureau of Economic Research and the National Industrial Conference Board.

[d] See the U. S. *Survey of Current Business,* Mar. 1943, p. 22; and Feb. 1946, p. 8; Feb. 1947, p. 8.

During the period 1923 to 1930, however, the ratios were unusually low. A possible explanation of this situation is that, during this period, the banks were making strong and successful attempts to induce employers to pay by check, and members of the working classes to open checking accounts instead of carrying around large sums in cash.

In one period, namely 1930–3, the volume of money in circulation increased by $1,199,000,000, despite the fact that the total compensation of employees was falling. Was this increase mainly due to hoarding?

Available banking statistics indicate that a factor other than hoarding was probably responsible for the increase. That factor was bank failures. Reports of the Federal Reserve Board show that total deposits in banks suspending operations in 1930–3 inclusive amounted to $6,859,000,000. Evidently the disappearance of this vast sum of deposit currency made the use of more pocketbook money essential. That the amount of new money actually coming into circulation was sufficient to offset only about one-seventh of the total shrinkage of deposits during the same period is revealed by Table IX. It also shows that total demand deposits diminished by more than eight billions at that time. In view of these facts, it cannot be said that the evidence thus far noted indicates the existence of any considerable amount of hoarding in the period 1930–3, even though individuals had on hand abnormally large supplies of pocketbook money. Since 1934, those habitually maintaining bank accounts appear to have settled down to their customary routines, and deposited as usual.

Between 1943 and 1946, the ratio of money in circulation to compensation of employees ran up sharply, and the demand for large denomination paper money increased. Did this indicate hoarding? Presumably not. There is every reason to believe that these happenings were both due to the rapid expansion of "black-market" operations. Since the use of checks in such illegal transactions was dangerous, it was necessary for the operators to carry with them large sums in pocketbook money, and, for this purpose, they found $100 to $1,000 bills to be much more convenient than were those of lower denominations.

In general, the table seems to indicate that the total volume of money in circulation has a very considerable degree of inertia. Thus, in 1920, in 1925–9, in 1934–5, and in 1937, it failed to expand in proportion to the expansion of wage payments. In 1946, after the termination of price control and hence of the black markets, the supply of pocketbook money shrank but slowly. Apparently inertia prevented the retirement of the excess supply of Federal Reserve notes.

Spendable Funds and the Demand for Goods

Those writers who attach great importance to the volume of "purchasing power" in the nation seem usually to assume that the presence of a large stock of spendable funds normally signifies the existence of strong demands for goods of all kinds. They can point out that, in boom times, money and deposit currency are both abundant, while in periods of depression both shrink in volume. They can emphasize the fact that possession of either money or deposit currency gives to the holder ability to select and secure any collection of goods purchasable for that sum of money. But this line of argument may be carried too far and prove too much.

Table IX shows that, even in 1933, when the depression was worst, the American people possessed nearly $22 billions of ready spendable funds. Suppose that, each day, the people decided to spend $20 billions. Someone else would receive every dollar spent. Therefore, on the next day, the population as a whole would still have $22 billions to spend. If they spent $20 billions on each day of the year, the total volume of business for the year would amount to $7,300 billions, or more than a hundred times the national income for that year. Would this not be a simple method of generating unheard-of prosperity? Since the Government could easily make more ready "purchasing power" by borrowing from the banks or printing more money, the sky would be the limit to the prosperity which could thus be conjured up!

The absurdity of the conclusions just reached makes it evident that the assumption that "purchasing power" is equivalent to a demand for goods is entirely untenable. In reality, the total amount of spendable funds on hand has very little influence indeed either upon the total demand for goods at any instant of time or upon the potential total physical volume of sales. All that the spendable funds total does is to place a ceiling upon the amount of buying which is likely to take place in a *very brief* period of time. It has no influence for any considerable period of time, for, as soon as money changes hands, it furnishes new "purchasing power" to the recipient.

Ordinarily, each well-to-do individual finds it imperative at all times to keep on hand checking accounts, money, or both, sufficient in amount to cover the balance required by his bank, to meet debts falling due, and to provide for possible emergencies. The sum of these items constitutes his reserve. Only *additional* funds are used to pay current bills and expenses. As regards cash reserves, what is true of the individual applies with equal force to business concerns. In both instances, only the cash on hand in *excess* of such reserves is ordinarily available to meet current expenses.

As a matter of fact, the total stock of spendable funds not held for reserves is probably but rarely large enough to cover the customary volume of buying for more than a few weeks or months at the most. It follows that, in buying goods for consumption or processing, the typical individual or concern is usually influenced but little by the size of his or its supply of spendable funds.

The fact remains, however, that, when the supply of circulating medium increases, prices tend to rise; when spendable funds dwindle, prices usually fall. Why is this? The forces producing such results are discussed in the next chapter.

Chapter X

THE EQUATION OF EXCHANGE
AND THE PRICE LEVEL

Note: Readers not interested in economic theory may prefer merely to skim this chapter.

The Value of Money in Terms of Other Goods

The fact is generally recognized that the value of one good in terms of another good is determined by the respective supplies of and demands for the two goods. Thus the value of corn in terms of eggs depends upon the supply of and demand for eggs as compared to the supply of and demand for corn. Since money, like corn, is a good, it follows naturally that the value of money in terms of eggs is similarly determined by the supply of and demand for money as compared to the supply of and demand for eggs.

However, money differs from other goods in that, as a rule, it is easily exchangeable for thousands of other goods, and is demanded mainly because of this ready exchangeability. The result is that people customarily evaluate other goods of all kinds in terms of the money unit. The value of another good in terms of money is referred to as its *price*.

For centuries, the fact has been observed that, at some times, there is a general tendency for the prices of most goods to rise, while, at other times, the tendency is for the prices of most goods to fall. This observation has led thoughtful persons to infer that something connected with the money is responsible for the general change in prices. Since investigation has shown that, as a rule, prices have risen in those times when money was becoming more abundant and fallen when its supply was diminishing, many persons have concluded that prices in general tend to vary directly with the supply of circulating medium.

At any given time, as Sir Josiah Stamp once pointed out, there is on hand a great mass of desirable things which have been produced by the joint efforts of Man and Nature. At the same time, human beings are in possession of numerous tokens which are readily exchangeable for these desired goods. These tokens consist of money and demand deposits.

One frequently-advanced hypothesis concerning the relationship between money and the price level is that, when tokens and goods balance, everything is in harmony. That this assumption is very far from the truth is brought out by the fact that, in 1936, as Table IX shows, our total circulating medium amounted to less than $27 billions, although, at that date, the value of private property in the United States was around $321 billions, or nearly twelve times as much.

A more common theory is that the more numerous the tokens in proportion to the aggregate of desired products, the larger tends to be the number of tokens which will be paid for the total supply of any good. Hence, when either the banks or the government create more tokens, and the supply of products is not increased proportionately, the average unit value of other goods, as measured in tokens, increases. It is contended further that this tendency is so strong that it commonly overcomes the most strenuous endeavors of governments to prevent it — "black markets" springing up and prices rising, despite legal restrictions backed by severe penalties.

However, the figures in Table XIII show that the assumption that changes in price averages tend to parallel closely increases in the volume of circulating medium sometimes is very far from the truth. Thus, between 1938 and 1944, the supply of money and demand deposits more than trebled, but the advances in the prices of commodities at wholesale or at retail and of the stocks of corporations ranged only from 15 to 32 per cent.

One thing which the just-mentioned theory clearly leaves out of account is the fact that the value of money, as measured in other goods, may be affected by the demand for it as well as by the supply of it. In reality, in studying changes in the value of money in terms of goods in general, one must evidently consider four factors:

1. The total supply of all other goods
2. The total demand for all other goods
3. The total supply of money
4. The total demand for money

However, as every mathematician knows, dealing with four variables at once is a very difficult task. Is there any way in which the problem can be made simple enough to be understandable by those not well versed in mathematics?

The Equation of Exchange

Recognition of the need for a readily comprehensible exposition of the relationships existing between circulating medium, goods volume, and the price level led that eminent physicist, astronomer, and economist, Simon Newcomb, to devise the "equation of societary circulation." Later this equation was analyzed by Edwin W. Kemmerer, and, still later, a more complete formulation was worked out and popularized by Irving Fisher under the title "the equation of exchange." The development of this new device for expressing economic relationships in mathematical terms has contributed greatly to a better understanding of the rôles of money and credit in our economy.

The Terms in the Equation of Exchange

The form in which the equation of exchange is customarily expressed today is

$$MV + M'V' = PT$$

To make this equation valid and meaningful, it is essential that each term be defined with precision. The following definitions are believed to fulfill this requirement:

M = the average number of dollars of pocketbook money in circulation during the period.

V = the average number of times during the period that each dollar of pocketbook money was paid out for commodities, securities, or services.

M' = the average number of dollars of deposit currency in existence during the period.

V' = the average number of times each dollar of deposit currency was checked out during the period in payment for commodities, securities, or services.

T = the number of units of commodities, securities, and services PAID FOR during the given period by transfer of either money or checks.

P = the average price in dollars per unit of all goods PAID FOR during the given period by transfer of money or checks.

From the definitions just given, it follows that, for the stated period in the nation

MV = the total of all *money* paid for commodities, securities, or services.

$M'V'$ = the total of all *checks* paid for commodities, securities, or services.

PT = the total value of all commodities, securities, or services paid for by the transfer of money or checks.

In considering the natures of the terms just defined, several cautions are necessary. For instance, it is difficult to say just what money is actually "in circulation." Statistics furnished by the Director of the Mint on "money in circulation" cover all money in the United States outside of the Treasury and the Federal Reserve Banks. Some of it changes hands frequently, some of it but rarely. M' covers all demand bank deposits. Every such deposit is counted as circulating, even though some accounts lie dormant for years. Moreover, when a man with a thousand-dollar bank balance checks out ten dollars, there is no way of connecting his check with any particular fraction of his credit balance at the bank. Under such circumstances, V', the average velocity of circulation of all demand deposits cannot be other than a purely mathematical concept. It represents total check payments, $M'V'$, divided by M', the average amount of demand deposits in existence during the period.

Some writers dealing with the equation of exchange have made the error of defining P and T in terms of goods BOUGHT during the given period. With these terms defined in that way, it will be a mere coincidence if $PT = MV + M'V'$, for goods bought in one period are often paid for in later periods. On the other hand, when P and T are made to apply to the goods PAID FOR in the given period, it is evident that PT must equal $MV + M'V'$; for, when the terms are thus defined, what the equation states is that total payments equal total receipts — a truth that cannot well be denied.

Difficulty of Measuring the Terms Statistically

The reader has doubtless noted that T is defined as the total number of *units* of commodities, securities, or services paid for in the given period, and that P is the average price per *unit*. The question at once arises as to what is to be called a *unit*. It is obviously absurd to add one horse to one apple and call the sum two units. For this problem, Irving Fisher appears to have offered the only practical solution proposed to date. It is to define as one combining unit the quantity of any good selling for one dollar at a particular date selected as "the base", and, AT ALL OTHER DATES, to keep this physical quantity UNCHANGED. Thus, if eggs were selling for 40 cents per dozen at the base date, 2½ dozens of eggs would, *at all dates*, constitute one combining unit. If coal were worth $10 per ton at the base date, 1/10 of a ton of coal would, *at all dates*, be counted as one *combining unit*.

The real difficulty of measuring statistically either T or P in the equation of exchange is that many of the commodities, securities, and services are not standardized, and hence it is impracticable to define clearly the size of the combining unit. For example, if a horse sells for $100 at the base date, the combining unit would evidently be 1/100 of that horse, but that horse may be very different indeed from other horses sold at the same or other dates. The difficulty of ascertaining the number of combining units of unstandardized commodities sold has confined the usefulness of the equation of exchange primarily to theoretical illustrative purposes. As long as a large proportion of articles sold are unstandardized, its usefulness will presumably continue to be so limited.

The Price Level

A concept which is of great importance in economic discussions is P, the average price of all units paid for, or, in other words, the *price level.* Irving Fisher devised an illustration which makes it easy to understand this concept. He imagined a lake in which both the inflow and outflow of the water are controlled by gates. The average elevation of the lake's surface above that of the sea represents the *price level*. Each square foot of the lake's surface may be thought of as representing the relative price of some specific article. When the wind blows, the elevations of the respective small units of the lake's surface will fluctuate. Such wave effects represent movements in individual prices. The fact to be noted is that, no matter how violent the wind, the average altitude of the lake's surface remains unchanged. For like reasons, individual price changes never affect the price level. If one wave is unusually high, that very fact means that some other parts of the lake's surface must be depressed sufficiently to offset the volume of the wave mentioned. Similarly, as long as the price level is unchanged, relatively high prices for some articles always mean relatively low prices for other articles. The underlying economic reason why this is true is that, if buyers spend more of their total combined income for one thing, they necessarily must spend less of their combined income for other articles.

Thus when, at the close of World War II, the Federal Government kept the prices of various goods below the levels which would have been established by competition, and also employed rationing to limit the buying of various necessities, individuals used larger than normal fractions of their incomes to buy luxuries and non-rationed goods. The natural result was that prices of such things as costume jewelry rose several hundred per cent. Had it not been for the fact that the regulations imposed by the Federal Government hampered production and thus affected T, and probably V and V', the effect of such regulations upon the general price level would presumably have been nil. Since, as we shall see later, trade and velocity of circulation tend to fluctuate in the same proportions, the probabilities are that the activities of the Office of Price Administration failed to affect materially the average of all prices. What this agency really accomplished was to raise non-controlled prices and drive a large part of the nation's trade into "black markets."

Basic and Derived Prices

The volume of trade, T, is made up of exchanges of two different types of goods:

1. Direct or consumption goods — for example, food, clothing, housing, and entertainment.
2. Indirect goods — for example, mines, factories, office buildings, raw materials, stocks, and bonds.

As previously indicated, P, the price level, represents the average unit price of ALL commodities, securities, and services paid for during the given period. We shall hereafter use the small letter p to indicate the average unit price of all DIRECT OR CONSUMPTION goods paid for during the given period.

It is well to keep in mind the fact that the only prices which are basic are those of direct goods. All other prices are merely more or less imperfect reflections of direct-goods prices which are expected to exist at later dates. Thus, flour prices represent, primarily, discounted anticipated future prices of bread. Wheat prices, in turn, are governed mainly by the anticipated future prices of flour. The value of a Saskatchewan wheat farm reflects guesses concerning the probable future course of wheat prices. Both potential buyers and potential sellers of indirect goods such as grains, livestock, raw materials, machines, buildings, and land, must usually pile guesses upon guesses about future supplies, future demands, and future interest rates. Under such circumstances, it is not surprising to find that, while the prices of direct goods are reasonably stable, the prices of indirect goods respond to rumors of all kinds, and swing up or down with changes of public sentiment from optimism to pessimism, or vice versa.

It follows that the amplitude of fluctuation is likely to be much larger in the case of P, the average unit price of ALL goods paid for in the given period, than in the case of p, the average unit price of the aggregate of CONSUMPTION goods paid for in the same period. The ratio of P to p will, therefore, vary in size, being larger in times of optimism and smaller in times of pessimism. Let us use the letter O to indicate this index of optimism. Then $O = \dfrac{O}{p}$ and $P = Op$.

While the cyclical swings of the ratio O are considerable in size, there is no reason to believe that this ratio has any long-time tendency either to rise or fall. Presumably, it merely fluctuates about a horizontal norm or trend.

The Quantity Theory of Money

As stated earlier in the chapter, observation led, long ago, to the conclusion that, other things being equal, prices tend to vary *directly* with the amount of money in circulation. During the Nineteenth Century, certain economists concluded that any given percentage change in the volume of money normally causes an equal percentage change in P, the general price level. This generalization came to be known as *the quantity theory of money.* This theory, if translated into the terms of the equation of exchange, would read as follows: *P varies directly and proportionately with M, and changes in P are caused by changes in M.*

At the end of the last century, this theory became a storm center of political controversy in the United States. Economists, as well as politicians, divided into two classes — defenders and opponents. Gradually, the issue faded into the background, but recently it has again been brought to the fore by the heated arguments between proponents and opponents of price control concerning the forces responsible for the price advances accompanying and following World War II.

The fact should be noted that, in the days when the quantity theory was first formulated, bank deposits constituted an unimportant fraction of the circulating medium. Now demand deposits make up the bulk of our currency supply. Does this change completely invalidate the quantity theory in its early form?

The answer is that it does not, for, as Irving Fisher has shown, the ratio of M' to M has a tendency to be reasonably stable, the two quantities being tied together by custom, by the necessities of trade, and by legal regulations.[1] Moreover, since the Federal Reserve System has been in existence, whenever M' increases, the spending of the newly-created deposit currency tends to strengthen the demand for Federal Reserve notes, and thus makes M tend to increase proportionally with M'. Under such circumstances, one would expect to find that, even though bank deposits came to make up the larger part of the circulating medium, the movements of M and P would still be directly and definitely correlated. Painstaking research [2] by Julius H. Spalding of New York University shows that such has been the case in most countries of the world. His findings are, of course, supported by the universally-known fact that monetary inflation has often resulted in skyrocketing prices.

However, Mr. Spalding's research also makes it clear that, in a country like the United States where credit currency makes up most of the circulating medium, the ratio of M' to M does vary somewhat with the passage of time. He shows further that, in such a nation, the correlation between M' and P is usually much closer than is the correlation between M and P. Furthermore, our experience in recent years with bank-deposit inflation demonstrates all too forcefully that an increase in M' tends to make prices rise. Under such circumstances, M' and not M is clearly the causal factor influencing P.

[1] *The Purchasing Power of Money,* The Macmillan Co. 1912 pp. 50–52.
[2] Unpublished manuscript.

The evidence seems, therefore, to prove that, whether changes are initiated in M or M', there is a marked tendency for the ratio of M to M either to remain roughly constant, or to change but slowly. It also indicates that variations in the quantity $M + M'$ (the total volume of circulating medium), do tend to cause proportional changes in P, the price level.

However, it would be erroneous to assume that changes in P are always at least approximately proportional to changes in M, M', or both, especially since recent experience in this country proves that such is far from being the case. For example, as Table XIII shows, the volume of money and deposits circulating in the United States rose between 1933 and 1946 from $21.79 to $126.28 billions, an increase of 480 per cent. Nevertheless, in the same period, wholesale prices rose but 84 per cent, the "cost of living" but 58 per cent, and stock prices, one of the most highly volatile constituents of P ran up only 83 per cent. Clearly, therefore, P (the price level) must have been influenced greatly by changes in V, V', or T.

Trade's Influence on the Price Level

Since T deals not with values but with units of services and material goods, there is a natural tendency to confuse it with production. As a matter of fact, however, the volume of trade is commonly far larger than the volume of production, for the typical product is likely to change hands several times before it is consumed. Furthermore, the number of times it turns over may differ under varying circumstances Moreover, many of the transactions entering into T, the volume of trade, pertain to such things as land and securities — things which are not what we usually class as "products."

Since $P = \dfrac{MV + M'V'}{T}$, it follows that, other things being equal, P must, perforce, vary inversely and proportionately with T, the volume of trade. It follows that T must always be regarded as an independent force affecting the size of P. Therefore, if, in any country, the volume of trade were to expand, and if both the volumes of money and demand deposits and their respective velocities of circulation were to remain constant, it is evident that P, the price level, would necessarily decline.

However, as a matter of fact, periods of increasing trade are not usually periods of falling prices. Why is this?

The explanation lies in the fact that the numerator and denominator of the fraction $\dfrac{MV + M'V'}{T}$ are not independent of one another. Carl Snyder showed [3] in a noteworthy study published a score of years ago that the oscillations of V' and T are closely correlated. For reasons which will be discussed in the next chapter, it seems certain that movements of V and V' are similar. It follows that there is a strong tendency for the fluctuations in V and V' to cancel those in T, thus allowing changes in M and M' to dominate P.

Inter-relationships in the Equation of Exchange

While the equation of exchange obviously balances, this mere fact tells us nothing whatever about causal relationships. Therefore, although the

[3] *Journal of the American Statistical Association*, Mar. 1924, pp. 36, 41.

Table XIII

RELATIVE FLUCTUATIONS
compared for
PRICES
and
THE VOLUME OF CIRCULATING MEDIUM

| Year | Price Indexes[a] | | | Total Circulating Medium (June 30) | |
	Wholesale (Base, 1926)	"Cost of Living" [b] (Base, 1923)	Stocks (Base, 1926)	Billions of Dollars[c] M"	Relatives (Base, 1926)
1919	138.6	102.3	70.7	$27.88	91.4
1920	154.4	118.2	64.2	29.38	96.2
1921	97.6	102.3	55.2	26.47	86.8
1922	96.7	97.4	67.7	26.09	85.3
1923	100.6	100.0	69.0	27.33	89.5
1924	98.0	101.3	72.8	28.22	92.5
1925	103.5	103.7	89.7	30.00	98.3
1926	100.0	104.3	100.0	30.52	100.0
1927	95.4	102.0	118.3	30.38	99.4
1928	96.7	100.6	149.9	30.71	100.8
1929	95.3	100.1	190.3	29.30	96.0
1930	86.4	96.7	149.4	28.92	94.8
1931	73.0	87.2	94.7	26.59	87.1
1932	64.8	77.9	48.6	22.64	74.2
1933	65.9	74.9	63.0	21.79	71.4
1934	74.9	79.4	72.4	24.63	80.8
1935	80.0	82.2	78.3	27.95	91.6
1936	80.8	84.1	111.0	32.79	107.6
1937	86.3	87.8	111.8	34.05	111.8
1938	78.6	85.7	83.3	32.91	107.9
1939	77.1	84.5	89.2	36.74	120.7
1940	78.6	85.3	78.1[b]	41.82	137.0
1941	87.3	89.0	66.1[b]	49.55	162.6
1942	98.8	97.7	69.8[b]	55.26	181.1
1943	103.1	103.3	84.4[b]	84.97	278.4
1944	104.0	104.6	96.4[b]	106.09	347.6
1945	105.8[b]	107.0[b]	128.5[b]	123.47[b]	404.6
1946	121.1[b]	118.4[b]	115.6[b]	126.28[b]	413.8

[a] Yearly averages. See the U. S. *Survey of Current Business,* 1940 Supplement, pp. 11–12, and 75; and Jan. 1941, p. 18, Feb. 1941, p. 58, and the Mar. issues for later years, p. S-3 in each.

[b] Extended from 1939 on the basis of the combined index given in the U. S. *Survey of Current Business,* Feb. 1945, p. 22, and Feb. 1947, p. S-42.

[c] See Table IX.

equation may be correctly written $P = \dfrac{MV + M'V'}{T}$, we are not justified in inferring from this form of statement that P is always the passive resultant of changes in the other five quantities in the equation. As a matter of fact, changes in P may give rise to changes in the other terms. Thus when, in 1933–34, the United States Treasury gradually marked up the paper money price of gold from \$20.67 to \$35.00 per ounce, there was an immediate and almost proportional rise in the paper-dollar prices of those commodities entering largely into or markedly affected by international trade, and there occurred no corresponding decline in the prices of other commodities.[4] Here we have, therefore, a definite instance of a change in P having forced changes in other factors in the equation of exchange.

Even if all of the other terms in the equation of exchange were entirely passive, optimism among speculators would tend to increase P, while pessimism on their part would tend to make it smaller. This would be true because, when people are optimistic, their estimates of the prospective future incomes to be derived from indirect goods such as stocks and real estate expand, while, at the same time, their estimates of the probability of future losses connected with the ownership of such goods shrink. In other words, as long as the boom psychology persists, most speculators look forward to increased dividend rates, higher rents, and few business failures. Hence their present valuations of these anticipated incomes expand, and they therefore raise their bids or asking prices for the real estate or securities in which they are interested. Such action naturally results in higher market prices for such indirect goods. Furthermore, at the same time, most people look for more building, plenty of plant expansion, and enlarged consumption. Hence raw materials and foodstuffs also tend to advance in price.

Such price advances during waves of optimism are almost invariably accompanied by speculation. Moreover, persons engaged in speculation nearly always desire to borrow from the banks in order to multiply their anticipated profits. Such borrowing increases M', the volume of demand deposits. The more money borrowed, the stronger is the demand for the goods in which speculation is rife, and the more do the prices of these goods rise. But as the speculative commodities, securities, or real estate become more valuable, the larger are the amounts which banks will lend thereon, hence M' expands further. The upward spiral usually continues until optimism gives way to doubt. Then the top heavy credit structure collapses. Throughout, however, M' has not, as the modernized quantity theory of money often assumes to be the case, been constantly the principal causal factor. Instead, it has intermittently caused price changes, and intermittently been the result of these changes.

The preceding discussion of the forces influencing the various factors in the equation of exchange makes two points clear:

1. The quantity theory of money offers only a partial explanation of the forces bringing about changes in P, the price level.

---

[4] See the present writer's article in the *Journal of the Amer. Stat. Assn.* for June, 1935, pp. 388 to 394.

2. The equation of exchange facilitates greatly an understanding of the relationships existing among money, deposit currency, trade, and the price level.

Forces Determining the Absolute Level of Prices

Since V, V', and T are to a considerable extent interrelated quantities, no one has been too sure as to exactly how the absolute level of prices is determined. While the evidence cited above shows that P tends to be determined primarily by M and M', it still leaves us in doubt as to how to answer the following baffling question: —Suppose that official Federal reports indicate that money and demand deposits in circulation total $50 billions; ought this quantity of circulating medium to make eggs sell at 40 cents or $10 per dozen? sugar at a nickel or a dollar per pound? Apparently, few students of monetary science have even attempted to unravel this mystery.

However, in his admirable pioneer work — *The Purchasing Power of Money,* pages 83 to 87, Irving Fisher gave the key to the solution when he called attention to the importance of the normal interval of time elapsing between successive receipts of income. He pointed out that a typical income recipient — for instance, a wage worker — tends to make his money supply last from one pay day to the next. However, Professor Fisher did not carry his analysis to its ultimate conclusion. When it is extended by the aid of a little relatively simple algebra, it becomes evident that p, the average level of prices of all the goods consumed during a given period depends upon the following four things: [5]

1. The quantity of cash in the hands of consumers.
2. The quantity of direct goods becoming available and being purchased by consumers.
3. The prevailing habits of the public regarding consuming and saving.
4. The average for all individuals of their respective time intervals between major receipts of income — for example wage or salary payments.

---

[5] Thus we know that, with various individuals, periods between customary dates of income receipt differ greatly. Some workers are paid weekly, some bi-weekly, others monthly. A Dakota wheat farmer may raise nothing but wheat, and sell his crop but once a year. Since wage and salaried workers make up the most numerous class of our population, and since they are usually paid once a week, or once a month, the probability is that, for the average American, the period intervening between regular receipts of income is somewhere between 7 and 30 days in length.

Fortunately, the problem can be analyzed algebraically without determining this figure statistically. We shall, therefore, hereafter merely use the letter i to designate this average time interval.

It appears that, in our endeavor to discover just what forces determine the absolute level of prices, our work will be simplified if we abbreviate the equation of exchange by using a single term for the entire circulating medium. Therefore, we shall let $M + M' = M''$. We shall also let V'' equal the number of times during any specified period that M'' was used in payment for goods. In this more compact form, the equation of exchange may be written $M''V'' = PT$. Transposed, it becomes $V'' = \dfrac{PT}{M''}$.

In addition, we shall let the letter m'' equal the sum of the money and demand deposits *in the hands of the consuming public*. It appears probable that the consuming public's share of the total circulating medium has a trend which is roughly horizontal. In a broad way, therefore, it seems reasonable to assume that $\dfrac{M''}{m''} = k$, a constant.

Since P, the general price level, is closely related to p, the average price of goods consumed, we seem justified in concluding that the only effective way to manipulate P, the general price level, is to make changes in the quantity of circulating medium or the volume of production, for the tendency of people to consume or to reserve cash for future use is something which it is difficult to control. This conclusion is entirely contrary to the widely prevalent view that the price level responds to manipulations of wage rates by labor unions or commissions. Labor leaders commonly assert that, if expenses of production are increased by raising wages or the prices of materials, and if, as a result, the business concerns affected are forced to increase

---

Obviously, a large part of this cash on hand is RESERVED for purposes other than the purchase of direct or consumption goods, being set aside, for example, to invest, to cover obligations falling due later, or to meet emergencies of one kind or another. We shall designate this *reserve fraction* by r. We shall also let the letter f stand for the *fraction* of their total cash on hand (including demand deposits) which consumers spend for consumable goods, either material or immaterial, before the respective dates when they next receive their cash incomes. Evidently $f + r = 1$, in other words the two fractions are complements.

We may illustrate the nature of these fractions by the case of the Smith family which possessed a checking account of $480 and $20 in pocketbook money. Mr. Smith earns $50 per week, and, on the average, spends the same amount weekly for living expenses. Therefore, for the Smith family,

$$r = \frac{\$450}{\$500} = \frac{9}{10} \text{ and } f = \frac{\$50}{\$500} = \frac{1}{10}$$

In the case of individual families, these fractions doubtless shift from day to day, but, for the nation as a whole, they probably have fair degrees of stability over any short period of time, even though they may possibly be materially different in times of pessimism from what they are in times of optimism.

Since, by definition, the interval i is one in which no income is received, it follows that, in that interval, expenses are normally paid out of money or bank deposits on hand. Therefore, the amount paid out during Period i for direct or consumption goods must be fm''. If we let q equal the number of physical units of direct or consumption goods paid for by consumers in Period i, and, if we let the average price per unit paid for all such direct or consumption goods in the same period be designated by the letter p, then, clearly, pq equals the total value of direct goods bought by consumers. Therefore pq must equal fm''.

For the convenience of the reader, the various terms just defined will now be summarized:

i = average period of time intervening between major receipts of income
M'' = total volume of circulating medium
m'' = total circulating medium in the hands of the consuming public
f = fraction of m'' spent in Period i for consumption goods
r = fraction of m'' not spent in Period i for consumption goods
q = number of physical units of consumption goods bought by consumers in Period i
p = average price per physical unit paid for all consumption goods bought by consumers in Period i
P = average price per unit of ALL goods paid for in Period i
O = $\dfrac{P}{p}$ = the index of optimism

As stated above $fm'' = pq$ = total amount spent for consumption goods in Period i. Hence, $p = \dfrac{fm''}{q}$, and $\dfrac{p}{m''} = \dfrac{f}{q}$. Furthermore, $P = Op$. Since f, m'', and q can all be expressed in absolute terms, the same is true of p.

Information concerning the absolute sizes of these quantities is lacking. However, the figures which follow probably have some resemblance to the actual sizes of f and m''. It will be observed that f is a very small fraction. This is, of course, due to the fact that the typical family keeps on hand a very sizable reserve of cash. Thus, for example, if it be assumed that:

m'' = $18,000,000,000
q = 1,500,000,000 physical units
f = 0.1

Then $p = \dfrac{0.1\,(\$18,000,000,000)}{1,500,000,000} = \dfrac{\$1,800,000,000}{1,500,000,000} = \$1.20$

In other words, the average price per unit of all goods consumed in Period i is $1.20, an absolute and not merely a relative number. The puzzle of what determines the *absolute* average unit price of direct or consumption goods has evidently been solved.

the prices of their products, this will cause no difficulty, inasmuch as higher wages and material prices will increase "purchasing power." This line of reasoning inevitably leads to the conclusion that the chief ultimate effect will be a higher price level. However, this conclusion is incorrect,[6] for, as indicated above, the price level, p, can, in practice, be pushed up only by increasing the supply of circulating medium or by cutting down production. But marking up wages or raw materials prices produces neither of these results. It appears, therefore, that, in the absence of inflation, attempts to pass on to customers increases in operating costs are foredoomed to failure.

Determinants of the Prices of Specific Goods

The respective prices of specific direct or consumption goods are determined by the way that consumers apportion their total consumption spending among the schedules representing respectively the demands for the various kinds of goods which they desire. To illustrate this fact let us take, for example, the case of John Smith. He brings home to his wife his weekly pay envelope containing $50. She lays aside $1 for insurance. This may increase very slightly the total family stock of cash held in reserve. She next sets aside $9 to pay for rent, and $2 for the gas bill. The remaining $38 she may apportion among thousands of possible articles of purchase running from awnings, beans, and butter to vinegar, yams, and zithers. Such tentative apportionments of income made by Mrs. Smith, Mrs. Jones, and millions of other potential buyers make up the demand schedules for the thousands of kinds of consumption goods offered for sale. These demand schedules, interacting with the millions of supply schedules of potential sellers of consumption goods, determine the market prices of all such goods, including the eggs and sugar mentioned above. If the demand for eggs happens to be particularly strong, or the eggs happen to be especially scarce, egg prices will rise, but the higher price for eggs will force housewives who buy eggs to reduce their demands for other articles.

But, as long as the nation's supply of circulating medium and the total volume of production both remain unchanged, any increase in the price of one article, say sugar, means that some other direct good must fall in price, for the average price, p, cannot change.

The above analysis not only assists us to solve the mystery of why sugar sells for a nickel instead of a dollar per pound, and eggs for forty cents instead of ten dollars per dozen; it also helps us to understand why the price of a dozen eggs equals that of eight instead of ten pounds of sugar.

Questions for Later Consideration

After wading through or skimming over this somewhat complex analysis of the price-determining mechanism, the typical practical-minded reader is likely to conclude that, while all this may be of interest to the monetary theoretician, it certainly has little bearing upon the problem of how to maintain prosperity in the United States of America. In reality, however, the purpose of this rather intricate algebraic treatment is to lay the foundation

---

[6] Thus, our equation $p = fm''$ shows that this line of reasoning is unsound, for p can advance only if f or m'' rises, or if q shrinks.

for an understanding of the fundamentals underlying some of the very practical economic issues which confront us from time to time.

For example, Dr. Townsend's disciples have always believed that the way to bring about prosperity is to make people spend their money more promptly. The use as currency of scrip which would diminish in value if not spent was advocated during the depression as a method of stimulating trade. Some theorists feel that bank deposits ought to be taxed in order to make them circulate faster. Do such proposals have any merit?

Whether they do or not depends primarily upon whether V'', the velocity of circulation, influences the volume of production. What is the rôle of velocity? Is it an active or a passive factor? Is velocity control one of the keys to prosperity? The next chapter constitutes an attempt to answer this question.

Chapter XI

THE VELOCITY OF CIRCULATION

Note: The first half of this chapter is intended primarily to help to clarify the thinking of students of economic theory. It is not essential to an understanding of the rest of the book that the reader master the algebraic formulae here presented.

Specialization and the Circulation of Non-Monetary Goods

In the preceding pages, much stress has been laid upon the rôle in our economy played by "circulating medium," the term here used to refer to money and demand deposits. It must, however, be admitted that, if other goods did not circulate, there would be little occasion for either money or bank deposits to circulate.

But why do other goods circulate? Evidently because the individual does not produce all the things which he and his family consume. And it is fortunate that he does not. As a matter of fact, the prosperity of the people of the United States depends largely upon the high degree of specialization prevailing here. The typical American adult works at a job for which he or she has been especially trained, and uses equipment particularly adapted to his or her needs. The products turned out by different persons are then exchanged. This method of production is far more efficient than is the system in which every family produces the things needed for its own use. It is, indeed, probable that, if each family in our nation were forced to become self-sufficing, a large proportion of our population would die of starvation.

Under the existing system of production for exchange, prosperity can be maintained only if goods can be kept moving steadily through the various stages of their preparation for use by consumers. When the products of farms, fisheries, and mines, flow regularly to the factories, and, after transformation, move on to wholesalers, retailers, and consumers, the nation flourishes. When, for any reason, the flow is impeded or retarded, prosperity declines.

The Essentiality of Money

This flow of goods would be practically impossible without the use of money or checks. Were there no circulating medium, our whole economic system would break down. For example, it would obviously be impossible for the minister to pay his light bill by doing a little preaching at the power plant, or for the weaver in a Massachusetts cotton mill to weave an hour or two to pay a Californian for a few oranges from his trees. Our nation's prosperity depends, therefore, upon the fact that goods in process move continuously through the productive mechanism toward the consumer, and that money and demand deposits move as continuously in the opposite direction.

The circulating medium flows around a complete circuit. As it is used to buy other goods, it generates a counterflow of these other goods, a counterflow which is capable of being continued indefinitely *as long as these other goods are not consumed.*

The flow of goods produced for consumption is, however, discontinuous, being broken by the act of using up or consumption.

The Two Broad Categories of Trade.

The nation's physical volume of trade, *T*, is not homogeneous, but is made up of two distinct segments:

1. Trade in goods not destined for consumption in the near future.
2. Trade connected with production and consumption.

These two types of trade differ greatly in their natures and behaviors. Thus stocks, bonds, and land move round and round the circuit indefinitely, for their purchase or sale has no tendency to lessen their quantity. In this respect, they differ radically from goods destined for consumption — for example, food and clothing. When goods of this latter type reach the hands of ultimate consumers, trading in them usually stops. Speculative activity centers about goods of the first type.

Forces Determining Turnover Rates for Goods.

The forces governing the numbers of turnovers of goods in process of production are very different from those governing the numbers of turnovers of speculative goods. The number of times that a speculative good may be exchanged in a year is unpredictable, being determined merely by the height of the speculative fever in the community. On the other hand, the number of turnovers of goods in process is rather closely defined by the degree of "roundaboutness" characterizing the system of production and trade prevailing in the nation at the time. Thus it is evident that, if every family used only its own products, there would be no turnover whatever. If every producer sold his products directly to ultimate consumers, each good would turn over but once. On the other hand, when products of mines are sold to jobbers who sell to manufacturers who sell to other manufacturers who sell to wholesalers who sell to retailers who sell to consumers, each good in process turns over at least half-a-dozen times.

It follows that the economic system prevailing in a region may greatly affect the average number of times that goods are turned over in that area. For example, in some nations, a large part of farm produce may be taken directly by farmers to ultimate consumers. In the United States, however, farm products may move through a chain of dealers consisting perhaps of commission firms, manufacturers, jobbers, wholesalers, and retailers, the last named finally selling the finished products to consumers. The number of exchanges depends, therefore, upon the way in which the nation's industries operate.

By contrast, the degree of specialization prevailing has practically no direct connection with the rate of turnover of speculative goods. A given share of stock or a specific piece of land may change ownership a dozen times in a year without affecting in any way the total supply of stock or land. Therefore, speculative goods may have turnovers which are very different from those applying to goods used in facilitating the productive process. These differences may be analyzed algebraically. If we let

a = the average aggregate number of units of goods participating in the productive process,

n = the average number of times that each unit of such goods was turned over during the period,

a' = the average aggregate number of units of speculative goods in the nation in the period,

n' = the average number of times that each unit of speculative goods was turned over during the period,

then, evidently

$$T = a n + a' n'.$$

Trade Composition a Determinant of Average Currency Velocity.

It was shown in the last chapter that $V'' = \dfrac{P}{M''} T$. Substituting for the value of T in this equation, we get $V'' = \dfrac{P}{M''}(a n + a'n')$.

This last equation helps us to understand why velocity is largely dependent upon the way in which the economy of the nation is organized. Thus, other things being equal, if every product of a farm or mine changed ownership ten times before it reached the consumer, the size of n would be twice as great as it would be if such goods turned over on the average only five times. It follows that the velocity of circulation of money and deposits is influenced materially by the degree of vertical integration existing in industry, for if one concern controls the entire productive process from its basic origin to the final consumption, there will be few changes of ownership, and this will tend to make n, and hence V'', small. If, on the contrary, there are many layers of middlemen, the velocity of circulation of both commodities and currency will be relatively high. Since the degree of vertical integration in industry prevailing in boom times is probably no larger than that existing when times are dull, there is no reason to believe that n is affected materially by cyclical variation in business activity; in fact, it probably changes but very slowly, responding merely to the gradual modifications of the industrial structure of the nation.

By contrast, n', the number of turnovers of speculative goods, doubtless fluctuates with every change in speculative sentiment. Here we have the factor primarily responsible for sharp fluctuations both in T, the volume of trade, and in V'' the velocity of circulation of money and demand deposits. This fact has been emphasized by Irving Fisher.

Why Trade and Velocity Fluctuate Similarly.

Since, as previously noted, Carl Snyder discovered that the fluctuations of V' and T are both very similar, the probabilities are that the oscillations of V'' and T greatly resemble one another. There are two reasons for believing that such is the case.

1. Since V'' includes V', and since check payments total far more than money payments, the natural result is that V' tends to dominate V''.
2. Monetary payments are largely duplicated by check payments. For example, the well-to-do citizen cashes a check, and gradually pays out the proceeds for goods. The employer also draws on the bank in order to get money to pay his employees.

The question now to be considered is how to explain the close relationship between trade and currency velocity which Carl Snyder found to exist. For reasons stated above, it seems probable that the cyclical variations in n are negligible. This being true, the correlation between V'' and T must be due to some relationship between V'' and one or more of the other components of T.

It has already been shown that, in the equation $V'' = \dfrac{P}{M''}(a\,n + a'n')$ the factor most influential in producing fluctuations in V'' is probably n'. In boom times, it usually runs up sharply. In such periods, new securities are usually issued in large volume, hence a', the volume of goods subject to speculation also expands. It follows that the quantity $a'n'$ usually varies directly with the degree of optimism prevailing.

Since production increases in times of prosperity, the term a will then be larger than in times of depression. Other things being equal, this will tend, in prosperous periods, to make the quantity $a\,n$ larger than normal. It will therefore reinforce the influence of $a'n'$ in making V'' larger in times of business activity than when business is dull.

However, in war time, this tendency may not prevail, for the increase in a may be partially or completely offset by a decline in n, a decline brought about by the fact that manufacturers sell huge volumes of goods directly to the Government, no middlemen being involved. This short-circuiting of trade evidently tends to lower n, and hence V''. Under normal circumstances, however, V'', the average velocity of circulation of money and deposits, tends to be relatively low in times of industrial stagnation. The analysis just set forth makes clear the respective effects of a, and a', n and n' upon the velocity of circulation of money and deposit currency. But the equation presented above shows that V'' varies not only with $(a\,n + a'n')$ but also with the fraction $\dfrac{P}{M''}$. How is this fraction affected by the fluctuations of business?

The Price — Currency Ratio and Velocity.

Observation seems to indicate that this fraction, as well as T, has a strong tendency to expand in times of optimism, and to shrink in times of pessimism. Apparently, it commonly so behaves because, in general, the average of prices, P, is more flexible than is the volume of circulating medium, M''. There are four reasons why the latter quantity tends to be the more rigid:

1. The volume of certain types of governmentally-issued money, for example, coins, treasury notes, and silver and gold certificates, are, in general, practically unaffected by shifts in public attitudes.
2. Deposits not originating in loans are not likely to vary greatly merely because people are becoming more optimistic or more pessimistic.
3. The volume of demand deposits outstanding against securities does not always respond promptly to changes in public sentiment.
4. In periods of recession, businessmen cannot pay off their indebtedness to banks until their notes fall due. This causes the decline in M' to lag behind the decline in P.

For these four reasons, it is evident that a sharp drop in prices is likely to cause the fraction $\dfrac{P}{M''}$, and hence V'', to diminish in size. It is also clear that, as business picks up after a depression, the supply of governmentally-issued money may well remain nearly stationary. Furthermore, those deposits based upon money or securities will not necessarily expand, and, in many cases, businessmen will not find it necessary to borrow at banks until the demand for goods has risen well above its depression level. Therefore P will grow faster than M'', and hence V'' will tend to rise. If we had at hand an accurate index showing the actual fluctuations of P, the general price level, it would be easy to test the validity of the above hypothesis. Unfortunately, no such index exists, and it is extremely difficult to construct one. However, there are available numerous index series showing the fluctuations of the prices of various classes of goods. The index numbers presented in Table XIII (in the previous chapter) cover three very important categories, commodities sold at wholesale, goods sold at retail to urban workers, and the stocks of more than four hundred large corporations. By aid of these indexes, we can see to what extent fluctuations in the fraction $\dfrac{P}{M''}$ conform to the premises laid down above. The data set forth in this table show that, in the 1920–21 recession, all classes of prices dropped decidedly more than did the supply of money and deposit currency. Between 1922 and 1929, both the volume of circulating medium and prices of tangible goods moved in narrow limits, but stock prices rose sharply. In the 1929 to 1933 collapse, wholesale prices and the "cost of living" declined in somewhat the same degree as did the volume of circulating medium, but the precentage drop in stock prices was more than twice as great. The statistics for the period 1919 to 1933 tend therefore to confirm the hypothesis advanced above that P fluctuates more widely than M''.

However, the fact must not be overlooked that all of these hypotheses refer solely to the *short-term* movements of the fraction $\dfrac{P}{M''}$. They do not cover *trend* forces. Therefore, it is not at all surprising to find that, during the inflationary period accompanying World War II, the commodity price rise did not keep up relatively with the expansion of the nation's supply of money and demand deposits, and that, between 1939 and 1941, stock prices actually fell. But since the trend as well as the fluctuations of the fraction $\dfrac{P}{M''}$

affect V'', we cannot completely analyze the problem of velocity until we go further into the relationships existing among P, M'', and V''.

Table XIV

AN INDEX OF THE VELOCITY OF MOVEMENT
OF OUR STOCK OF CIRCULATING MEDIUM

Year	A Debits to Individual Accounts in 141 Cities[a] (Billions) (Index of M'V')	B Total Amount of Deposit Currency[d] (June 30) M' (Billions)	C Index of Velocity $\dfrac{A}{B}$
1919	$455	$23.00	19.7
1920	483	23.91	20.2
1921	399	21.56	18.5
1922	439	21.63	20.2
1923	464	22.51	20.6
1924	492	23.37	21.1
1925	570	25.18	22.6
1926	608	25.63	23.7
1927	674	25.53	26.4
1928	806	25.91	31.1
1929	935	24.65	37.9
1930	662	24.40	27.1
1931	481	21.77	22.1
1932	322	16.95	19.0
1933	300[b]	16.07	18.7
1934	332	19.26	17.3
1935	374	22.38	16.7
1936	429	26.55	16.1
1937	433	27.60	15.7
1938	374	26.45	14.1
1939	390	29.69	13.1
1940	409	33.97	12.0
1941	492	39.94	12.3
1942	553[c]	46.34	11.9
1943	688[c]	67.55	10.2
1944	776[c]	83.59	9.3
1945	850[c]	96.72	8.8
1946	907[c]	98.04	9.3

[a] *Statistical Abstract of United States:* for 1934, p. 257 and 1942, p. 329.
[b] Rough estimate.
[c] United States *Survey of Current Business,* March 1943, p. S–14, Sept. 1943, p. S–15, March 1944, p. S–15, and March 1945, p. S–14; March 1946, p. S–14; March 1947, p. S–15. (adjusted to the basis of earlier years by dividing by 1.04).
[d] See Table IX.

Relation of Velocity to Currency Supply.

The fact was brought out in the previous chapter that P does not always vary directly and proportionally with M'', the total supply of money and demand deposits. This lack of close correspondence in the movements of P and M'' has led a school of writers on monetary problems to conclude that an increase in M'' is usually offset by a decrease in V'', leaving P practically unaffected, and hence that inflation is innocuous, and can be indulged in with impunity. They also contend that, because of this offsetting tendency, any attempt to regulate the price level by varying the quantity of money or deposit currency is doomed to failure. In support of their position, they can cite the data in Table XIII. Reference to this table shows that, between 1926 and 1944, M'', the volume of circulating medium, increased by 247.6 per cent, yet prices of stocks, and of commodities at both wholesale and retail were not very different in the two years.

By referring to Table XIV, they can show further that the total volume of check payments was materially smaller in 1944 than in 1926, hence the failure of prices to rise can scarcely be ascribed to an increase in the volume of trade.

Why Velocity Remained Low from 1933 to 1937

Since movements of V' and T have, in the past, shown marked correlation, and since, during the late depression, trade was in the doldrums, it was not at all surprising to find velocity declining sharply from 1929 to 1933. But between 1933 and 1937, the Federal Reserve Board's index of industrial production moved up from 76 to 110,[1] and, in addition, speculation increased markedly. It therefore appears certain that, during this period, T expanded greatly. Under such circumstances, one might expect that V' would have risen sharply. However, in fact, the reverse was true, for Table XIV shows that, instead of rising, the index of velocity continued its decline — falling from 18.7 to 15.7. How is this behavior to be explained? A careful algebraic analysis[2] indicates that, for one reason or another, the period

---

[1] U. S. *Survey of Current Business,* 1940 Supplement, p. 7.

[2] The figures in Table XIV deal exclusively with deposit currency, and Column C of that table is an index of V', the velocity of demand deposits, and gives no record of V'', the velocity of all currency. However, for reasons stated earlier in the chapter, it seems probably that the movements of V' and V'' are very similar.

It will be remembered that, for Period i,

T = the number of units of services, commodities, and securities paid for in the given period.

P = the average price paid per unit for all goods

q = the number of units of consumption goods paid for in the given period

p = the average price paid per unit for consumption goods

O = $\dfrac{P}{p}$ = the index of optimism

Therefore, $P = Op$

M'' = the total volume of circulating medium

m'' = the volume of circulating medium in the hands of consumers, and that $\dfrac{M''}{m''} = k$, and,

therefore, $M'' = km''$

f = the fraction of m'' paid for consumption goods in the given period

$fm'' = pq$. Therefore, $\dfrac{p}{m''} = \dfrac{f}{q}$.

Substituting in the equation $V'' = \dfrac{P}{M''} T$ we get $V'' = \dfrac{Op}{km''} T = \dfrac{O}{k} \dfrac{p}{m''} T$. Since $\dfrac{p}{m''} = \dfrac{f}{q}$ it

1933 to 1937 was marked by a tendency on the part of consumers to increase the proportions of their respective cash holdings reserved for future use. Now an increase in such reserves may indicate the presence of hoarding. On the other hand, the fraction of available cash not spent for purposes of consumption may be invested promptly by putting it into the savings bank or using it to purchase life insurance, securities, war bonds, or other income-yielding property. Therefore, the evidence thus far presented does not enable us to determine whether or not the relative increase in reserves indicated a tendency to hoard rather than to invest. This question will be taken up in a later chapter. All that we have proved is that there was an increase in reserves at the expense of spending for consumption. This change may have been caused by distrust of New Deal policies, by pessimism concerning the investment outlook, by caution brought on by the prevalence of unemployment, or by some other reason.

Why Velocity Remained Low After 1937

The index of velocity recorded in Table XIV shows that the tremendous production expansion connected with World War II failed to stop the decline in V', the velocity of circulation of bank deposits. As previously pointed out, one reason why V' continued to slide down was that the Federal Government bought directly from manufacturers vast quantities of supplies.[3] During the war period, rationing, accompanied by the persistent pressure to buy war bonds, was another force keeping velocity low. It had this effect for two reasons:

---

follows that $V'' = \dfrac{O}{k}\dfrac{f}{q}T = \dfrac{O}{k}\dfrac{T}{q}f$. But $T = a\,n + a'n'$ (See preceding chapter; definition of letters are repeated below). Therefore $V'' = \dfrac{O}{k}\dfrac{f}{q}(a\,n + a'n')$. It will be remembered that the quantity k is assumed to be constant.

This equation, then makes it evident that in the absence of restriction by government, the speed with which money and demand deposits flow around the circuit is dependent primarily upon

O, the prevailing degree of optimism or pessimism.

f, the relative readiness of the public to spend cash for consumption goods instead of investing it or saving it for future use.

q, the quantity of goods purchased for consumption.

a, the volume of goods in the process of production.

n, the average number of turnovers of goods in the productive process. This quantity is governed by the degree of division of labor, and the state of integration prevailing in industry.

a', the stock of speculative goods on hand.

n', the average rapidity of turnover of speculative goods. This quantity reflects the presence or absence in the nation of speculative enthusiasm.

We are now ready to attempt to solve the problem of why, between 1933 and 1937, V', the velocity of circulation of demand deposits, declined instead of rising. In this attempt, we shall use the equation $V'' = \dfrac{O}{k}\dfrac{T}{q}f$ and shall assume that the index of V' presented in Table XIV serves satisfactorily as a measure of the movements of V''. What we know of the period 1933 to 1937 makes us almost sure that O increased. Since speculation also increased, it seems practically certain that the fraction $\dfrac{T}{q}$ likewise grew larger. If these assumptions are correct, it follows that the fall in V'' must have been explained by a shrinkage in f, the fraction of available cash spent for consumption goods.

[3] Such direct purchasing would obviously reduce n, the number of turnover of goods, and hence, since $V'' = \dfrac{O}{k}\dfrac{f}{q}(a\,n + a'n')$, would decrease the size of V' and V''.

1. Every purchase of a bond would increase reserves at the expense of consumption.
2. A thousand dollars spent for such bonds would not generate as many monetary transactions as would a thousand dollars spent for food or clothing.

Is Monetary Expansion Normally Offset by Velocity Retardation?

We now come to the consideration of a very important practical question: — *"Is it or is it not true that an increase in the outstanding quantity of money and demand deposits normally brings about an offsetting shrinkage in the velocity of circulation, so that the price level remains about the same whether we have $10 billions or $100 billions of money and deposits in circulation?"*

From the equation of exchange, we know that $P = \dfrac{M''V''}{T}$. If, in time of unemployment, new money or deposits are issued and used to buy goods, the first effect is to set people to work. This soon increases T. Until full employment is attained, there is then a very definite tendency for the increase in M'' to be offset by the increase in T, and hence P, the price level, does not rise. Eventually, however, everyone who can be induced to work is employed, and T stops growing. If, thereafter, M'' continues to expand, will its rise be offset by a decline in V'', with the result that prices will remain stationary?

It is not easy to answer this question categorically.[4] Abundant evidence in all countries indulging in runaway inflation proves conclusively that, whenever new money is created in large enough quantity, the price level invariably rises. However, where inflation is moderate in extent, there appears to be some tendency for people to increase the proportions of their respective incomes saved. In so far as this happens, the price level will not increase by as large a percentage as the increase in the supply of circulating medium.

---

[4] The question may be resolved into the following form — *After the unemployed have been set to work, will further expansions in M'' be offset by adjustments in O, f, or q, with the net result that P will not rise?*

In answering this question, a few more equations will help. One of these equations, $V'' = \dfrac{O}{k}\dfrac{f}{q}T$ appearing earlier in the chapter, becomes, when transposed, $\dfrac{V''}{T} = \dfrac{O}{k}\dfrac{f}{q}.$ We also know that $P = M''\dfrac{V''}{T}.$ Clearly, therefore, $P = M''\dfrac{O}{k}\dfrac{f}{q}.$ It will be remembered that k is assumed to be roughly constant, and it is improbable that increasing M'' will cause O to *shrink*. Since there are no more persons to be set to work, further increases in M'' are not likely to be offset by a growth of q. Therefore, if a further increase in M'' is to be offset at all, it must be brought about by a decline in f, the fraction of cash on hand spent for consumption, and hence an increase in r, the fraction of cash carried to reserves.

To secure dependable statistical evidence on this point is not easy. Reasoning abstractly, it seems probable that, in so far as increases in M'' cause rather sudden and marked increases in the money incomes of the people, there probably is a definite tendency to save a larger proportion of current income. In other words, it seems likely that, under such circumstances, r does increase at the expense of f. The reverse relationship probably holds when M'' is being rapidly contracted in volume. To the extent that such is the case, it obviously follows that large variations in M'' may be offset in whole or in part by changes in f. Since f is a component of V'', this means that changes in M'' may be counterbalanced to some extent by changes in the velocity of currency circulation.

Can Inflation be Indulged in With Impunity?

A second very practical question now emerges: *If there is a tendency for changes in M'' to be offset by changes in V'', does it follow that the danger that currency expansion will cause the price level to rise materially is too slight to justify any worry about it?* The answer is that, as the previously-mentioned studies by Julius H. Spalding of New York University show, such a conclusion runs counter to the actual experience at various times of most of the countries of the world. Inflation has wrecked the economy of nation after nation. In the United States, in spite of all offsets, the inflation accompanying World War II gradually pushed the price level upward, thus practically nullifying the strenuous endeavors of thousands of Federal and local officials to keep prices from rising. Everywhere, illegal increases offset in large measure legal restrictions. Everywhere legal price ceilings were forced to yield before the irresistible force of an increasing supply of spendable funds in the hands of the public.

Is Price-Level Control by Currency Manipulation Impracticable?

The third intensely practical question to be considered in this connection is: *Does the tendency for changes in V'' to offset changes in M'' make unworkable any attempt to regulate P, the price level, by varying the amount of circulating medium?*

The answer is that world-wide experience proves conclusively that changes in M'', if sufficiently large, will always force similar, though not necessarily proportional, changes in P. Therefore, the contention that it is non-feasible to regulate P by controlling M'' cannot be sustained.

Is Velocity a Causal Factor?

A point much disputed among students of the money problem is whether or not velocity is a causal factor or, instead, plays a purely passive rôle. Some of those who assume that it can influence the other factors in the equation of exchange have devised elaborate schemes for promoting the nation's welfare by manipulating V, V', or both. The indications are, however, that velocity is normally a resultant rather than a causal force,[5] but, as we shall see later, there is some evidence that governmental manipulation of velocity may exercise a causative influence on other factors in the equation of exchange.

Can Production be Controlled by Manipulating Velocity?

We now come to the fourth of the highly important practical problems which our excursion into the field of algebra will help us to solve. The problem may be stated thus: — *Can production, employment, and prosperity be increased or diminished by regulating V'', the velocity of circulation of money and deposit currency?* The belief is certainly widespread that any influence

---

[5] As we have seen, $V'' = \dfrac{O}{k}\dfrac{f}{q}(an + d'n')$, and since every one of the variables on the right-hand side of equation is determined by forces independent of V'', it appears that, in the absence of direct governmental regulation of V'', it must be regarded as a strictly dependent or passive variable having no causative characteristics whatever.

which makes money circulate rapidly is socially beneficial. It is, of course, true that, when currency velocity is high because of much speculative activity, brokers tend to prosper. However, the buyers and sellers of the speculative goods are "out of pocket" all the commissions paid to the brokers. Probably, therefore, the trading adds very little to the nation's prosperity. As a matter of fact, in times of undue speculative activity, it may even reduce the prosperity of the nation by using up the time of persons who might be engaged in more productive activities.

The fact that speculation is most active in times of prosperity indicates merely that, when people are optimistic and have large incomes, they are inclined to speculate more than they do in times of depression. The belief that the trading causes the prosperity is, therefore, easily explained, even though it has no foundation in fact.

The notion that prosperity could be restored by making money and deposits circulate more rapidly was especially prevalent in the earlier years of the 1930–1940 depression — a time when many persons became much worried about the general paralysis of business and the shrinkage in the volume of circulating medium. After 1933, as Table IX shows, the Federal Government pumped into circulation a steady stream of new money and demand deposits, yet business remained in the doldrums. Moreover, as Table XIV indicates, the velocity of deposit circulation, which was at a record-breaking low, not only did not rise, but continued to drift downward. Many economists, both of the conservative and radical schools, concluded that here lay a real cause of trouble. They decided that what prevented prosperity from returning was the fact that the newly issued money was being hoarded. The obvious conclusion was that the thing necessary to overcome the lethargy which had gripped the nation was to pry loose the hoarded funds. Several able economists sponsored "Buy Now" campaigns, oblivious of the fact that the people who respond to such a slogan and buy more this month, curtail next month's purchases by a like amount — the reason being that all the oratory and pleading have brought them no more income, and income can be spent only *once*.

Is Forced Spending for Consumption Sound Policy?

Inherent in many of the proposed plans was the dangerous idea that, in time of depression, anyone who has cash ought to use it to purchase consumption goods, the fact being overlooked that the man who so employs his accumulated savings will have nothing left for the rainy day which is all too likely to come to everyone.

The thrifty person, realizing this fact, normally invests sizeable sums in income-producing property. When he retains a considerable cash balance, it is either because he needs the cash for working capital, or because he expects prices to fall and hence considers immediate investment to be unwise. These facts are apparently overlooked by those who believe that the accumulation by individuals of substantial reserves of money and bank deposits is indefensible from the social standpoint.

Whatever their lines of reasoning, the fact remains that many persons, including some very competent authorities, have concluded that depressions are brought on by the hoarding of money and deposits, and, therefore, that, to prevent or to cure depressions it is necessary to find some method of stopping hoarding. They usually also hold that this end can be attained by speeding up V''', the velocity of circulation.

Schemes for Increasing Velocity

As previously mentioned, this theory appears to have been the basis of Dr. Townsend's plan, for he provided that the pensions which he sought for the aged were to be cancelled unless they were spent promptly. Presumably, the same point of view actuated those who advocated the issuance of stamped scrip which, by diminishing in value two per cent weekly, would be assured of rapid circulation. It seems also that the detailed plan to tax cash balances, worked out by C. William Hazelett, and presented in his book *Incentive Taxation,* rests upon a similar line of reasoning.

The Probable Effects of Forced Spending

The question now to be considered is what the actual effect of compulsory speeding up of velocity would be. It certainly seems most unlikely that compulsory spending would have any tendency whatever to increase the rate of turnover of goods being produced for market,[6] but it might speed up greatly the process of exchanging stocks, bonds, and speculative commodities. This, in fact, would probably be the primary result of any artificial regulation of V or V', for it appears evident that, if every owner of money or deposits were compelled to spend within a brief time all the cash he possessed, his natural defense would be to buy either securities or those commodities which could readily be resold. Several persons could easily agree to exchange securities as often as necessary, and, by so doing, they could comply with the demand for spending, and yet not affect materially their respective financial positions.

Mr. Hazelett has foreseen this likely method of evasion, and hence proposes to tax at the rate of 2 per cent all cash balances above $300 turned over less than 8 times during the year, and to exclude from the legal list of expenditures everything except the purchase of newly-created goods or services or *new* issues of securities.[7]

If such a law were to be put into operation in a period of recession, its effects would probably be somewhat as follows:

1. It would increase the average fraction of cash holdings spent; in other words, it would encourage some of the less thrifty to dissipate their cash reserves, and hence would increase the number of persons appearing on the relief rolls at a little later date.
2. It would temporarily cause a spurt of commodity buying, but this

[6] As previously noted, $V'' = \frac{O}{k} T \frac{f}{q}$ and $V'' = \frac{O}{k} (an + d'n') \frac{f}{q}.$ When one considers the nature of the terms involved, it seems highly improbable that the mere forced speeding up of V'' would tend to enlarge O, the index of optimism, increase a, the number of units of goods in process, or n, the rate of turnover of goods in process. It could scarcely change a, the amount of speculative goods in existence, but it might and presumably would stimulate n', the rate of turnover of speculative goods.

[7] C. William Hazelett, *Incentive Taxation,* p. 3.

tendency might be promptly offset to a considerable extent by a reduction in the volume of circulating medium, this reduction being brought about by the fact that business men would be stimulated to devise new ways of reducing their borrowings from banks, and hence their average deposit balances at banks. By so doing, they would, of course, lessen the total volume of circulating medium in the nation.

3. It would produce an artificially strong market for new issues of securities. As a result, the public would lose money in unseasoned and risky new ventures.

4. Existing corporations would take advantage of the situation to retire bonds and preferred stock, and to issue great volumes of short-term notes. This would weaken their financial structures.

5. Governments, too, would find it very easy to float short-term notes, and the net result would probably be to sink the governments deeper into debt.

6. If the Federal Government used the proceeds of note sales to retire its indebtedness to banks, the supply of deposit currency would be greatly reduced, thus accentuating the decline in business.

7. To evade the tax, people would convert their bank deposits into pocketbook money and would report to the authorities only part of their cash holdings. Reduction in checking balances would make the process of debt-payment less convenient, and the stocks of hidden money would enhance the profitableness of burglary.

8. The whole process would represent another encroachment on the institution of private property, for the Government would be taking away the right of the individual to spend his money when and as he chose — and this is a fundamental part of freedom. Already, our individual liberty has been curtailed far too much.

Clearly, therefore, plans to engender prosperity by speeding up velocity are fraught with many and serious dangers. What they really seem to offer is an opportunity to jump out of the frying pan into the fire. This opportunity, once understood, is not likely to appeal to thoughtful Americans.

The avowed aim of most of those who seek to eliminate depression by speeding up the velocity of circulation of our currency supply is to *stop hoarding,* thereby stimulating the demand for goods, and increasing production and employment. But just what do they mean by hoarding? Has it really been responsible for preventing prosperity? This subject will be discussed in the next chapter.

Chapter XII

HOARDING

Flows in an Ideal Economy

Under ideal economic conditions, buyers would receive a *steady* flow of income, they would spend their receipts regularly, and the flow of money and deposits would move around the circuit without a cross current. As it moved, it would generate a *steady* counterflow of goods, and the demand for these goods would give rise to a *steady* volume of production. As long as crops were good and peace prevailed, we would have perpetual prosperity.

Retardations of Circuit Flows

But this is not the way our economic machine really works. Just when our agriculture is flourishing, our factories humming, our railways operating near capacity, buying begins to slacken. When buying declines, our great industrial machine slows down. Unemployment appears. Profits decline. Idleness, with no pay envelopes, brings misery. What starts this disastrous chain of events? As already noted, the answer given, not only by popular writers but also by many economists, is that potential buyers have decided to "hoard" their money instead of spending or investing it. But exactly what is "hoarding"? How, if in any way, does it differ from saving?

The Nature of Hoarding

It is usually assumed that hoarding is a practice to be condemned as anti-social. However, one does not need to ponder the subject long before one discovers that any attempt to define hoarding on the basis of ethical significance is doomed to fail. To some, the man who lays away a goodly part of his income for a rainy day is commendably thrifty. To others he is a miser. The housewife who fills 200 cans with vegetables and stores them in her cellar is cited as a paragon of virtue who ought to be imitated by all her neighbors. Her sister, who buys up 20 cans because she foresees a shortage, and rationing, is condemned as a hoarder. We can be sure that practically every person who lays aside for the future money, or bank deposits, or material goods believes that he is doing the sensible, logical thing, and, in most cases, he is doubtless correct in his assumption, for, as we have seen, it is the saver rather than the spendthrift who not only forges ahead himself but who brings prosperity to the nation.

The discussion in earlier chapters has made it entirely clear that an increase in the volume of money or deposit currency is no indication whatever of the existence of "over-saving" or "under-spending." We have also learned that the paucity of new security buying since 1930 has not been due to any tendency to hoard. Must we then conclude that the amassing of money or other goods is never anti-social, and that all of the dither about "hoarding" and "under-spending" is a case of "tilting at windmills"? Are hoarding and saving really identical? As we have seen, saving has no tendency to

126

lessen the volume of spending. Does hoarding differ from spending in this respect? Before attempting to answer these questions, it may be worth while to consider a hypothetical situation which brings out some of the possibilities.

How Hoarding Might Produce Depression

Let us suppose that, owing to fear of famine, rationing, or some other untoward situation, each family in the nation had accumulated and now possessed food, clothing, and fuel sufficient to last for several months. Let us suppose, further, that the necessity for providing safeguards against future emergencies now seemed so imperative that every family decided that, for the immediate future, buying would be confined to the indispensable necessities. Since the future outlook was black, they would make no investments. What would be the result?

Evidently, most retail establishments would find themselves practically without customers. Therefore, they would order no goods from wholesalers. The wholesalers, in turn, would curtail their buying from manufacturers. The latter, lacking orders, would lay off help, or close down. Within a brief time, the whole industrial system of the nation would be paralyzed. And this paralysis would have been caused entirely by the failure of the people to continue *spending their incomes at their customary rates.*[1]

The term *hoarding,* when thus defined, is clearly not at all synonymous with *saving,* for hoarding, unlike saving, reduces the total volume of spending. From what has just been said, we must, then, conclude that the belief that under-spending may bring on a depression is not *necessarily* fallacious, for if, at any time, the total volume of spending in the nation shrinks, the flow of money and deposits around the circuit will diminish, and such diminution will almost certainly reduce the counterflow of goods, and soon cause unemployment.

Has Hoarding Generated Depression?

The fact that a thing is possible does not, however, prove that it is likely to happen. Has hoarding ever really been responsible for a depression? To this question various supposed authorities give absolutely contradictory answers. What are the facts?

The very common assumption that the depression of the 1930's was accompanied by widespread hoarding rests almost entirely upon the fact that, as Table XIV shows, bank balances were steadily rising, although people were curtailing their spending. It is taken for granted that, normally, a family tends to spend its entire cash balance in some brief, but never clearly specified, period of time. As noted in an earlier chapter, this assumption is far from the truth. While available statistics are not adequate to enable one to determine the facts accurately, it appears that, in the

[1] In the algebraic terms presented in the last chapter, they would have diminished f, the fraction of their cash spent for consumption goods, and they would not only have increased r, the fraction of their cash held in reserve, but they would have refrained from investing the sums added to this reserve. Since investing is one form of spending, it is clear that they would have reduced their total volume of spending below the customary level, and such a reduction seems to typify the situation commonly thought of as *hoarding.*

average interval of time elapsing between major receipts of income — an interval probably between 9 and 15 days in length — the typical American family spends only about a tenth of its cash balance.[2]

It is a bit surprising to learn that, even in 1933, a depression year in which most people were supposed to be living a hand-to-mouth existence and subsisting partly on savings, the average American family spent in a typical income period only about a tenth of its supply of money and demand deposits. Evidently, the typical family's spending for direct goods is very different indeed from its supply of ready cash — in other words, the amount of spending and the amount of available purchasing power are two different things, the latter being far larger than the former. Clearly, the typical family sets aside for definite purposes relatively large reserves, and, only in case of emergency, does it draw upon these reserves to buy such things as food, clothing, or incidentals.

Granted that this is true, it does not follow that a *shrinkage* in the typical fraction of cash on hand spent in a given interval of time may not result in depression. Was it such an uncompensated shrinkage in spending — that is, a shifting of cash from spending money to *idle* reserves — which prevented recovery during the 1933–1937 pump-priming era? A theoretical analysis of the facts gives no support to the theory that hoarding — that is a slowing down in spending — was a major factor either in causing the Great Depression, or in preventing escape from it.[3] Fortunately, however,

---

[2] A rough approximation to the magnitude of this fraction is easily obtained by substituting in the equation, $pq = fm''$, numbers bearing some resemblance to the actual data applying to the United States in 1933. It will be remembered that

q = the physical quantity of direct or consumption goods marketed in Period i
p = the average price per unit of all direct or consumption goods marketed in Period i
m'' = the average amount of money and bank deposits in the hands of consumers in Period i
f = the fraction of their cash (m'') which consumers spent in Period i for direct goods, and that
Period i = the average time elapsing for the average individual between receipts of income.

Figures on Page 13 of the United States *Survey of Current Business* for June, 1944, indicate that, in 1933, the people of the United States spent for direct goods $46.55 billions. Let us assume for the purpose at hand that Period i equalled approximately one-thirtieth of a year. Table XIII shows that, on the average in 1933, total circulating medium was probably not far from $22 billions. Let us assume, further, that $15 billions was in the hands of the consumers of the nation. This quantity is represented by m''. Since $pq = fm''$, it appears that, in 1933, f, the fraction of available cash spent in Period i, amounted to roughly 0.10.

[3] If we are to have the circuit flow of money and deposits, and the counterflow of goods running smoothly, it is clear that pq must not fluctuate widely. Since $pq = fm$, any shrinkage in f, with m'' remaining constant, will obviously force pq downward. Since prices (including wage rates) are influenced by custom, contracts, union requirements, and governmental regulations, p is very "sticky." Therefore, a shrinkage in f is likely to result in a decline in q. If this decline in q is offset by increased investment, expansion in the production of indirect goods may counterbalance the diminution in the production of direct goods. If this happens, no untoward results will follow. If, however, the reduction in the size of q is not so offset, the result will be a falling off of trade, in other words a business recession.

That such a shrinkage in f might have been the obstacle which caused difficulty is indicated by a conclusion reached in the last chapter, namely, that a decline in the size of f is one of the principal forces which, ever since 1933, has kept V'' low. The subject, therefore, seems worthy of further analysis.

As noted above $fm'' = pq$. Evidently, a reduction in f can cause a decline in pq only in case m'' does not rise sufficiently to offset the decline in f. However, Table XIII shows that, from 1933 to 1937, M'' rose rapidly. In all probability, m'' did the same, for there is no reason to believe that the *proportion* of circulating medium in the hands of consumers diminished. It appears therefore, that actually, although consumers found their incomes and cash holdings gradually expanding, they tended to keep their purchasing of direct or consumption goods on a fairly ever

e do not need to rely solely upon theoretical analysis to ascertain whether,
ring the "Thirties," the public at large did or did not engage in hoarding
a vast scale. Data are now at hand which enable us to compare roughly
r the pre-War decade the realized national book income with both spend-
g for consumption goods and spending for investment. These figures
ve been entered in Table XV.

lation of Spending to Income

If there is any point concerning spending which is made plain by com-
on observation, it is that the typical family does not reduce materially its
y-by-day spending for direct goods unless its income is reduced. The first
fect of a shrinkage of income is to cut down current saving. Only when
is shrinkage of income is greater than the usual saving, does a curtailment
ordinary direct expenses occur.

On the other hand, if the family income expands, the first effect is likely
be to increase the percentage of income saved. Ordinarily, the next effect
to stimulate the buying of expensive durable goods such as refrigerators,
tomobiles, and houses. Since, for the most part, increased savings are in-
sted promptly in savings bank accounts, life insurance, real estate, building
d loan stock, or other securities, it seems logical to suppose that, in both
od times and bad, almost the entire realized income of the people of the
tion is spent promptly. How does this conclusion — based as it is solely
on general observation and deductive reasoning — conform to such
atistical evidence as is available?

In compiling the data appearing in Table XV, it was necessary to keep
mind certain facts:

1. "Total consumption expenditures," as reported by the United States
   Department of Commerce and recorded in Table XV, Column 2, do
   not include purchases by government of buildings, ships, equipment,
   munitions, etc., hence, in comparing the total incomes of consumers
   with expenditures for consumption goods, it is logical to deduct from

---

el. Apparently, then, the decline in f came about mainly because of increases in income and m'',
d therefore was merely an offsetting factor.

Moreover, it seems improbable that changes in the size of f are likely to be either large
ough or persistent enough to interfere seriously with the course of business activity. Since the
erage person tends to spend most of his current income promptly, it is scarcely conceivable
at, in time of depression, with income abnormally low, any degree of misgiving concerning
e future would lead the population as a whole to reduce spending for consumption goods by
much as one-fifth. Suppose, nevertheless, that, in 1933, intense pessimism in some Period i
used a reduction in f from 0.10 to 0.08. Since $fm'' = pq$, it is evident that, if m'' remained un-
anged, pq would be reduced from $1.5 to $1.2 billions — a cut of $0.3 billions. In a !nation
ving a $46 billion annual volume of sales of consumption goods, can one imagine a $0.3
llion cut in orders throwing business into a tailspin? That such could happen seems most
likely.

But this hypothetical contraction in orders applied merely to one Period i, assumed to be
out 12 days in length. What about the next 12 days, and the next 12 days, and the next? Would
t the fraction f, having once been cut, tend, automatically, to stay smaller than formerly?

The answer to this question is that exactly the reverse is true. There is a strong tendency for
duced spending for consumption to give rise to shortages of direct goods in the hands of con-
mers, and these shortages are likely to be made up in the next Period i. If spending (fm'')
m $1.5 to $1.2 billions in one twelve-day period, it would be far more likely to go to $1.8
llions in the next period than to remain at $1.2 billions, for many people would seek to re-
enish their depleted larders.

the total income received by individuals most of the taxes which the
pay. The figures entered in the fifth column of Table XV represen
therefore, after-tax income only.

2. The spendings of individuals do not comprise merely amounts pai
out for consumption — they also include amounts spent for saving
bonds, for life insurance, for savings-bank deposits, for building an
loan shares, and for numerous other classes of investments. Most o
the money so paid out does not find its way into the buying of th
consumption goods listed by the Department of Commerce an
entered in Column 2 of Table XV. Instead it is used to purchas
production goods, or to cover governmental expenditures for thing
other than goods consumed directly by individuals. To find tota
spending, it is, therefore, necessary to add the items in Columns
and 3.

3. The items entered in Column 3 represent only four classes of inves
ment by individuals — namely life insurance, savings-bank deposit

Table XV

TOTAL SPENDING BY INDIVIDUALS
compared for the pre-War years with the
TOTAL AFTER-TAX INCOME OF INDIVIDUALS

| Year | Billions of Dollars Spent for | | | After-tax Realized Book Income of All Individuals [e] (Billions) | Ratio of Spending to Income |
	Consumption Goods [a]	Four Important Recorded Items of Saving and Investment [b]	Total		
1929	$78.43	$0.95	$79.38	$80.0	0.99
1930	71.08	1.01	72.09	71.2	1.01
1931	61.42	−1.85	59.57	61.3	.97
1932	49.67	−4.04	45.63	46.6	.98
1933	46.55	−1.37	45.18	45.6	.99
1934	51.99	1.34	53.33	52.3	1.02
1935	56.45	2.22	58.67	57.8	1.01
1936	62.27	2.78	65.05	67.4	.97
1937	66.22	2.41	68.63	69.2	.99
1938	63.30	2.08	65.38	63.3	1.03
1939	66.47	2.87	69.34	68.3	1.01
1940	70.81	3.34	74.15	73.7	1.01

[a] U. S. *Survey of Current Business*, June, 1944, p. 13.

[b] Includes net *increases* in claims against insurance companies, savings bank deposits, build
ing and loan assets, and holdings of U. S. savings bonds. The net increases in claims
policy holders against insurance companies have been calculated by subtracting "unpai
premiums" and "premium notes and loans" from the sum of "reserves" plus "unpaid div
dends." Savings bank deposits data have been obtained by averaging the figures for th
various pairs of fiscal years. The figures on U. S. savings bonds represent excesses of issu
over redemptions. The data have been extracted from various issues of the *Statistical A
stract of the U. S.*

[e] Net taxes paid by individuals have been subtracted from the total income receipts of ind
viduals, as reported in the *Statistical Abstract of the U. S.* for 1942, p. 358. The tax paymen
subtracted are those estimated by Richard M. Bissell of the U. S. Dept. of Commerce, an
published in his article in *Fortune* entitled *The Anatomy of Public Spending*.

building and loan securities, and Federal savings bonds. Had records of other investments been available, they would have been added to the items recorded in Column 3. But the four categories are the only ones for which reasonably complete data are at hand.

4. Due to necessary omissions and some overlapping, the figures in neither Column 4 nor Column 5 can be considered as being exactly what we need. However, it is believed that, respectively, they do at least roughly approximate the disposable income of consumers and the volume of spending by consumers.

The probabilities are that the small fluctuations shown in the last column of Table XV have no particular significance as they may well be due mainly to imperfections in the data. What Table XV really seems to indicate is that, in peace time (just as we assumed on the basis of general observation) people do, as a rule, spend practically their entire after-tax incomes either for consumption goods or for investments. When spending equals income, there obviously is no hoarding. The indications are, therefore, that, although it is hypothetically possible for hoarding to bring on business stagnation, there is no evidence that hoarding had anything to do either with causing or intensifying the 1930–1940 depression. Apparently, then, all the elaborate plans devised for inducing hoarders to disgorge hoarded funds have rested upon foundations no firmer than the stuff that dreams are made of.

What Accounts for Declines in Buying?

But one important question still remains to be answered. If extensive hoarding is a mere figment of the imagination, how are we to explain the collapses in demand that have appeared all too frequently? Business may be running on an apparently even keel, with factories, mines, and farms turning out goods rapidly, and with these goods being regularly taken off the market by consumers. Then demand disappears, stocks accumulate, factories and mines shut down, and lines of the unemployed appear before the soup kitchens. Such was the course of events in later 1929 and again in 1937. If hoarding was not responsible for the shortage of demand, what brought it about?

Before attempting to answer this question, it seems desirable to look into the nature of "demand." What are its characteristics? These will be analyzed in the next chapter.

Chapter XIII

DEMAND AND ITS REPLENISHMENT

Demand Defined

As we have seen, one school of writers on economics holds that depressions are caused by lack of "purchasing power," or, in other words, by lack of spendable funds. Other writers contend that business collapses because of lack of *demand* for its products. Many assume that "purchasing power" and demand for goods are practically synonymous. However, in an earlier chapter, the fact has been pointed out that, in reality, the two are not even closely related. Our stock of "purchasing power," that is, of spendable funds, has been shown to be practically equivalent to our stock of circulating medium. But what do we mean by *demand?*

Economists define *demand* as want coupled both with willingness to buy and ability to pay for the article desired. One must always be on guard against the fallacy that mere want is equivalent to demand. After the Germans were driven out, the people of Naples had urgent wants for American goods of almost every kind imaginable; but, at the same time, their demands were as weak as their wants were strong, for they lacked not only spendable funds but the ability to get such funds.

It is also erroneous to assume that want coupled with ability to buy makes demand. In reality, demand measures the extent to which some other good is preferred to money. Several million Americans doubtless possess funds sufficient to enable each of them to pay for a trip around the world. Yet few make such a tour. Why? Obviously because they prefer to use their purchasing power for other purposes. *Unless one has ability to pay for a good and also wants it more than any other good selling for the same amount of money, he has no demand for the good, no matter how much he may want or need it.*

Since, in the United States, most purchases are made on a money basis, almost the only persons capable of creating *demand* are those holding either money or bank deposits. As a rule, therefore, the total *immediate* demand of any person for goods is limited by the amount of circulating medium in his possession at the moment. It would, however, be highly erroneous to assume that his demand for a good either approximates or is closely related to the size of his holdings of money and deposits.

Demand Schedules

An individual's demand for a good is usually expressed in terms of price per unit. He may desire but one unit of the good, or, instead, he may be willing to buy many units of the good if he can get it cheap enough. Thus a man may order his broker to buy ten shares of United States Steel stock at $55, ten more shares at $50, twenty additional shares at $45, and forty

132

more shares at $40. His *demand schedule* for this stock would therefore be:[1]

10 shares at $55
20 shares at $50
40 shares at $45
80 shares at $40

One can imagine collecting from all brokers in the country schedules recording the demand, at a given instant of time, of all individuals desiring to buy this stock, and then adding together all these schedules. The result would be the *composite demand schedule* for United States Steel stock at one instant of time. It might appear as follows:

80,430 shares at $56
91,650 shares at 55
102,720 shares at 54
108,960 shares at 53
and so on

This schedule might be plotted on cross-section paper, using the number of shares for the horizontal scale and the price for the vertical scale. The result would be a curve sloping downward to the right. Such a graph could correctly be referred to as the curve of demand for United States Steel stock. Both the schedule and the curve would show, *for that given instant of time,* the respective numbers of units of the given commodity which could be sold at various prices.

Since the necessary data rarely exist, it is usually difficult to measure accurately the demand for even one given article at any single instant of time. The demand curves for different commodities and for the same commodity at different instants of time, are all likely to have different shapes. To construct a series of demand curves showing *changes* in the demand for the same given article is usually entirely impracticable. To build up such a series of demand curves for any considerable number of articles would be a monumental task. Since different articles are measured in different units and sell at different unit prices, it is obviously out of the question to construct a total demand schedule for goods in general by combining the separate demand schedules for the various classes of goods.

Effective Demand

As every well-trained student of economics knows, in any given market for a given commodity at a given time, there is likely to be a supply curve as well as a demand curve, and the price at which these two curves intersect is the market price, in other words, the price at which the good is selling at the moment.

Only those fractions of the demand which are at prices higher than the market price constitute *effective demand.* Thus, if the market price for wheat is $1.20 per bushel, all demand at prices below $1.20 is ineffective, for it produces no sales.

[1] Note that the demand schedule is always cumulative, for those who would pay $55 or $50 are still more ready to buy at $45 per share.

The statement is often made that lowering the price of a commodity increases the demand for it. This is a careless usage which often leads to erroneous reasoning. A better way of stating the idea is to say that lowering the price increases the quantity which can be sold.

In reality, an increase in demand means that, at the same given prices, it is possible to sell more of the good. Thus if, at the opening of the market, only 5,000 bushels of wheat could be sold at $1.29, but, later, 8,000 bushels could be sold at the same price, one could correctly say that the demand had strengthened. Graphically, this change would be indicated by a movement of the demand curve to the right.

Producers and dealers in general have ever sought to discover ways and means of increasing their prices without decreasing their respective volumes of sales. However, unless their efforts or other forces cause shifts to the right in the positions of the curves representing respectively the demands for their products, they are always doomed to disappointment, for, otherwise, sales always decline as prices rise.

Regardless of whether demand is strong or weak, it is usually true that the entire available stock of a product can be sold, provided it is offered at a price sufficiently low. Since this is true, certain economists have concluded that the way to extricate a nation from depression is for producers to lower their prices sufficiently to make possible sales of all the products their respective plants can turn out. Undoubtedly, such lowering of prices would cause production to expand to the degree desired. Why then do not producers follow this plan?

The answer is that each producer must sell goods at prices high enough to cover his expenses of production or else he will soon become bankrupt and be out of business. He usually cannot reduce greatly expenses per unit of output unless he can reduce radically wage rates per piece. Ordinarily, this cannot be done without precipitating a strike. Furthermore, minimum wage laws may prevent such action.

In time of depression, any producer who increases output in the hope that other producers will do the same and thus increase the buying power of the public is gambling on something not likely to happen under free competition. To obtain such unanimity of action it is necessary to have production controlled by an all-powerful central authority. This proposed remedy for depression appears therefore to be decidedly chimerical in nature.

The Dynamics of Demand

Whenever some individual's demand price for a given good happens to be higher than the market price, demand tends to turn from a static to a dynamic force — in other words, there is action — the individual buys the good. This act of purchasing ends his demand for the particular unit or units of the good bought. Furthermore, since he has spent part of his purchasing power, his demand for all other goods is curtailed by the amount of the purchase. Thus, the possession of a $9,000 bank account enables its owner to demand at the same time a new home, a fine motor boat, a trip around the world, and a hundred shares of stock in any one of a large number of corporations. If, however, he spends the $9,000 for a trip around the world, his demand for all the other goods disappears. He cannot both "eat his cake and have it." Therefore, every dollar spent destroys the individual's demand for a dollar's worth of goods. Demand schedules are, therefore, inter-related phenomena.

Within a short time after any market opens, each individual buyer present at the opening is likely to have completely satisfied his effective demand for the good being marketed. Such being the case, it is evident that the entire effective demand existing when the market opens will probably disappear within a few minutes thereafter, for all persons having effective demands — that is, demands at prices above the market — are able promptly to satisfy such demands by purchases at the market price. Once such purchases are all made, the market is cleared. One might expect that, this clearing process having been accomplished, trade would be at an end. In reality, however, it continues indefinitely. Why is this true?

The answer is that demand is constantly being replenished. How does this come about? Obviously, after the market is cleared, the buyers and sellers of goods will readjust their respective supply and demand schedules to correspond to their new situations, and this readjustment may lead to more sales. Even so, it would seem reasonable to suppose that, after a few hours, all persons preferring other goods to circulating medium would have acquired the goods desired; that all persons preferring circulating medium to other goods would have acquired money or deposits; and that, therefore, trade would come to a standstill. Why does this not happen?

There are four reasons why trade never stops:

1. Always some prospective buyers and sellers are changing their minds concerning the relative desirability of owning money as compared to owning other goods.
2. Because of arrangements and contracts already in effect, circulating medium is ever moving from one owner to another owner.
3. New goods are ever being produced and sold, and the proceeds of such sales enable the sellers to increase their demands for other goods.
4. New prospective buyers, sellers, or both may appear in the market.

The net result is that, over and over again, the market is cleared, and, over and over again, new effective supply and new effective demand come into the market. This process normally continues as long as the market is open. Therefore, the shape of the curve representing the demand for a good is ever changing.

As previously pointed out, the total amount of buying by any individual in any given period is, as a rule, influenced but slightly by the size of his cash holdings but is governed primarily by his receipts during the period of money or demand deposits. In other words, his demand is replenished mainly through *accessions* to his spending power. How are such accessions brought about?

The answer is that the usual way of generating additional demand, as expressed in monetary terms, is to sell something. However, the effect produced depends upon the type of goods sold.

Two Types of Demand Replenishment

As indicated in an earlier chapter, sales in a nation are divided into two very different segments:

1. Sales of speculative goods such as land, stocks, grains, and cotton
2. Sales of goods which are being processed as they move from the farm or mine to the ultimate consumer.

Forces Controlling Speculative Trading

Speculators buy goods because they hope to be able to sell them soon at prices higher than those which they have paid for the goods. A large part of the trading in real estate, stocks, bonds, metals, cotton, and grains is speculative in nature, and has little or nothing to do with the movements of such goods necessarily incident to either further processing or consumption. The speculative purchaser buys because he believes that the price of the good will go higher. The speculative seller sells because he believes that the price will fall.

In considering speculative activity, it is well to note the fact that, if all speculators had the same opinions about the future course of the market price of any good, there would be very little trading in the goods. Thus, if prospective buyers of wheat and owners of wheat all felt that the price was going to rise sharply, the owners would be as reluctant to sell as the potential buyers would be anxious to purchase the wheat. Under such circumstances, few sales would occur. Activity in trading results, therefore, from the fact that different speculators disagree as to the price outlook for the given good, rather than from any general increase or decrease in "liquidity preference."

Replenishment of the Demand for Speculative Goods

In the case of speculative goods, demand is replenished automatically, for every sale provides the wherewithal to make another purchase. Therefore, the demands for such goods tend to change with every shift in public sentiment. Thus, if traders generally become more optimistic concerning the outlook for corporate earnings, the demands for various stocks will grow stronger and the prices of securities will advance. Higher prices will have but little tendency to reduce the number of shares traded in, for the trading does not diminish the total buying power of the traders. High prices will, of course, increase the total value of shares sold, but the larger payments can be accommodated by increasing the velocity of circulation of bank deposits. This is what happens in the case of the typical bull market.

As long as goods are not used up, they can flow from owner to owner indefinitely at any speed required by the degree of speculative enthusiasm prevailing. One may think of them as flowing around a circuit in one direction while money and bank deposits flow around the circuit in the opposite direction.

How Merchants' and Manufacturers' Demands Are Replenished

In many respects, the ordinary transactions of a merchant resemble those of a speculator, for, in each case, sales of goods tend, more or less automatically, to provide the seller with the cash needed to replenish his stock. A given good may, in fact, pass through the hands of a series of merchants, each sale providing the funds to restock the shelves. As long as the goods are not destroyed or consumed, the flow may continue indefinitely.

However, merchants and manufacturers are merely middlemen engaged in passing along demands having their origins in the wants and incomes of the ultimate consumers of goods. Eventually, directly or indirectly, the products of mines and factories and the stocks on merchants' shelves arrive in the hands of purchasers who consume them or radically change their forms. Once goods are used up, there is no chance of selling them and thus obtaining funds to replenish the demand for other goods.

However, though a manufacturer cannot replenish his demand by selling fuel or materials which have been used up, he ordinarily does replenish it by selling the finished products brought into being by the using up of the fuel and materials. As a rule, his total sales bring in funds sufficient to cover all of his operating expenses.

The Demands of Consumers

A change in psychology may change the demands not only of speculators but also of consumers. As we have seen, the typical family has on hand a sizable reserve of money or deposits. If, in a period of optimism, a widespread tendency to buy consumption goods develops, demands for such goods may strengthen, and heavy purchasing may result. The prices of such goods will, therefore, rise, and production will expand. If men are idle, this will tend to set them to work. Once those are employed who will accept existing wage rates, the expansion in the available supply of goods will practically cease. If added buying is speeding up the transfer of finished products to the hands of consumers, the market prices of direct goods will climb rapidly. Since, as noted in an earlier chapter, the respective velocities of circulation of such goods and of the money used for their buying are governed by the existing technology of production, the velocities will not increase. Therefore, higher prices will tend to terminate the buying spree.

That consumption will quickly eliminate any potential demand based upon accumulations of liquid savings, no matter how great such accumulations may be, is illustrated by the following example. Suppose that, at the end of World War II, potential consumers had on hand $100 billions of cash savings, that the supply of consumption goods available for purchase was 40 billion units worth $1 per unit, and that newly produced consumption goods were coming on the market at the rate of 10 billions of units per month, also worth $1 per unit. Suppose further, that, in the next month, the possessors of the savings proceeded to buy for consumption 30 billion units of direct goods. Such buying would cut the stock of old goods in the hands of dealers to 10 billion units. With the new units produced in the month, the total stock would now be 20 billion units. Since most of the sellers would also be potential consumers, the cash available at the end of the month for purchasing direct goods would still be approximately $100 billions but the quantity of goods available for purchase would have shrunk from 40 billion to 20 billion units. Presumably, therefore, the prices of the goods on hand would be at least twice as high as at the beginning of the month, and this price increase would drastically reduce the tendency to buy. Moreover, if the rate of buying in the first month were not curtailed, but were continued for a second month, the merchants' shelves would be practically empty, and prices would skyrocket as would-be consumers fought for the scanty new supplies appearing on the markets. Clearly, therefore, any tendency to spend accumulated savings destroys itself promptly.

The thing to be kept constantly in mind is that, while sales of speculative goods automatically replenish demand, sales of direct goods to consumers do nothing of the kind. The food purchased by a workingman's family is almost never sold in order to replenish his demand for more food. However, the food which he eats enables the workingman to perform more labor, and for it he obtains money. This money enables him to replenish his demand for edibles.

In general, the demands of ultimate consumers must be replenished either by the sales of the services of themselves or of members of their families, or else by the sales of the *services* of such of their possessions as lands, houses, or securities. Receipts from the sales of such services are known as wages, salaries, profits, dividends, interest, or rent. Together they make up the consumer's realized income.

Types of Income

At this point, it may be worth while to digress and describe briefly four different ways of defining income.

1. The total *book income* of an individual is that shown by his books if properly kept. It takes account not only of current receipts but also of gains or losses in the value of capital assets or durable goods held. Since it is measured in terms of money, this concept is commonly but inaccurately referred to as "money income."
2. The *realized book income* refers to only that part of total book income *realized* during the period, and ignores changes in the value of property held.
3. The *goods income* of an individual refers to the physical quantity of goods obtainable for his book income. It is usually calculated by dividing his book income by an appropriate price index.
4. The *real or psychic income* of an individual represents the amount of pleasure which he gains or pain which he escapes during a given period. While this concept is intangible, nevertheless everyone spends his life trying to make his psychic income as large as possible.

Factors Limiting Demand

It is an axiom among all but the most thriftless that an individual's annual consumption must not exceed his annual realized income. The thrifty ordinarily endeavor to conserve their capital gains, spending for direct goods not more than their normal current realized income, hence it is this last mentioned quantity which primarily accounts for the replenishment of the demand for direct or consumption goods.

Income is not, however, a controlling factor in the case of the demand for speculative goods. The individual speculator's ability to make a purchase is usually dependent primarily upon his possession of money or deposit currency, hence his volume of buying is generally influenced more by the size of his bank balance than by the amount of his current income.

Production and Demand Not Necessarily Identical

Economists commonly assume that production automatically generates demand. In so assuming, they are usually correct. However, production, *in itself,* does not replenish spending power. The pianist may render a wonderful sonata. The "victory gardener" may grow an abundance of vegetables. The farmer may cut and store hay for his livestock. Each of these acts constitutes production, but none of them necessarily adds a single dollar to the total market demand for newly produced goods.

It follows that, if the one using up goods is to reconstitute his demand, it is essential for him not only to produce something for sale, but also actually to sell sufficient of it to cover the value of the goods used up. Therefore, sale as well as production is essential if spending power and demand are to be properly replenished.

Schedules Showing Estimated Buying Potentials

As noted earlier, the ordinary demand schedule refers to the situation existing at an instant of time. Such a schedule is not infrequently confused with another decidedly different type of schedule — one showing not demand at the moment but, instead, the quantities of a particular good which it is estimated would be bought during a given period of time at each of a series of prices. This may be referred to as a schedule of estimated *sales* volumes. One can also construct a schedule showing for a given individual the estimated *dollar volume of purchases* which he may be expected to make in a specified period of time. A third type of schedule presents an estimate of the *total volume of buying* which is likely to be done in a given period by all of the individuals in a nation. This may be called a schedule of *actual spending.* A fourth type of schedule sets forth an estimate of the *net volume of new spending power* available in the nation during a period of time. Table XIV shows that, for most years, the last two estimates, if correctly made, are likely to be approximately identical.

Replenishment of Total Demand

The total demand for goods on the part of all the individuals in a nation is, as a rule, determined mainly by the size of their aggregate realized income. True, when they happen to be over-optimistic, they borrow at the banks, and therefore are able, for a time, to spend somewhat more than their incomes. When they are pessimistic or when bankers are calling loans, they spend a bit less than their incomes. However, in most years, these changes are small in proportion to the sizes of their respective incomes. Therefore, in ordinary times, it is the amount of realized national income which determines the rate of replenishment of total demand.

Before the close of World War II, the papers and magazines were studded with articles telling of enormous savings in the hands of the public and inferring that these constituted a huge pent-up demand for goods that would be released as soon as the war ended. As noted in an earlier chapter, the war-time net saving for the nation as a whole was probably *negative*. Therefore, any post-war increase in total demand was due either to currency inflation or to a tendency on the part of individuals to increase their spending in proportion to their cash reserves — a tendency generated largely by a lack of realization of the fact that their nominal savings were partly or wholly offset by prospective future tax burdens.

Another very widely held illusion is that the advent of a great war greatly intensifies the *demands* for goods in general. As a matter of fact, war, in itself, does nothing of the kind. Obviously it greatly magnifies the *wants* for certain types of goods, but intensifying *wants* does not increase *demand* in the least. The ratio of aggregate demand to aggregate supply ordinarily increases in war time solely because the government is inflating the currency in order to get money to pay expenses. By creating more money, the government translates wants into demand.

How Prosperity and Depression Affect Demand

Whenever the national income increases, or people in general become optimistic and tend to go into debt and use the resulting borrowed funds to buy goods, demand curves for all kinds of luxuries and conveniences shift to the right. When the national income drops, when banks call loans, and when people generally become pessimistic concerning the future outlook, demand curves for all things except necessities tend to shift well to the left. These alternating simultaneous movements in thousands of demand curves constitute the phenomenon commonly referred to as the business cycle.

Transferring versus Generating Demand

As pointed out in an earlier chapter, the mere buying and selling of goods already on hand does not generate any real addition to the NET total of demand at any given instant of time, for every dollar added to the seller's spending power is subtracted from the buyer's spending power. Thus, while Jones can increase his demand by selling a block of securities to Smith, the money paid by Smith to Jones reduces Smith's demand by a like amount.

It is equally true that shifting the demand from one person to another or from one group to another does not increase the total demand for goods over any given period. Thus the new buying power acquired by a pensioner or charity recipient is offset by an equivalent loss of buying power on the part of taxpayers or donors. Similarly, it is impossible for government, by spending, to increase the total demand in the nation for labor or other goods unless it secures funds by currency inflation or by borrowing abroad. If it levies taxes or sells bonds to citizens, it cuts private demand by the same

New York City — a product of economic freedom.
{See page 22.}

amount that it increases governmental demand. This principle holds just as truly in war time as in peace time.

Were a government to finance a major war without resorting to inflation, the normal result would be great shrinkages in the demands for civilian goods. Hence, the prices of such goods would fall, their production would shrink, and workers would be forced out of civilian industries and into industries turning out war goods. Under such circumstances, there would be no tendency for the national average of either wages or other prices to rise. The total dollar expense of financing the war would, therefore, be far less than that of financing it by the use of inflation.

The same principle applies when an employer is forced by government or by a labor union to pay higher wages to his employees. If total employee working time is not reduced, the immediate effect is, of course, to increase their demands for goods, but, for every dollar added to the demand schedules of the employees, a dollar is subtracted from the demand schedules of the employer. Total demand remains unchanged.

It follows that the total NET demand for newly-produced goods can be increased only if the net total of new spending power in the nation is enlarged.

Quack Nostrums Recommended to Cure Depression

As pointed out above, if an individual uses any dollar of his income to buy one good, he cannot use the same dollar to buy another good. Therefore, the notion that, in time of depression, high-pressure advertising and salesmanship may help to increase total sales, and thus lift the nation out of depression, is obviously a fallacy.

As Adam Smith long ago made so clear, all restrictions on either domestic or foreign trade burden both buyers and sellers. Tariffs, quotas, export bounties, cartel arrangements, exchange controls, and restrictions on the free movement of money or precious metals are all pernicious. Eventually, they injure all parties concerned.

Active foreign trade is desirable, but lending to foreigners money with which to buy American goods is not likely to stimulate trade. If they have the wherewithal to pay for the goods, they will not need to borrow. If they are not able to pay now, they will probably not be willing to pay later, and, if Uncle Sam then requests payment, they will denounce him as Uncle Shylock demanding his pound of flesh.

Furthermore, if we lend to foreigners a billion dollars of existing money to pay for goods which they buy from us, we lessen by a billion dollars the buying power of our own citizens, and hence do not increase by a penny the total volume of orders placed with American business concerns.

If, instead of lending existing dollars, we employ some International Bank, Monetary Fund, or other device to *create new money* for foreigners to borrow from us and use to purchase goods from us, it is undoubtedly true that the demand for the products of our industries is temporarily strengthened. However, the same would be true if our Government printed new money and distributed it by broadcasting it from airplanes. For at least two reasons, this bizarre device would, from our standpoint, be better than making the loans to foreigners:

1. When we trade tangible goods to foreigners in return for promises to pay, we are minus the goods and are not likely ever to get anything of value in return. Were we to distribute money from airplanes, our own citizens would still possess the products of our industries.
2. When we lend money to foreigners and later ask them to pay what they owe us, we not only undertake a troublesome and irritating task, but transform our debtors into enemies instead of friends. The airplane distribution method would not lead to either of these troubles.

Obviously, scattering money from airplanes would be a highly unscientific way of promoting recovery from depression, but it would not lead us into the error of believing that exchanging our valuable possessions for foreign promises is trade, when in reality it is nothing but camouflaged alms-giving. When we give to foreigners, the proper procedure is to do it openhandedly as good neighbors, and do it without any thought of trying to collect payment in the future. This method might gain for us good will instead of ill will. Moreover, such giving, if financed by taxation, would not involve inflation and the manifold evils arising therefrom.

The Economic Spiral

In explaining how to maintain continuous prosperity, some writers on economics have stressed the importance of production. Others have emphasized spending. Many have centered their attention upon purchasing power. Recently, it has been fashionable to talk of the national income as a causal factor. In this chapter, we have described the rôle of demand, and have mentioned new spending power. The truth is that all of these factors are essential to a solution of the problem, but how each is related to the other is something that has rarely, if ever, been explained. What are the causal connections involved?

The truth seems to be that these factors follow one another around an endless spiral in the following sequence:

A   INCOME furnishes
B   NEW SPENDING POWER which makes possible
C   DEMAND which leads to
D   SPENDING which gives rise to
E   PRODUCTION which generates
A'   INCOME which furnishes
B'   NEW SPENDING POWER which makes possible
C'   DEMAND which leads to
D'   SPENDING which gives rise to
E'   PRODUCTION which generates
A'' INCOME etc., etc.

A common error which it is essential to avoid is the assumption that, because A, A', and A'' all represent income, they must be identical. Such is far from being the case, for every step in the sequence is subject to modification by outside forces, and any such modification tends to affect the sizes of all subsequent items. The whole process is an ever-changing spiral.

The Spiral Flow and the Importance of Its Stability

The normal flow around the spiral may be illustrated by the following example:

Suppose that, this week, employees receive a billion dollars in wages and salaries. They therefore proceed to buy from retail merchants, landlords, and others a billion dollars' worth of goods. These recipients buy from wholesalers, employees, and others a billion dollars' worth of services and material goods. Wholesalers and other recipients now buy from manufacturers, railways, and others a billion dollars' worth of goods. Manufacturers and the other recipients of the billion dollars buy from farmers, miners and others a billion dollars' worth of goods. All employers next pay out from their receipts wages and salaries amounting to a billion dollars.

The circuit flow of the money and bank deposits around one loop of the spiral is complete. Evidently the flow of circulating medium in one direction has generated a counter-flow of goods in the other direction. Furthermore, the flow of circulating medium and the counter-flow of services and material goods are both equal in money value. This is true because, normally, the national income resulting from a given volume of production approximately equals the value of the goods turned out in producing that income.

However, as we have seen, net new spending power may exceed the realized national income either because the national government is printing new money or because it or its citizens are borrowing from the banks. The appearance of such excess spending power strengthens the total demand for goods and hence tends to raise the prices of the goods. If, at the time, part of the nation's labor force is unemployed, the higher prices will usually increase the volume of employment, production, and hence income. If, however, all who are willing to work already have jobs, the principal result will be an advance in the general price level.

In an ideal social economy, the flow might be represented by a spiral band ever growing wider as technical improvements caused production to expand, but the band would be free from indentations. Unfortunately, however, in our economy, as it actually exists, the spiral band is deeply scalloped, for the flow of spending, production, and income has fluctuated tremendously from time to time.

It is well to note that, in most instances, this variation has not been caused by war's destructiveness, by drouth, or by other natural disasters. Instead, depressions have often appeared (as for example in 1929) at times when our economy seemed to be in excellent balance, and when, apparently, everything favored continuous prosperity. What was the trouble-making factor? Where did it enter the spiral?

The answer is that, in almost every case, the trouble has arisen because of the tendency of people in general to shift their outlooks simultaneously, and more or less rhythmically, from optimism to pessimism, and then back to optimism. These oscillations in public sentiment have given rise in turn to changes in the net volume of new spending power, of demand, and of actual spending.

Any irregularity in the spending of circulating medium generates a corresponding irregularity in the flow of other goods. Any stoppage in spending quickly brings a stoppage in production. Therefore, there is little chance of assuring continuous prosperity unless new spending power is generated at an approximately constant rate, and unless the volume of buying can be kept stable.

This is true because wages, and many other prices, being fixed by custom, or contract, or set by labor unions or government, have a high degree of rigidity. If all potential sellers were at all times willing to accept for their goods the best prices obtainable, then any amount of goods could be bought with any amount of new buying power, and trade might flow along smoothly regardless of fluctuations in the volume of new spendable funds appearing in the markets. But we do not live in that kind of a world. In our world, prices have no such flexibility. Therefore, whenever the total dollar volume of new spending power varies noticeably, it causes disturbances in the volume of trade and production. It is, indeed, not going too far to say that, in our modern economy, whether we have depression or, instead, active business and full employment, depends largely upon the *regularity* of the *replenishment* of the total stock of spending power in the hands of all individuals combined, for it is this replenishment which generates the demand necessary to keep goods flowing smoothly and production active.

Our attempt to gain passage through the gates leading to abiding prosperity taught us that one of the keys is *sustained demand for new products.* Now we find that such sustained demand depends upon the maintenance of a smooth flow in the supply of new spending power. What this *new spending power* is, and how it can be maintained, will be discussed in the next chapter.

Chapter XIV

NET NEW SPENDING POWER

The Sources of New Spending Power

Earlier chapters have made clear the fact that the realized book income of the people of the nation is the one *fundamental, dependable, continuing* source of net new spending power. However, realized book income is not the *only* fountainhead of additional purchasing power. New spendable funds may also be secured by creating new money or by borrowing from the banks.

In so far as the effect upon the net volume of new spending power is concerned, borrowing from the *banks* is entirely different from borrowing from *individuals or non-banking concerns.* For example, when Jones borrows from Smith, the spending power of the latter is diminished exactly as much as the spending power of the former is increased. However, when Jones borrows from a *bank,* he increases his spending power, but, unless the bank is short on reserves, its tendency to spend to buy goods is probably not diminished in the least. Total spending power in the nation has, therefore, been increased by the amount which Jones borrowed.

The effect is the same when a *government* borrows from the banks. It can use the deposits obtained to buy goods. The borrowed dollar buys neither more nor less than does a dollar taken from a taxpayer.

Likewise, the Federal Government can obtain new spending power by stamping out or printing money. Such is the case because of the fact that the newly created dollars are just as effective for buying goods as are the dollars issued at earlier dates.

Just as *additions* to the supply of new spendable funds may arise through the creation of new bank deposits or paper money, so the total volume of spending power, and hence of demand for goods, may shrink on account of the paying off of bank loans, or through the retirement by the Government or the Federal Reserve banks of outstanding pocket-book money.

From what has just been said, it is evident that the nation's demand for newly produced goods is replenished primarily from the following sources:

1. The sale of newly produced services and material goods. This source is roughly equivalent to the realized national income.
2. The creation of new circulating medium:
   (a) By private borrowing from banks
   (b) By governmental borrowing from banks
   (c) By governmental creation of new pocketbook money

The second group of sources is erratic and intermittent in nature, and may be negative as well as positive.

In brief, *the net new spending power accruing in any period of time approximately equals the algebraic sum of the national realized income and the*

Table XVI

CONSTITUENTS OF NET NEW SPENDING POWER
(Billions of Dollars)

| Year | Demand[a] Deposits, Dec. 31 | | | | Money in Circulation[g] Dec. 31 | Total Circulating Medium | | Realized National Book Income[h] | Net New Spending Power[j] |
| | Other than Federal | | Federal[f] | Total | | Dec. 31[j] | Change During Year | | |
	Nat'l Banks	Other Banks[c]							
1918	8.99[b]	11.15[d]	0.31	20.45	5.24	25.69			
1919	10.29[b]	14.47[d]	.45	25.21	5.38	30.59	+ 4.90	62.94	67.84
1920	9.50[b]	12.45[d]	.30	22.25	5.61	27.86	− 2.73	68.43	65.70
1921	8.57[b]	10.80[d]	.26	19.63	4.69	24.32	− 3.56	56.69	53.13
1922	9.53[b]	12.04[d]	.18	21.75	4.82	26.57	+ 2.25	57.17	59.42
1923	9.55[b]	12.96[d]	.19	22.70	5.04	27.74	+ 1.17	65.66	66.83
1924	¹10.33[b]	14.00[d]	.15	24.48	5.05	29.53	+ 1.79	67.00	68.79
1925	11.11[b]	14.19[d]	.17	25.47	5.10	30.57	+ 1.04	70.05	71.09
1926	10.73[b]	12.67[d]	.19	23.59	5.10	28.69	− 1.88	73.52	71.64
1927	11.23[b]	12.95[d]	.21	24.39	5.00	29.39	+ .70	73.97	74.67
1928	11.78[b]	13.40[d]	.25	25.43	4.97	30.40	+ 1.01	75.90	76.91
1929	11.09[b]	13.30[d]	.25	24.64	4.86	29.50	− .90	79.50	78.60
1930	10.64[b]	12.39[d]	.33	23.36	4.89	28.25	− 1.25	72.40	71.15
1931	9.07[b]	9.84[d]	.44	19.35	5.61	24.96	− 3.29	60.20	56.91
1932	8.28[b]	8.39[d]	.64	17.31	5.41	22.72	− 2.24	46.71	42.47
1933	8.34[b]	7.45[d]	1.30	17.09	5.52	22.61	− .11	44.71	44.60
1934	10.39[b]	9.40[d]	1.28	21.07	5.58	26.65	+ 4.04	51.56	55.60
1935	12.58[b]	11.40[d]	.99	24.97	5.90	30.87	+ 4.22	56.49[i]	60.71
1936	14.52[b]	13.38[e]	.95	28.85	6.54	35.39	+ 4.52	65.28[i]	69.80
1937	13.83[b]	12.36[e]	.83	27.02	6.55	33.57	− 1.82	69.03[i]	67.21
1938	15.08[b]	13.00[e]	.87	28.95	6.86	35.81	+ 2.24	62.76[i]	65.00
1939	16.65[e]	14.34[e]	.83[e]	31.87	7.60	39.47	+ 3.66	68.50[i]	72.62
1940	20.27[e]	17.09[e]	.79[e]	38.15	8.73	46.88	+ 7.41	76.24[k]	83.65
1941	22.70[e]	18.71[e]	1.89[e]	43.30	11.16	54.46	+ 7.58	92.73[k]	100.31
1942	29.16[e]	22.67[e]	8.44[e]	60.27	15.41	75.68	+21.22	117.28[k]	138.50
1943	35.95[e]	27.62[e]	10.31[e]	73.88	20.45	94.33	+18.65	143.13[k]	161.78
1944	39.13[e]	30.36[e]	20.81[e]	90.30	25.31	115.61	+21.28	156.79[k]	178.07
1945	44.15[e]	35.01[e]	24.67[e]	103.83	28.51	132.34	+16.73	160.77[k]	177.50
1946	58.60[m]	43.28[m]	2.99[m]	104.88	28.95	133.83	+ 1.49	165.12[k]	166.61

[a] Includes demand deposits of individuals, partnerships, corporations, States, and local governments.
[b] For data, see the *Statistical Abstracts of the U. S.* for 1929, p. 269; 1938, pp. 249–51; 1940, p. 261; and 1942, p. 296. Alaska, Hawaii, and the Philippines are excluded.
[c] Data estimated or taken from the various *Annual Reports* of the U. S. Comptroller of the Currency. All unspecified deposits have been taken to be demand deposits. In the first decade here covered this item was large enough to be of importance. In later years, it is negligible in size.
[d] Estimated by calculating the ratio of demand deposits in all other banks on June 30 to the same item for national banks on June 30, interpolating for the Dec. 31 ratio, and then applying the interpolated ratio to the Dec. 31 deposits of national banks.
[e] Data taken from the various *Annual Reports* of the U. S. Comptroller of the Currency.
[f] For most years figures are available for June 30, only. The estimates here entered have been obtained by averaging the mid-year figures for the various pairs of years.
[g] For data, see the various issues of the *Statistical Bulletin* issued by the Standard Statistics Co. and various issues of the U. S. *Survey of Current Business.*
[h] Data up to 1934 from page 7 of the report of the National Industrial Conference Board entitled *National Income in the U. S. 1799–1938.*
[i] Revised figures secured by telephone from the National Industrial Conference Board.
[j] Equals the algebraic sum of the items in the two preceding columns.
[k] U. S. Dept. of Commerce estimates recorded in the U. S. *Survey of Current Business,* Feb. 1946, p. 32; Feb., 1947, p. S–42; Mar. 1947, p. S–1.
[l] Preliminary estimate.
[m] Letter from the Comptroller of the Currency — dated Aug. 1, 1947.

CHANGE in the total volume of circulating medium in the nation. The computation of this aggregate is shown in Table XVI.

The Net Volume of New Spending Power

While, in any given year, the volume of buying of newly-produced goods does not necessarily equal the volume of net new spending power, available statistical evidence indicates that, as a rule, the two quantities are very similar in size. If, therefore, we really want to find the cause of underspending during a depression, the thing to study is the net volume of NEW spending power.

Inspection of the data in Table XVI makes it obvious that the net volume of new spending power is dominated by the realized national income. Nevertheless, in some years, especially those during World War II, changes in the volume of circulating medium were large enough to be decidedly significant. It is also clear that the total of new spending power is a distinctly unstable quantity, and that its instability is due not merely to fluctuations in some one constituent, but is, instead, brought about by variability in every component making up the total.

Spending Power and the Price Level

While, as noted in an earlier chapter, the existing level of prices is determined by the equation $P = \dfrac{M''V''}{T}$, the commonest cause of a shift in the price level is a variation in the size of the ratio $\dfrac{\text{Net New Spending Power}}{\text{Volume of Goods Produced}}$. Since, ordinarily, production generates income, and since income is normally the chief constituent of net new spending power, there is a strong tendency for the ratio to remain constant.

When, however, new circulating medium is created by the Government or by the banks, the usual result is for the total amount of new spending power to outrun the total value, at existing prices, of the nation's output of goods. Under such circumstances, possessors of the expanded volume of spending power bid against one another for the limited supply of goods, and hence prices rise.

The increase in spending-power volume usually affects not only the prices of newly created goods, but also the prices of goods already in existence. One reason why this is true is that the prices are related. Consider, for example, the prices of the services of houses — in other words, house rents. Such services are newly produced goods. If the values of such services increase, it is obvious that the values of houses will also rise, for the latter values represent the present worths of anticipated future house rents. For similar reasons, an increase in the price of copper raises the market prices of the stocks of copper-mining corporations.

Individual Price Controls and the Price Level

During war time, the typical government pays part of its expenses by inflating the currency. In recent years, this unsound method of finance has usually been accompanied by the enactment of laws placing "ceilings" upon the prices of services and material goods. In the United States, for example, the Office of Price Administration listed hundreds of goods the sale of which at "above-ceiling" prices was forbidden.

In a large proportion of all cases, the "ceiling prices" were lower than those which would have resulted under free competition. Whenever this was true, the quantity of goods demanded exceeded the amount supplied, and shortages developed. Price controls are usually effective in two respects: first, they compel people to buy less of the things they want most; second, they lead them to buy more of the things they want less.

One result of the inability of would-be customers to buy the goods which they most wanted was to increase total purchases of war savings bonds. Such purchases reduced the volume of inflation by cutting down the amount of Federal borrowing from the commercial banks. To the extent that inflation was thus reduced, the efforts of the O.P.A. to keep prices down were successful. However, despite the effects of savings-bond purchases, inflation went on at a rapid rate, the amount of circulating medium more than doubling before the war ended.

Since the prices of most necessities were held down by law, and since, as a result, the supplies of such goods were inadequate to meet the demands therefor, the public found itself in possession of billions of dollars of surplus new spending power. Part of this was utilized to buy goods in the "black markets." Part was used to purchase goods the prices of which were unregulated. Examples of such goods were furs, jewelry, diamonds, real estate, and stocks.

Since previously-presented figures indicate that, in general, hoarding is a myth, and that, when our people have spending power they spend it, it seems almost certain that, under the O.P.A., the price-level rise per billion dollars of inflation was neither more nor less than it would have been had the O.P.A. never existed. The holding down of the prices of goods in the regulated legitimate markets accentuated the increases of the prices of "black-market" and unregulated goods. On the whole, the two influences cancelled out, making the net effect on the price level zero.

Demand Deposits — Their Origin and Import

As brought out in the last chapter, if we are to prevent depressions, it seems essential to stabilize the circuit flow of money and deposits. Does this mean that people must never pay off their indebtedness to banks? To arrive at this conclusion would be ominous, for if such indebtedness is never to be liquidated, the burden of debt will, of course, grow and grow and grow. Clearly, therefore, this conclusion is unwarranted. How then can the volume of demand deposits be stabilized? To answer this question, we need to consider how demand deposits originate.

A large volume of deposits is generated by taking to banks pocket-book money and exchanging it for credits on the books of the banks. Additional deposits are created when merchants, manufacturers, farmers, and other producers borrow in order to facilitate the production of goods. Such loans are normally paid out of the proceeds of the sale of the goods. While both of the just-mentioned classes of loans fluctuate with the volume of business activity, neither has any marked tendency to generate those great oscillations known as business cycles. The same cannot be said of another type of bank loans — namely, those loans obtained to facilitate speculation.

Borrowing, Speculation, and Business Activity

In every wave of speculation, whether its object be tulip bulbs, stocks, land, or something else, the lure of quick and easy profits leads the speculators to borrow heavily from the banks. As the prices of the articles dealt in rise, bankers become willing to lend larger and larger amounts on the same property. Thus, the volume of bank loans — and hence of deposits and ready buying power — climbs steadily as speculative enthusiasm grows stronger. As a result, speculative margins become thinner and thinner.

If, at all times, all speculators either operated on a cash basis or carefully segregated funds used for speculation from funds used for other purposes, a boom and the collapse that normally follows might come and go without noticeably affecting either production or consumption. In reality, however, such speculation is largely dependent upon bank credit, and complete segregation of speculative from non-speculative funds is far from being the rule. For example, when prices are rising, many speculators cut down on consumption, and employ their resulting savings to provide margin necessary to cover speculative accounts. At the same time, other speculators are using parts of their "paper profits" to make payments on new homes, furniture, jewelry, and miscellaneous luxuries.

When the crash comes and brokers and bankers call for more margin, those speculators who are over-extended can ordinarily meet the calls only by reducing radically their customary expenditures for consumption goods. Homes are often sacrificed in order to prevent complete bankruptcy. Thus, during both the boom and the ensuing collapse, the effects of speculative and non-speculative undertakings become much intermingled. The net result is that speculative forces often exert a very real influence upon the volume of bank credit used in non-speculative activities.

Instalment Buying

An important force giving rise to an expansion of bank loans — and hence of bank deposits — is borrowing to buy durable goods such as homes, automobiles, and refrigerators. When people are optimistic, millions buy things which they had long wanted but had not before dared to purchase. Payment for the goods is made partly in cash and partly in promissory notes. The recipients of these notes commonly trade them to banks in exchange for deposit accounts. In this way, instalment buying enlarges the volume of bank loans, deposits, and new spendable funds.

Why Bank Credit Fluctuates

The reasons just set forth make it obvious that, in times of optimism, lending by banks tends to increase the aggregate buying power of the people of the nation. At such times, it enlarges very materially the amount of new spendable funds becoming available for the purchase of goods, and hence influences markedly the volume of buying. Bank credit expansion is, indeed, the major mechanism responsible for booms.

As long as such expansion continues, prosperity usually persists. Eventually, however, the aggregate of private loans from the banks stops growing. Why?

There are five reasons why the volume of bank loans does not expand indefinitely:

1. Federal or State laws are likely to limit deposits to a certain multiple of "reserves" of some kind.
2. The number of persons whom bankers feel to be satisfactory credit risks is limited.
3. The amount of bank credit which the banks are willing to extend to any one of such individuals is limited.
4. After a year or two of active buying on credit, practically every family that can possibly afford it has a new car, a new refrigerator, new furniture, and perhaps a new house. It will not need to replace these for several years, and one of the main reasons for borrowing is to purchase durable goods.
5. More important still is the fact that, having mortgaged its future income, the family is in no position to buy, in accustomed amounts, goods of any kind. The net result is, of course, to curtail the total demand for goods, and to make the demand for durable consumption goods especially short. This shortage tends to bring on depression in the industries producing durable goods.

The Effect of Bank-Credit Contraction

Ordinarily, the expansion of bank deposits which accompanies the typical boom stops as soon as pessimism begins to creep over the nation. In this connection, a fact which is often overlooked is that the mere cessation of the loan-expanding process tends to curtail business activity. Thus, if, in a given year, the net new spending power in the nation has been made up of $90 billions of realized income and $10 billions of deposit inflation, and if inflation stops, total new spending power will shrink from $100 billions to $90 billions, and this 10 per cent curtailment in the volume of new spendable funds may well be sufficient to throw business into the descending spiral which leads to serious depression.

As soon as it becomes evident that new orders for goods are falling off and that profits are likely soon to decline, speculators become frightened, prices of land, stocks, and commodities fall, and brokers call for additional margins. Putting up more margin reduces the ability of the customer to buy goods. When retail sales fall off, orders to wholesalers decline, and such merchants, in turn, cease buying from manufacturers; hence production soon shrinks. As production diminishes, profits fade away. Men are laid off. This frightens other employees, and they stop buying goods on credit, and tend to reduce their indebtedness. Their cessation of buying of course makes production decline still further, and this decline leads to diminished employment. As employment shrinks, the national wage total becomes smaller, and this curtails buying by wage workers. Such curtailment causes a further fall in sales, profits, and the national income.

Moreover, the advent of pessimism leads bankers to press many borrowers for payment, and to hesitate about making new loans. The result is that loans, and hence deposits, diminish, and this causes the volume of new spending power to decline, and brings about additional shrinkage in the volume of goods bought. All the other phenomena characterizing business recessions soon follow.

Borrowing as the Cause of Depressions

The principal conclusion to be drawn from the analysis just given is that the actual villain in the depression drama is borrowing. Here, at last, we have discovered the real action giving rise to stoppage of buying and hence to depressions. If people generally refrained from going into debt in times of widespread optimism, they would not be compelled later to curtail current purchasing in order to meet their obligations.

Since, when business is active and prices are rising, the general tendency is to yield to temptation and over-expand debt, it seems that the safest method of preventing the depression, which nearly always follows a boom, is for government to take measures to eliminate that expansion of bank credit without which the boom could never develop. If the total volume of bank loans were prevented from expanding far above normal in times of optimism, there would be little tendency for them to drop far below normal in the following period of pessimism.

The shrinkage in the total volume of demand deposits may well be thought of as a reliable gauge recording the extent to which the necessity of paying off debts is curtailing the ability of the public to buy currently produced goods.

Table XVI shows that, from 1929 to 1932, a period of only three years, net new spending power fell from $78 to $42 billions, a decline of 46 per cent. In the face of such a huge drop in ability to buy, it is obviously superfluous, in explaining the origin of depression, to conjure up some hypothetical additional force such as hoarding. The reason why people bought less in 1932 than in 1929 is extremely simple — they did not have the necessary new spending power.

Reasons for Shrinkage in Spending Power

But why did their buying power collapse? Table XVI indicates that there were two reasons:

1. Demand deposits declined from $24 to $17 billions — a shrinkage of $7 billions.
2. Realized income fell from $80 to $47 billions — a drop of $33 billions.

Clearly the major immediate cause of the meager spending in 1932 was income shortage. A minor immediate cause was the paying off of debts owed to the banks. Since the shrinkage in income was so much greater than the shrinkage in the volume of demand deposits, the question of course arises as to whether the contraction in the volume of circulating medium was anything more than a minor factor in bringing about the decline in the volume of net new spending power.

Were it not for the snow-balling effect of any change in the flow of circulating medium, one would certainly be compelled to answer this question in the affirmative. One must remember, however, that many prices, including wage rates, are notoriously "sticky," and that, therefore, a billion-dollar drop in circulating medium tends to reduce immediately the total volume of goods bought, and hence production, by something like a billion dollars' worth. Such a reduction soon causes workers to be laid off, and orders for raw materials to be cancelled. This process, in turn, reduces the incomes both of the workers and of the producers of raw materials. When they stop buying, the result is to curtail employment and production still further. It was this series of steps which, between 1929 and 1932, pulled down the national income so radically. It was this process in reverse which made the national income expand so tremendously after 1938.

Governmental Finance and the Demand for Privately Produced Goods

Now that a large fraction of the total income of the people of the nation has come to be absorbed by government, either through taxation or borrowing, the question of how such absorption affects net aggregate spending power, and also the total demand for privately produced goods, is a matter of major interest.

If a government raises ten billions of dollars either by taxation or by non-bank borrowing, and pays out to its citizens ten billions in the form of bond interest, pensions, relief, or unemployment insurance, the total buying power of the population remains unchanged, for what the taxpayers and bond buyers have lost, other inhabitants have gained.

It is likewise true that money extracted from the pockets of the people and used by government to purchase goods from private sellers does not materially diminish the total volume of buying of privately-produced products. In this case, the government is merely acting as a buying agent for the taxpayers and bond buyers. For example, if government collects ten billions in taxes and uses the money thus obtained to buy airplanes built in private factories, the total volume of sales of privately produced goods is not greatly diminished, for the increases in plane sales will roughly offset the shrinkage in the sales of goods for ordinary consumption.

On the other hand, if government employs labor and equipment to produce the airplanes *in its own factories*, the volume of sales of privately produced goods and the total income of persons employed in private industry will diminish. The volume of orders in industries other than airplane production may, however, remain undisturbed.

The Effect of Public Spending

At present, the most popular panacea for unemployment is to have government hire people to construct public works. Clearly, if the funds to pay for the public works are raised either by taxation or by borrowing from non-bank lenders, the demand for labor used in producing other goods will tend to be reduced by the same amount that the demand for labor on public works is enhanced; hence the number of employees laid off in other fields will tend to equal the number hired for public construction projects. Therefore, unemployment will be as prevalent as before the public works were started. Government employment is, then, a remedy for unemployment only to the extent that it is financed by creating new circulating medium, either by borrowing from the banks or by printing new money. Each of these procedures has the same result — it lessens the value of the dollar, and hence robs the thrifty of their hard earned savings. Since these savings are the major source of new capital, anything discouraging their accumulation tends to wreck the private enterprise system. Therefore, those who believe they can preserve private enterprise by using public works to take care of unemployment in time of depression are doomed to disappointment.

Liquidation of Government's Debt to the Banks

The huge debt now owed by the Federal Government to the banks hangs over the nation's business like the sword of Damocles. If in a period of business recession any considerable fraction of this debt were to be transferred to non-bank holders, or if, at such a time, the Government were to make sizable payments on this debt, the result would be to reduce the net total of demand deposits outstanding, cut down total net new spending power, and, in all probability, bring on a first-class depression. The moral is that the Government should take advantage of every period of business expansion to reduce its indebtedness to the banks, and should refrain from such reduction in times of business recession.

Spending Power and Manufacturing Activity

How variations in spending power control the activities of industry is well illustrated by the case of manufacturing — a field concerning which statistical data have, for a long time, been especially abundant. For many years, the United States Census of Manufactures has published figures showing the "Total Value of Products" turned out by all manufacturing establishments. These totals cannot, however, legitimately be used to measure the value of the net product of the manufacturing industry in the nation, for the value of products depends largely upon the costs of materials and services bought from agriculture, mining, transportation, and other industries. Furthermore, the products of some factories constitute the raw materials used in other plants, hence the total reported value of products may include several valuations of the same materials.

In order to picture better the activities of the manufacturing industry itself, the Census Bureau also reports for each manufacturing industry a quantity called the "Value Added by Manufacture." This quantity is arrived at by deducting from the gross "Value of Products" the total cost of materials, containers, fuel, purchased electric energy, and contract work. The remainder furnishes the best existing measure of the amount of money available to pay for the services of the employees and capital engaged in the manufacturing industry. Table XVII and Chart 6 make it possible to compare readily the relationship between the nation's volume of net new spending power and the aggregate value of manufacturing activity. In Chart 6, these two variables are plotted against one another in the form of a scatter diagram.

Table XVII

DEPENDENCE OF THE TOTAL VALUE ADDED BY MANUFACTURE UPON THE NET TOTAL OF NEW SPENDING POWER ACCRUING DURING THE YEAR IN THE UNITED STATES

	A	B	C	D	E
Census Year	Net New Spending Power (Billions)		Value Added by Manufacture (Billions)		Error of Estimate (Per Cent)
	Actual[a]	Minus 20 Billions[b]	Estimated $\frac{B}{2}$	Actual[c]	$100 \frac{C-D}{D}$
1919	$67.84	$47.84	$23.92	$23.74	+ 0.8
1921	53.13	33.13	16.56	17.25	− 4.0
1923	66.83	46.83	23.41	24.57	− 4.7
1925	71.09	51.09	25.54	25.67	− 0.5
1927	74.67	54.67	27.33	26.33	+ 3.8
1929	78.60	58.60	29.30	30.59	− 4.2
1931	56.91	36.91	18.45	18.60	− 0.8
1933	44.60	24.60	12.30	14.01	−12.2
1935	60.71	40.71	20.35	18.55	+ 9.7
1937	67.21	47.21	23.60	25.17	− 6.2
1939	72.62	52.62	26.31	24.68	+ 6.6
					Av. 4.9

[a] See the last column of Table XVI.
[b] Reasons for the subtraction and division are discussed in the text.
[c] *Statistical Abstract of the U. S.,* 1942, p. 885. The figures for 1935-7-9 are slightly smaller than they should be to be exactly comparable with those for earlier years; for, in the later years, the value of contract work has been subtracted. Were the figures made comparable, the errors in Column E would be reduced for 1935 and 1939, and increased for 1937.

It requires only a glance at the chart, to see that the two variables are closely correlated, for the points representing the various years all lie close to the diagonal line. It will be observed that the diagonal cuts the vertical axis at $20 billions. This indicates that, between World War I and World War II, the people of the United States spent, as a rule, about $20 billions per annum for essentials, the remainder of their net new spending power being paid out for things which were bought more freely in prosperous years than in times of depression. It is for this reason that Column B of Table XVI shows net new spending power minus $20 billions.

It will also be observed that the triangle in Chart 6 is $66 billions high while the base is $33 billions — exactly half of the altitude. This ratio explains why the figures in Column C of Table XVII are half the size of those in Column B.

Reference to the figures in Table XVII makes it evident that the relationship between net new spending power and the value added by manufacture is such that, if the former is known, the latter can be calculated with the

CHART 6

DEPENDENCE OF THE
VALUE ADDED BY MANUFACTURE
UPON THE
NET VOLUME OF NEW SPENDING POWER▾

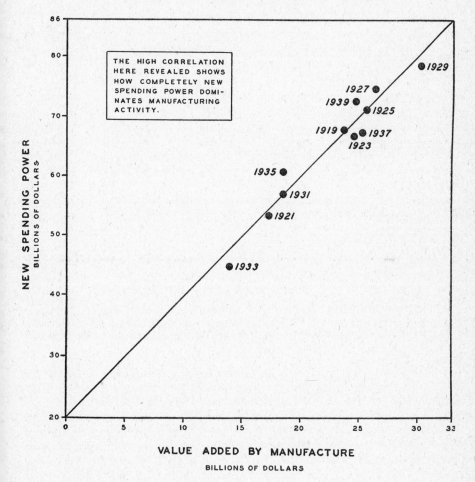

THE HIGH CORRELATION HERE REVEALED SHOWS HOW COMPLETELY NEW SPENDING POWER DOMINATES MANUFACTURING ACTIVITY.

NEW SPENDING POWER
BILLIONS OF DOLLARS

VALUE ADDED BY MANUFACTURE
BILLIONS OF DOLLARS

▾FOR DATA, SEE TABLE XVII

greatest of ease. All that is necessary is to subtract $20 billions from the new spending power total and divide the remainder by 2. Columns C, D and E show that the differences between the results thus estimated and the true totals are surprisingly small, the average error of estimate being slightly less than 5 per cent. The figures seem to prove conclusively that, in general, new spending power is very promptly translated into manufacturing activity.

But is this conclusion sound? Does it not place the cart before the horse? Is it not more logical to conclude that, in reality, it is the manufacturing activity which creates the new spending power?

It is undoubtedly true that wages, interest, rent, and dividend payments result from manufacturing production, and that these form an important part of the national realized income, and hence of net new spending power. It is also clear, however, that, in the 1919 to 1921 period, the $6 billion shrinkage in the value added by manufacture could not account for the $14 billion drop in new spending power taking place in that period. Similarly, in the 1921 to 1929 interval, the $13 billion increase in value added by manufacture was manifestly not responsible for the $25 billion net growth in new spending power. The same principle applies to the later periods covered. If value added by manufacture is the motivating force, the tail must wag the dog in a remarkable way!

Furthermore, no one has explained clearly how an increase in manufacturing activity can account for changes in buying power brought about by borrowing from banks or by paying off bank loans, but, at times, this factor of bank loans has had a marked influence upon the total ability of the population to buy goods. Thus, in late 1929, when optimism gave way to pessimism, the total volume of brokers' loans declined from $6,540,000,000 in September to $3,391,000,000 in December, a drop of 47 per cent in three months.[1] To assume that this drop was caused primarily by a decline in factory activity would be absurd. On the other hand, it is clear that those persons who paid off $4,149,000,000 of indebtedness had their ability to buy manufactured products seriously curtailed.

In 1937, between February and October, the loans and investments of reporting "member banks" declined $1,064,000,000, but the sharp break in manufacturing production did not begin until September.[2] Obviously, therefore, the autumn drop in factory output could not have caused the credit decline occurring earlier in the year. The evidence just presented shows how untenable is the belief that factory production dominates changes in the net volume of new spending power.

On the other hand, Table XVI makes it equally clear that the major source of new spending power is the realized income of the people of the nation, and we know that this income arises from the *combined* production of manufacturing and other industries, a number of which tend to fluctuate in unison. Therefore, the question of whether new spending power gives rise to production, or production gives rise to new spending power, is as puzzling as the old problem of which comes first, the hen or the egg.

[1] *Standard Statistical Bulletin*, June Supplement, 1930, p. 5.
[2] U. S. *Survey of Current Business*, 1940 Supplement, pp. 8; 50–51.

In reality, the situation does parallel almost exactly the case of the hen and the egg. The hen lays an egg which hatches, and the resulting chick may eventually grow into a hen; but it certainly is not the same hen that laid the egg! Similarly, as pointed out in the preceding chapter, industrial production today gives rise to sales tomorrow or next week. Such sales furnish the cash to pay at a still later date wages, salaries, rent, interest, profits, and dividends. These constitute the bulk of the nation's realized income, and realized income is the major item in net new spending power. Next, the net new spending power is used to buy industrial products and this purchasing stimulates new production by the nation's industries. This production, however, is not the same production mentioned in the first instance — it is on the next round of the spiral.

It follows that knowledge of the value of production at any given date enables one to predict the value of the realized income at a LATER date. Knowledge of the income at that later date helps greatly in forecasting the value of production at a STILL LATER date.

It must, however, be remembered that the net volume of new spending power is determined, not only by the size of the realized income, but also by additions to or subtractions from the nation's stock of circulating medium. Such additions or subtractions may or may not be related to the volume of production in the nation.

From what has just been said, it appears that the highest degree of correlation would be found between net new spending power at one date and value added by manufacture at a later date. However, the time difference is probably only a few weeks or months. Censuses of the manufacturing industry are taken only once in two years. Therefore, it is impracticable to make comparisons on the precise time basis which would presumably show the closest relationship. The percentages of error shown in the last column of Table XVII are, however, so small that better timing could scarcely be expected to cause any material reductions in their size.

One of the reasons why the "Value Added by Manufacture" is correlated so closely with the national net new spending power total is that a large part of the goods consumed in the nation have passed through the factories in the nation. Therefore, when the consumer buys almost anything, the resulting restocking of the merchant's shelves tends to set in motion factory wheels somewhere.

The relationship may also be viewed from another angle. There are ordinarily but two reasons leading manufacturers to produce goods:

1. They have orders for goods.
2. They believe that, if they produce goods, they will be able to sell them at a profit.

But why do they expect to be able to sell products at a profit? Clearly, it is because their products are in demand. But what makes such demand possible? As we have learned from an earlier chapter, the strength of demand depends upon the rate at which new spending power accrues. Such being the case, it is not surprising to find that the total volume of sales of all manufactured products depends upon the net volume of new spending power originating in the nation in the same year.

Agriculture's Dependence Upon New Spending Power

That the same principle applies to other industries as well is shown by the figures appearing in Table XVIII. The figures in the last column show that, in the period 1922 to 1929, the portions of new spending power used

Table XVIII

VALUE OF TOTAL FARM MARKETINGS
compared with
NET NEW SPENDING POWER IN THE NATION

Year	Value of Farm Marketings[a] (Billions)	Net New Spending Power[b] (Billions)	Per Cent of Spending Power Used to Pay for Farm Produce
1919	$14.60	$ 67.84	21.6
1920	12.61	65.70	19.2
1921	8.15	53.13	15.3
1922	8.59	59.42	14.5
1923	9.56	66.83	14.3
1924	10.22	68.79	14.9
1925	10.99	71.09	15.4
1926	10.56	71.64	14.7
1927	10.76	74.67	14.4
1928	11.07	76.91	14.4
1929	11.30	78.60	14.4
1930	9.02	71.15	12.6
1931	6.37	56.91	11.2
1932	4.74	42.47	11.2
1933	5.31	44.60	11.9
1934	6.33	55.60	11.4
1935	7.09	60.71	11.7
1936	8.37	69.80	12.0
1937	8.85	67.21	13.2
1938	7.69	65.00	11.8
1939	7.88	72.62	10.8
1940	8.34	83.65	10.0
1941	11.16	100.31	11.1
1942	15.32[c]	138.50	11.1
1943	19.34[c]	161.78	12.0
1944	19.79[c]	178.07	11.1
1945	20.80[c]	177.50	11.7
1946	23.93[c]	166.61	14.4

[a] *Statistical Abstract of U. S.* for 1943, p. 617.
[b] See Table XVI.
[c] U. S. *Survey of Current Business,* June 1946, p. 15 and Mar. 1947, p. S–1.

to purchase the products of farms fell within a remarkably narrow range, averaging 14.6 per cent, or slightly more than one-seventh. After 1930, the fraction of new spending power going for farm produce dropped closer to one-ninth, the average for the years 1931 to 1945 inclusive being 11.5 per cent. The drop to this lower level may have been brought about by the fact that, in the depression, the fall in agricultural prices was far larger than the

CHART 7

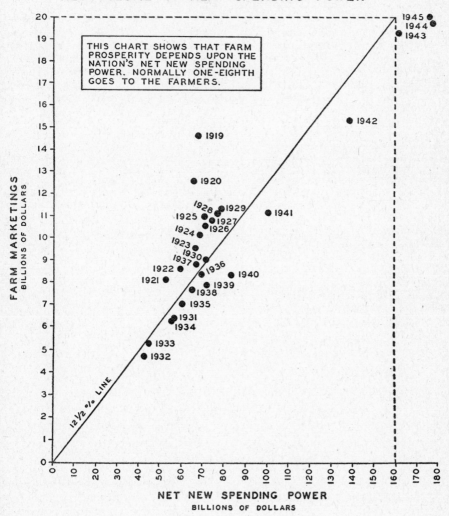

DEPENDENCE OF THE
TOTAL VALUE OF FARM MARKETINGS
UPON THE
NET VOLUME OF NEW SPENDING POWER▼

(●1946

THIS CHART SHOWS THAT FARM PROSPERITY DEPENDS UPON THE NATION'S NET NEW SPENDING POWER. NORMALLY ONE-EIGHTH GOES TO THE FARMERS.

FARM MARKETINGS
BILLIONS OF DOLLARS

NET NEW SPENDING POWER
BILLIONS OF DOLLARS

▼FOR DATA, SEE TABLE XVIII

decline in the prices of urban products. Perhaps it shows that, per unit of output, farm expenses shrank more than did expenses in other industries. Whatever the cause, the results indicate that the net volume of new spending power is the dominant force determining whether, in any given year, the cash income of our agricultural population will be large or small.

Chart 7 shows graphically in which years farm cash income lay above, and in which years it lay below, the 12½ per cent line.

The evidence presented makes it difficult to avoid the conclusion that stability in the accrual of new spending power is a prerequisite essential to abiding prosperity. Without it, no industry can continuously flourish. Without it, neither employers nor employees can avoid hard times.

Chapter XV

THE SOURCE OF WAGES

The Wage Total and National Prosperity

The majority of adults in the United States are employees. Wages or salaries constitute their chief sources of income. It follows that the prosperity of the majority of Americans depends primarily upon the size of the wage and salary total.

Note that, from the standpoint of the general welfare, it is the total that is really significant. High wage rates coupled with very few working hours per week may leave the working class with plenty of leisure, but with scanty cash to pay rent and grocery bills. High annual pay for an employed minority, with the majority unemployed, does not spell general prosperity. It is obvious to everyone that those out of work are not likely to be prosperous. What may be overlooked in this connection, however, is the fact that, in time of depression, those fortunate enough to have good jobs are often compelled to share their incomes with those who are idle, thus reducing their own economic welfare. It follows that, if we are to solve the problem of how to assure widespread and enduring prosperity, we must study the forces that govern the size of the nation's wage and salary total.

Net New Spending Power and Payments to Employees

Economists have long pointed out that the only *real costs* of production are *labor* and *waiting*. Labor gets its pay in the form of wages, salaries, and profits. The payment for waiting is interest.

The *expenses* of production include not only payments for labor and waiting, but also payments for natural resources and their services. In most advanced nations, payments comprised in this third category make up but a minor fraction of all expenses. Interest charges are also relatively unimportant. It follows that payments for labor make up the bulk of all the expenses of production.

Manual workers and the less educated classes of mental workers ordinarily receive *wages*. Technicians, administrators, and executives commonly draw *salaries*. Farmers and merchants usually get their pay in the form of *profits*.

Since the nation's supply of neither natural resources nor waiting tends to vary greatly from year to year, and since the proportion of the labor force depending for its pay upon profits changes but slowly, it is not surprising to find that wages and salaries tend to absorb a fairly constant share of the net total of new spending power. However, Table XIX and Chart 8 show a stability in this percentage which is remarkable. Even the siphoning off by Government of nearly half of the nation's income left the percentage virtually unchanged. The great unionizing campaign of the Congress of Industrial Organizations, backed by the Wagner Act, apparently did produce a ripple, but soon the percentage dropped back to its normal level. The indications are, indeed, that, whether the labor supply is free or monopolized,

Table XIX

THE SHARE OF THE EMPLOYEES
IN THE NATION'S NET NEW SPENDING POWER

Year	A Total Net New Spending Power[a] (Billions)	B Total of Wages, Salaries and Other Compensation of All Employees in the U. S.[b] (Billions)	C Per Cent of Net New Spending Power Going to Employees $\frac{100 \text{ B}}{\text{A}}$
1919	$67.84	$35.40	52.2
1920	65.70	42.28	64.4
1921	53.13	36.21	68.1
1922	59.42	37.70	63.5
1923	66.83	42.89	64.2
1924	68.79	44.49	64.7
1925	71.09	46.85	65.9
1926	71.64	48.50	67.7
1927	74.67	48.20	64.6
1928	76.91	49.00	63.7
1929	78.60	50.73	64.5
1930	71.15	46.39	65.2
1931	56.91	39.32	69.1
1932	42.47	30.90	72.8
1933	44.60	29.24	65.6
1934	55.60	33.92	61.0
1935	60.71	36.90	60.8
1936	69.80	42.39	60.7
1937	67.21	47.42	70.6
1938	65.00	44.48	68.4
1939	72.62	47.60	65.5
1940	83.65	51.57	61.6
1941	100.31	64.5	64.3
1942	138.50	84.1	60.7
1943	161.78	106.3	65.7
1944	178.07	116.0	65.1
1945	177.50	114.5	64.5
1946	166.61	109.8	65.9
			Median = 64.65

[a] See Table XVI for computation of data.
[b] Does *not* include allowances made by proprietors to themselves. For sources of data, see Table XII.

whether government plays a major or a minor rôle, whether industry is prosperous or in the depths of depression, the nation's wage and salary total tends to absorb about 64½ per cent of the aggregate of net new spending power available. Presumably this constancy is accounted for by the fact that, as long as freedom and private property exist, owners of natural resources demand and get pay for the use of these things; accumulators of capital demand and get pay for waiting; and farmers, merchants, and small businessmen generally demand and get pay for their productive efforts. It appears, furthermore, that, under such circumstances, struggles by employees

CHART 8

DEPENDENCE OF THE TOTAL PAY OF EMPLOYEES UPON THE NATION'S NET VOLUME OF NEW SPENDING POWER▼

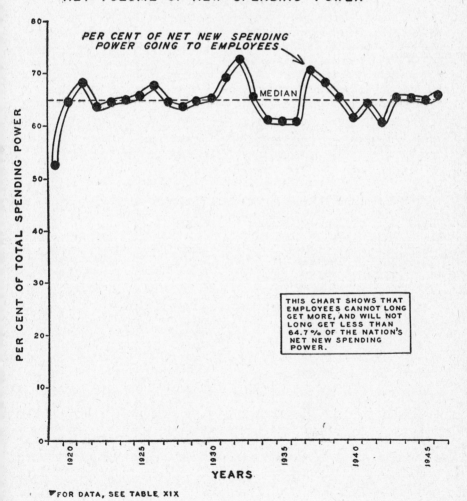

PER CENT OF NET NEW SPENDING POWER GOING TO EMPLOYEES

MEDIAN

THIS CHART SHOWS THAT EMPLOYEES CANNOT LONG GET MORE, AND WILL NOT LONG GET LESS THAN 64.7% OF THE NATION'S NET NEW SPENDING POWER.

PER CENT OF TOTAL SPENDING POWER

YEARS

▼FOR DATA, SEE TABLE XIX

to enlarge their percentage of the nation's supply of new spending power are foredoomed to failure, and succeed only in creating strife and hatred, and lowering the national income and with it their own total pay.

Relationship of the Wage Total for All Industries to the Net Total of New Spending Power.

The evidence presented in Table XIX seems to show conclusively that the total pay of all employees in all industries depends primarily upon the aggregate of new spending power generated in the nation. Is the relationship of this last-mentioned aggregate to the wage total alone as close as it is to the total of wages and salaries combined?

Statistics of the type required to make possible an answer to this query are decidedly scanty. The United States Department of Commerce and other agencies studying income usually fail to separate salary payments from wage payments. Apparently the only available continuous record of wage payments covering any considerable period of years is that prepared by the present writer and published by the National Bureau of Economic Research in the volume entitled *The National Income and Its Purchasing Power.* Table XXII in that report shows the estimated total of wages paid in the United States in each year from 1909 to 1928 inclusive. The figures for the last three years of this period were prepared before final Census reports were published, and hence are less reliable than are the figures for earlier years.

Table XX

THE WAGE TOTAL FOR ALL INDUSTRIES IN THE UNITED STATES
compared with
TOTAL NET NEW SPENDING POWER

Year	A Total New Spending Power[a] (Billions)	B Total Wage Bill[b] (Billions)	C Percentage of Available Funds Going to Wages $\frac{100\,B}{A}$
1919	$67.84	$23.03	33.9
1920	65.70	29.54	45.0
1921	53.13	23.35	43.9
1922	59.42	24.55	41.4
1923	66.83	28.69	42.9
1924	68.79	29.05	42.2
1925	71.09	30.76	43.3
1926	71.64	32.60	45.5
1927	74.67	32.88	44.0
1928	76.91	32.23	41.9

[a] See Table XVI, last column.
[b] See Table XXII of the National Bureau of Economic Research report entitled *The National Income and Its Purchasing Power.*

The net result is that the only years for which we have at hand data both on total net new spending power and total wage payments are the years 1919 to 1928 inclusive, and the data for 1926 to 1928 are not highly dependable, though the data for 1926 and 1927 are believed to be fairly close to the truth. The figures for 1919 to 1928 inclusive are presented in Table XX.

The entries in Table XX indicate that, for the years 1919 to 1928 inclusive, approximately 43 per cent of all net new spending power found its way into the pockets of wage workers. The only year in which there was a wide departure from this percentage was 1919. In that year, war influences continued to affect wage payments. In the early part of the year, many men were still in the army where the wage level was much lower than in civilian life. Furthermore, the price level was rising rapidly, and wages, being influenced by custom and contract, probably lagged somewhat behind prices of finished products, thus giving very temporarily to the employees an abnormally small share of the net value product of industry.

Although the period covered by Table XX is too brief to justify positive conclusions, the data in the table indicate strongly that the size of the total wage bill depends mainly upon the net volume of spending power available in the nation.

The Source of Factory Wages

As stated in the preceding section, up-to-date figures showing for industry as a whole over a considerable period of years a separation of wage and salary data are not available. However, such information is furnished by the Federal Government for one of our major industries — namely, manufacturing.

That the relationships prevailing in manufacturing are typical of those governing other industries seems highly probable for two reasons:

1. The manufacturing field is so large and varied that it is almost certain to be representative of labor in general.
2. It is highly competitive, and, before the advent of the New Deal, suffered relatively little from governmental interference.

Before proceeding with a study of the available data, it seems worth while to analyze some of the relationships controlling the demand for factory products, and hence for factory labor.

Table XVII and Chart 6 show that the total value of manufactured goods sold depends upon the net new spending power accruing in the nation. Similarly, the total value of all purchases made by manufacturers depends upon the total value of factory products sold; for the manufacturer must, in the main, rely upon the proceeds of sales to get the wherewithal to make purchases. Out of such receipts, he must, of course, pay not only for all the materials obtained from other factories, from farms, and from mines, but also for the fuel and power furnished by the mining and electrical industries. As noted in the preceding chapter, the residue remaining from gross receipts, after meeting the payments just mentioned, is recorded by the Census of Manufactures under the caption "Value Added by Manufacture."

Clearly, it is out of this residue that, in general, the money necessary to meet the factory wage bill must be obtained. In other words, wages must be paid out of the "value added by manufacture."

Relation of Wage Total to Value Added by Manufacture

The next question to be considered is whether the wage bill represents a fairly constant or, instead, a highly variable fraction of this value. Has the growth during the last decade in the power of the labor unions tended to increase the relative share of the laborer in the "value added by manufacture"? The facts in the case as regards the period 1919 to 1939 are shown definitely by figures extracted from the Federal Census of Manufactures and recorded in Table XXI.

The lower graph in Chart 9 shows that factory labor tends to get an almost constant share of the gross value of the products of American factories. The figures in Table XXI and the upper graph in Chart 9 make it clear that, on the whole, the factory wage bill comprises a fairly constant fraction of the total amount remaining to manufacturers out of receipts from sales after they have paid for materials, containers, contract work, fuel, and

Table XXI

RELATIONSHIP OF THE
TOTAL FACTORY WAGE BILL
TO THE
TOTAL VALUE ADDED BY MANUFACTURE

	A	B	C
Census Year	Total Factory Wage Bill[a] (Billions)	Total Value Added by Manufacture[a] (Billions)	Ratio of Wage Bill to Value Added $\frac{A}{B}$
1919	$9.61	$23.74	0.405
1921	7.45	17.25	.432
1923	10.15	24.57	.413
1925	9.98	25.67	.388
1927	10.10	26.32	.384
1929	10.88	30.59	.356
1931	6.69	18.60	.359
1933	4.94	14.01	.352
1935	7.31	18.55[b]	.394[b]
1937	10.11	25.17[b]	.402[b]
1939	9.09	24.68[b]	.368[b]
Total	$96.31	$249.15	0.3866

[a] *Statistical Abstract of the U. S.* for 1942, p. 885.
[b] For 1935 and later years, the cost of contract work has been subtracted in arriving at these figures. For earlier years, this subtraction has not been made. To be strictly comparable, the 1935 to 1939 figures for "Value Added" should be slightly larger and the ratios slightly smaller than those here entered.

power. The proportion disbursed as wages has ranged from a low of 35 per cent in 1933 to a high of 42 per cent in 1921.

CHART 9

LABOR'S SHARE IN THE VALUE OUTPUT OF MANUFACTURING
(UNITED STATES)

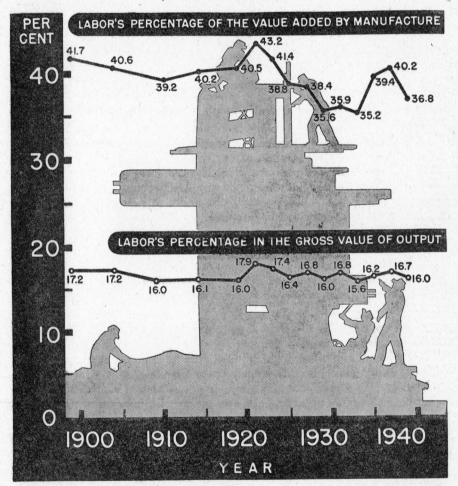

Year in and year out, labor receives a nearly constant share of the customer's dollar and a nearly constant share of the product of all our factories. The balance must go to pay for materials, taxes, salaries, depreciation, interest, insurance, rent, power, etc.

Percentages computed from data in the *Statistical Abstract of the United States* for 1941, page 845.

The nature of the forces causing the percentage to fluctuate is not known. Extensive unionization by the C.I.O. in 1936 and 1937 did not prevent the ratio of wage totals to value added by manufacture from being as low in 1939 as in 1935. In the steel and automobile industries, the two outstanding ones organized by the C.I.O. in 1936 and 1937, the figures were as follows:

Census Year	Steel	Automobile
1935...............................	48.4	48.5
1939...............................	44.5	48.8

These figures show that, in the steel industry, the percentage going to wages declined, and that, in the automobile industry, the percentage remained almost constant.[1] Apparently, then, even the most powerful unions are unable to increase noticeably the share of the value product paid out in wages. If workers stay on the job, competition among employers assures them of as large a share of the sales dollar as they can secure by any amount of struggling. Strikes serve only to diminish the size of the pie to be divided.

Relation in Manufacturing of Real Hourly Earnings to Physical Output per Man-Hour

In the days when each family produced the larger part of the goods which it consumed, it was plain to everyone that returns depended upon production. Nowadays, however, the relationship between pay and production has become so involved that most workers probably see little connection between the two. Strangely enough, some writers who consider themselves to be trained economists expound the doctrine that the wage level prevailing in a nation depends upon the comparative bargaining strengths of employers and employees.

A study by Charles E. Young, Manager of the Statistical Research Department of the Westinghouse Electric Corporation shows the fallacious nature of this point of view. His findings are presented in Table XXII and Chart 10.

Merely a glance at Chart 10 is required to show that, on the average, real hourly earnings are tied closely to physical productivity. Clearly, therefore, bargaining avails the working class little or nothing. Only by producing more can the workingman hope to raise his scale of living. Under free competition, if he produces more, this happens almost automatically. No matter how efficiently organized the workers may be, they and their families will suffer if production declines. Labor's share of the product is determined by forces beyond its power to control.

Forces Controlling Labor's Share of the Product

Why is it that labor cannot increase its percentage of the value of the product? The chief reasons appear to be as follows:

1. Payments for newly produced goods are partly payments for *direct* and partly payments for *indirect* labor. For example, in a textile factory, it is necessary for the customer who buys cloth to pay not only for the services of the weavers but also for the services of the clerks,

[1] *Statistical Abstract of the U. S.* for 1940, p. 826 and for 1942, pp. 908 and 915.

Table XXII

REAL HOURLY EARNINGS IN MANUFACTURING
compared with
PHYSICAL FACTORY OUTPUT PER MAN-HOUR *
Data for 1939 = 100

Year	Average Hourly Earnings in Manufacturing[a]	"Cost of Living" Index[b]	Real Hourly Earnings	Output Per Man-Hour in Manufacturing[c]
	A	B	100 (A ÷ B)	
1914	33.5	72.7	46.1	44.2
1919	71.3	125.3	56.9	43.8
1920	86.8	144.1	60.2	48.6
1921	76.1	128.5	59.2	52.7
1922	71.0	120.4	59.0	58.8
1923	78.3	122.6	63.9	57.3
1924	81.8	122.9	66.6	61.0
1925	81.7	126.2	64.7	65.1
1926	82.3	127.2	64.7	67.2
1927	83.1	124.7	66.6	69.3
1928	84.2	123.3	68.3	73.1
1929	85.1	123.2	69.1	75.5
1930	83.1	120.1	69.2	78.0
1931	77.8	109.4	71.1	81.5
1932	71.1	98.2	72.4	77.7
1933	70.0	93.0	75.3	82.9
1934	84.0	96.3	87.2	85.8
1935	86.8	98.7	87.9	91.0
1936	87.6	99.7	87.9	92.1
1937	98.4	103.3	95.3	90.9
1938	99.1	101.4	97.7	91.9
1939	100.0	100.0	100.0	100.0
1940	104.3	100.7	103.6	106.4
1941	114.3	105.8	108.1	108.3
1942	132.0	117.2	112.6	110.9
1943	149.2	124.2	120.1	111.6
1944	158.2	126.3	125.3	113.8
1945 (p)	157.7	129.0	122.2	119.8

* Table prepared by Charles E. Young of the Westinghouse Electric Co.
[a] United States Bureau of Labor Statistics data on Average Hourly Earnings in Manufacturing. Figures prior to 1932 are based upon BLS Payrolls Index and Census Reports.
[b] Compiled by the U. S. Bureau of Labor Statistics. It shows price changes in the goods bought by typical urban working-class families.
[c] Derived by Charles E. Young from estimates made by Solomon Fabricant of the National Bureau of Economic Research for the years up to 1939 and from later data prepared by the Federal Reserve Board.
(p) Preliminary.

the bookkeepers, the technicians, and the officials who devote their time to making the affairs of the producing concern run smoothly. If these persons are not paid, they will quit work, and production will bog down.

2. The money paid for the finished cloth goes partly to pay for *present* labor, and partly to pay for *past* labor. Thus, it is present labor that is tending the machines which weave the cotton into cloth; but it was past labor that helped to produce the cotton out of which the cloth is made; it was past labor that dug out the iron ore, that smelted it, and that made it into the intricate machines which do the actual work of weaving. If those plantations which grow cotton, if those concerns which provide machines find that present labor seizes more than its share of the buyer's dollar, no more cotton and no more machines will be forthcoming, and, when the present supply of cotton is exhausted, or the present machines are worn out, production will stop.

3. As pointed out earlier in the chapter, the inability of wage workers to increase their percentage of the value product results in part from

CHART 10

REAL HOURLY WAGES vs. OUTPUT PER MAN HOUR IN MANUFACTURING

1939 = 100

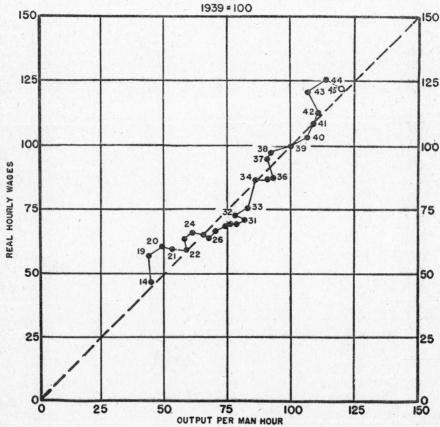

the fact that the services of capital and of farmers and other proprietors cannot be obtained free. If those who devote their efforts to

Table XXIII

ESTIMATES OF THE TOTAL FACTORY WAGE BILL IN THE UNITED STATES

Year	A Factory Wage Totals Reported by the Census of Manufactures[a] (Millions)	B Factory Payrolls Index[b] B	C $\frac{A}{B}$	D Estimated Factory Wage Total for U. S.[b] (Millions) B × C
1919	$9,611	98.0	98.07[f]	$9,611
1920		117.2	98.25[g]	11,515
1921	7,451	75.6	98.55[f]	7,451
1922		81.2	98.19[g]	8,006
1923	10,149	102.9	98.63[f]	10,149
1924		96.0	98.69[g]	9,472
1925	9,980	101.1	98.71[f]	9,980
1926		104.2	98.66[g]	10,280
1927	10,099	102.4	98.62[f]	10,099
1928		103.5	98.61[g]	10,206
1929	10,885	110.4	98.60[f]	10,885
1930		89.4	98.63[g]	8,817
1931	6,689	67.8	98.66[g]	6,689
1932		46.7	98.62[f]	4,606
1933	4,940	50.1	98.60[f]	4,940
1934		64.5	98.63[g]	6,361
1935	7,311	74.1	98.66[f]	7,311
1936		85.8	98.66[g]	8,465
1937	10,113	102.5	98.66[f]	10,113
1938		78.5[c]	98.63[g]	7,742
1939	9,090	92.2[c]	98.59[f]	9,090
1940		105.6[d]	98.57[g]	10,406
1941		154.4[d]	98.56[g]	15,221
1942		226.1[e]	98.55[g]	22,279
1943		308.3[e]	98.54[g]	30,382
1944		318.7[e]	98.53[g]	31,404
1945		270.5[e]	98.52[g]	26,651
1946		245.6[e]	98.51[g]	24,196

S=*U. S. Survey of Current Business.*
[a] *Statistical Abstract of the U. S.* for 1942, p. 885.
[b] S. Supplement, 1940, pp. 40–44.
[c] S. Mar. 1941, p. 18.
[d] S. Feb. 1945, p. 22.
[e] S. Oct. 1945, p. 20; Feb. 1947, p. 32; and May, 1947, p. 24.
[f] Computed.
[g] Estimated by aid of a smooth curve.

management are not paid for their time, if those who save and accumulate the capital necessary to finance the concern's operations are not compensated for their trouble, the new funds needed if the business is to be expanded cannot be secured.

The net result is, therefore, that the wage-working class in the manufacturing industry is compelled to content itself with approximately 39 per cent of the total receipts taken in to pay for the services of the manufacturing industry to the buyers of manufactured products. Occasionally its share drops to 35 per cent; occasionally it rises to 42 per cent; but rarely does it get outside these limits.

Relation of Factory Wage Bill to New Net Spending Power

Figures presented by the United States Bureau of Labor Statistics make it possible to estimate rather closely for each year from 1919 to 1942 the size of the total factory wage bill in the United States. Such estimates appear in Table XXIII.

If the total value added by manufacture bears a definite simple mathematical relationship to the net total of new spending power, and if it also maintains a roughly constant ratio to the total factory wage bill, it follows that there must likewise be a simple relationship between the factory wage bill and the net volume of new spending power. Such being the case, it must be possible to estimate the approximate size of the factory wage bill if the net volume of new spending power is known. Table XXIV presents an estimate made on the basis of the principles just established.

Since it seems reasonable to suppose that, as population grows, the *total* volume of relatively fixed expenses will also increase, Column B has been calculated on the basis of the assumption that fundamental necessities cost the average inhabitant $162 per year. This gives an average for the entire period equalling approximately the twenty-billion-dollar annuity derived from Chart 6.

Column F shows that, on the basis of the assumptions made, it is possible to approximate, by using records of population and new spendable funds alone, the total factory wage bills for all the years from 1919 to 1946 inclusive — the average error of estimate being but 6.9 per cent. That such is the case is remarkable especially in view of the fact that the period covered is one characterized by violent fluctuations in both new spendable funds and employment.

Clearly, however, the volume of new buying power becoming available in the nation and population growth are not the sole determinants of the factory wage total, for, as Table XXIV, Column F, shows, estimates based upon these criteria alone sometimes differ from the truth by nearly 20 per cent. Among the reasons accounting for such errors are the following: —

1. Estimates of the realized national income are likely to be in error by several per cent.
2. In some years, the volume of factory orders, and hence of factory employment, is likely to be affected noticeably by orders from

abroad. Such orders are not necessarily reflected in the volume of new spendable funds in the hands of Americans.

Table XXIV

DEPENDENCE OF THE TOTAL FACTORY WAGE BILL UPON THE TOTAL NET VOLUME OF NEW SPENDING POWER

Year	A	B	C	D	E	F
	Net New Spending Power (Billions)			Total Factory Wage Bill (Billions)		Error of Estimate (Per Cent)
	Total[a]	Non-Variable Expenses[b] ($162 per capita)	Disposable Funds A−B	Computed[c] 0.19C	Actual[d]	$100 \dfrac{D-E}{E}$
1919	$67.84	$16.94	$50.90	$9.69	$9.61	+0.8
1920	65.70	17.25	48.45	9.23	11.51	−19.8
1921	53.13	17.59	35.54	6.77	7.45	−9.1
1922	59.42	17.85	41.57	7.92	8.01	−1.1
1923	66.83	18.15	48.68	9.27	10.15	−8.7
1924	68.79	18.51	50.28	9.57	9.47	+1.1
1925	71.09	18.77	52.32	9.96	9.98	+0.2
1926	71.64	19.02	52.62	10.02	10.28	−2.5
1927	74.67	19.32	55.35	10.54	10.10	+4.4
1928	76.91	19.53	57.38	10.92	10.21	+7.0
1929	78.60	19.73	58.87	11.21	10.88	+3.0
1930	71.15	19.98	51.17	9.74	8.82	+10.4
1931	56.91	20.14	36.77	7.00	6.69	+4.6
1932	42.47	20.22	22.25	4.24	4.61	−8.0
1933	44.60	20.36	24.24	4.62	4.94	−6.5
1934	55.60	20.50	35.10	6.68	6.36	+5.0
1935	60.71	20.63	40.08	7.63	7.31	+4.4
1936	69.80	20.79	49.01	9.33	8.46	+10.3
1937	67.21	20.87	46.34	8.82	10.11	−12.8
1938	65.00	21.03	43.97	8.37	7.74	+8.2
1939	72.62	21.20	51.42	9.79	9.09	+7.7
1940	83.65	21.39	62.26	11.83	10.41	+13.6
1941	100.31	21.59	78.72	14.96	15.22	−1.7
1942	138.50	21.79	116.71	22.17	22.28	−0.5
1943	161.78	22.10	139.68	26.54	30.38	−12.6
1944	178.07	22.38	155.68	29.58	31.40	−5.8
1945	177.50	22.63	154.87	29.43	26.65	+10.4
1946	166.61	23.00	143.61	27.29	24.20	+12.8
Total						Av. 6.9

[a] See Table XVI.
[b] The $20 billion total mentioned in Table XVII, Column B averages about $162 per capita. The figures here entered are obtained by multiplying by $162 the population estimates given in the U. S. *Statistical Abstract* for 1942, p. 11, and later census estimates.
[c] The multiplier, 0.19, is the ratio of the total of Column E to the total of Column C for the peace years 1919 to 1941, inclusive.
[d] See Table XXIII, Column D.

3. The ratio of factory wages to factory sales is not exactly constant, for it takes time to adjust wages to changing conditions.

4. The assumption that the average American requires each year exactly $162 for fixed charges is evidently subject to a wide margin of error. The amount actually needed for such expenses is dependent upon the rent level, interest rates, the amount of debt outstanding, railway fares, postage rates, prices of various other necessities, the volume of taxation, and many other things.

Since the factory wage total is so definitely dependent upon the national volume of new spending power, it appears that those manufacturers who assert that, in making wage payments, they are merely acting as the agents of their customers, are closely approximating the truth. Given the net volume of new spending power in the nation, the factory wage total is approximately determined. The employer can do little to make it either larger or smaller. He is at the mercy of powerful forces over which he has no control. Unless he yields to them, his business is soon defunct.

Apologists for labor monopolies frequently contend that, before the advent of unionization, labor was ground down and "exploited" by ruthless employers, and that the unions are to be credited with rescuing labor from this sorry plight. They also assert that, in view of the fact that employers so long took advantage of helpless labor, it is only poetic justice if labor, now that it has grown powerful, tends to ride roughshod over employers.

There can, of course, be no doubt about the fact that most employers have bought labor at the lowest price obtainable. However, the figures which we have presented show that, for many decades, wages have borne nearly constant mathematical relationships both to net new spending power and to the volume of productivity. In view of this evidence, the assumption that, before the days of unionization, employers were able to depress wages below competitive levels appears to be nothing more than a figment of the imagination. The truth seems to be that, then as now, the inexorable inter-action of supply and demand compelled employers to turn over to labor its share of the total product — a share determined by forces beyond their control. It follows that the assumption that labor monopolies have been a necessary development to overcome the ruthless "exploitation" of labor appears to be a hypothesis contrary to fact.

As pointed out in earlier chapters, the amazing increase in the average real hourly wages of American workers has been due to increasing physical productivity per man hour, and this increasing efficiency has, in turn, been brought about by inventions and discoveries implemented by vast amounts of new capital originating in the savings of the thrifty. It appears, therefore, that the assertion that labor's upward progress is the result of unionization and collective bargaining rests upon a foundation just as firm as that underlying the cock's claim that his crowing made the sun rise.

Moreover, as long as the net volume of new spending power does not vary, employees are as powerless as the employers to change the wage total materially, for, no more than the employer, can they successfully combat the forces of the market. However, by affecting the costs, selling prices, and hence the volume of sales of factory products, they can change the net volume of new spending power and hence can modify the wage total *obtainable at a later date.*

The evidence presented in Table XXIV throws an interesting side light upon a topic much discussed by economists in the Nineteenth Century — namely, the doctrine of "the wage fund." The figures in this table seem to prove that, although the Classical Economists were not entirely accurate in their views concerning its origin, they were correct in stating that the total of wage payments is determined by the size of the existing "wage fund." From our study, it now appears that the chief source of that wage fund is the realized income of the people of the nation, but that this source may be augmented or diminished by changes occurring in the volume of the circulating medium.

But realized income depends upon production volume. Therefore, as pointed out by economists of the Classical School, production automatically generates demand; and this is as true in the case of the demand for labor as in the case of the demand for any other good.

How Wage Rates and Employment Influence Employee Income

During the early 1940's, all political parties were especially vociferous in their demands for full employment. Since the prosperity of the working class is measured by the total of wages received, and since the wage total is the product of the number of hours of work times the average hourly wage rate, one might assume that, to the workers, a high average hourly wage rate is just as important as is full employment. For any instant of time, this conclusion is correct. However, this line of reasoning is sadly misleading in its implications, for it fails to take into account the fact that the *future* volume of new spending power depends largely upon the *present* physical volume of production, and that the present volume of production depends mainly upon the present volume of employment. It follows that prosperity cannot continue long unless most of the nation's potential working force is actively engaged in turning out goods.

In practice, moreover, when new spending power shrinks, employment also shrinks. However, it must be remembered that, if wages and other prices were all perfectly flexible a shrinkage in the volume of new spending power would cause no decline in either the volume of physical production or the volume of employment. Under such hypothetical conditions, all the goods on earth might, indeed, be bought for a single dollar!

In reality, however, no such flexibility does exist. Production does stop. Unemployment does appear, and with it comes hard times for the working class. Therefore, if our population as a whole is to be made prosperous, it is necessary to prevent mass unemployment. How is this goal to be achieved?

Chapter XVI

EMPLOYMENT DETERMINANTS

"Full Employment"

After the flood of Governmental buying accompanying World War II had set most of the idle to work, there poured forth from platforms, pulpits, and presses a veritable torrent of pronouncements to the effect that, in the future, the American people were not going to tolerate mass unemployment. In the 1944 campaign, the typical politician felt it imperative to promise that, after the war, his party, if put into power, would assure "full employment." Committees of businessmen and public-spirited citizens worked diligently over the problem of how actually to provide "full employment." Unfortunately, however, in most instances, those in charge of these worthy movements were completely in the dark as to the nature of the forces giving rise to mass idleness. As a result, their efforts to prevent unemployment were as likely to be crowned with success as would have been the case had they been directed toward the prevention of earthquakes or tornadoes!

One of the things which annoyed these public-spirited citizens was that "Doubting Thomases" persisted in raising the question as to just what was meant by the phrase "full employment." The "man in the street" could see no difficulty whatever in defining the term. In his opinion, full employment signified merely that whoever wanted work could find a job. However, many economists were not satisfied with this definition, and hence they asked for answers to such questions as the following: —

1. When persons normally working at skilled jobs are selling shoe strings on the street corner or shovel leaning on a W.P.A. project, are they to be counted as employed?
2. When a plant, because of shortages of orders for its products, is operating but 30 hours per week instead of the customary 40 hours, are its workers fully employed?
3. Is the carpenter who is idle because he can find no work at the union scale of $2.00 per hour, but who can readily obtain employment at $1.00 per hour to be counted as one of those wanting work, but unable to find it?

Estimates of the number of jobs required to give "full employment" to all potential workers in the United States might well vary by as much as 20,000,000 persons merely because the different estimators did not give identical answers to these three questions.

The third question in the above list makes it obvious that unemployment does not entirely depend upon forces external to the potential employee, but is, to a considerable extent, a matter of volition. This fact complicates tremendously the difficulty of deciding whether a man is or is not unemployed. It is, therefore, impossible to determine at any time either how many people

176

Table XXV

THE TOTAL VOLUME OF EMPLOYMENT OF WAGE WORKERS IN ALL SIZABLE FACTORIES IN THE UNITED STATES[d]

	A	B	C	D	E	F	G
Year	Average Number of Wage Earners Employed [a] (Thous.)	Index of Employment in Mfg.[b]	$\frac{A}{B}$	Av. No. of Wage Earners Employed (Thous.) B × C	Av. Hours Worked per Yr. by Av. Employee[c]	Billions of Hours of Employment D × E	Percentage Change from Preceding Year In Employment
1919	8,424	1,067	7895[e]	8,424			
1920		1,071	7895[f]	8,456	2,265	19.15	
1921	6,475	820	7896[e]	6,475	2,143	13.88	−28
1922		907	7895[f]	7,161	2,312	16.56	+19
1923	8,194	1,038	7894[e]	8,194	2,312	18.94	+14
1924		964	7891[f]	7,607	2,204	16.77	−11
1925	7,871	998	7887[e]	7,871	2,266	17.84	+6
1926		1,017	7887[f]	8,021	2,261	18.14	+2
1927	7,848	995	7887[e]	7,848	2,242	17.60	−3
1928		997	7892[f]	7,868	2,251	17.71	+1
1929	8,370	1,060	7896[e]	8,370	2,270	19.00	+7
1930		924	7894[f]	7,294	2,063	15.05	−21
1931	6,163	781	7891[e]	6,163	1,899	11.70	−22
1932		663	7888[f]	5,230	1,636	8.56	−27
1933	5,788	734	7885[e]	5,788	1,711	9.90	+16
1934		857	7888[f]	6,760	1,631	11.03	+11
1935	7,204	913	7890[e]	7,204	1,748	12.59	+14
1936		990	7889[f]	7,810	1,856	14.50	+15
1937	8,569	1,086	7888[e]	8,569	1,819	15.59	+8
1938		897	7892[f]	7,079	1,612	11.41	−27
1939	7,887	1,000	7895[e]	7,895	1,767	13.95	+22
1940		1,075	7895[f]	8,487	1,812	15.38	+10
1941		1,321	7895[f]	10,429	1,937	20.20	+31
1942		1,540	7895[f]	12,158	2,023	24.59	+22
1943		1,777	7895[f]	14,029	2,117	29.70	+21
1944		1,691	7895[f]	13,350	2,142	28.60	−4
1945				12,437[g]	2,075	25.81	−10
1946				11,630[g]	1,885	21.93	−15

[a] *Statistical Abstract of U. S.* 1942, p. 885.
[b] U. S. *Survey of Current Business*, 1940, Supp. p. 31, and Feb. 1946, p. 32.
[c] See the U. S. *Survey of Current Business*, 1940, Supp. p. 39, and later issues for March in each year. The National Industrial Conference Board's estimates of average hours worked per week have been multiplied by 47, because the Census Bureau's factory wage figures indicate that this is the average number of weeks worked per year by the average "full time" worker.
[d] Factories producing respectively in the Census year less than $5,000 worth of goods are not covered.
[e] Computed.
Interpolated or extrapolated.
U. S. *Survey of Current Business*, May 1947, p. 24.

are unemployed or what constitutes "full employment." One can, however, hope to measure CHANGES in the total volume of employment.

The Actual Volume of Employment

The volume of employment in an industry is better measured in terms of hours than in terms of the total number of persons on the pay roll, for, because of "work spreading," the latter quantity may, in time of depression, fail to give much indication of the amount of time devoted to work.

As it happens, figures furnished by the Bureau of the Census, the United States Department of Labor, and the National Industrial Conference Board enable one to estimate, independently of wage-payment data, the total number of hours of employment given by all factories in the United States in each of the years 1919 to 1946 inclusive. Figures thus derived appear in Table XXV.

In general, any decline in the total number of employee-hours worked in a given unit of time means reduced production, and less goods-income both for the working class and for the people of the nation as a whole. The question now to be considered is the nature of the forces which, from time to time, give rise to sharp declines in the aggregate volume of employment. Obviously, until these forces are clearly understood, it is folly to attempt to draft a program to provide "full employment."

For a generation, theorizing on the causes of unemployment has been a favorite occupation among students of labor problems. This theorizing has been intensified by the chronic mass unemployment prevailing in the "Thirties." It seems worth while to consider at this point some of the most popular of the theories evolved.

The Inequality Theory of Unemployment

Certain writers have contended that the wholesale idleness of the "Thirties" was brought about by growing inequality in the distribution of wealth and income. That this contention is without foundation is strongly indicated by figures appearing in Monograph No. 4 prepared by Adolph J. Goldenthal under the general supervision of Robert R. Nathan, and put out by the Temporary National Economic Committee headed by Senator Joseph C. O'Mahoney. The data in this monograph show clearly that there has been no persistent tendency for wealth or income concentration to increase. Evidently, therefore, one must look elsewhere for the cause of mass unemployment.

The Overproduction Theory of Unemployment

Probably the most naive, but nevertheless one of the most widely held hypotheses as to the cause of unemployment, is the overproduction theory. Its weakness is made obvious by the fact that, before the collapse of 1930, production was running but slightly above normal.[1] Furthermore, one of the most marked characteristics of the 1930–1940 debacle — as indeed of all other depressions — was a striking decline in the physical volume of pro-

[1] See the present author's book *The Causes of Economic Fluctuations* (Ronald Press), Chap. 4, for evidence on this point.

duction. If overproduction caused the trouble, reduced production should certainly have remedied it. In reality, however, the more that production fell off, the worse the depression became, and the larger was the number of people out of work.

The Over-stocking Theory of Unemployment

Many people ascribe depressions and mass unemployment to the over-stocking of durable goods — a situation which usually characterizes a boom. Doubtless this factor does tend, in post-boom periods, to cause idleness among the producers of such goods. However, the theory is not adequate to explain a long period of mass unemployment, for, at any time that production of durable goods is at a low ebb, the usable stocks of such goods are rapidly depleted. For example, automobiles wear out, and machines become obsolete. Buildings deteriorate, and, as population is steadily increasing, the supply of satisfactory structures soon becomes inadequate.

Furthermore, wants are multitudinous, and, if spending power is unimpaired, the only effect of the over-stocking of one good is to lead to the purchasing of other goods. It therefore seems improbable that either over-stocking of durable goods or accumulation of inventories ever has had any noticeable tendency to diminish total sales volume and thereby to bring on a business depression.

The Under-Investment Theory of Unemployment

Another theory which, among orthodox economists, has found far more favor than has either of the hypotheses just mentioned is the view that depressions are brought on by underinvestment. While, undoubtedly, this theory has in it an element of verity, its proponents have carried their inferences much farther than the facts justify.

As shown in an earlier chapter, the high productiveness of American labor today is due mainly to the abundance and quality of the equipment at its disposal. This equipment is the result of very heavy capital investment per worker. With a smaller investment, production would be less, and wage rates would necessarily be lower. Therefore, *if present wage rates are to be maintained,* an average of five or six thousand dollars' worth of new investment is required for each worker added to the nation's labor force. If wage rates are to be advanced, the investment per employee must be even larger. On the other hand, if wage rates were lowered sufficiently, any number of workers could be employed without the addition of any new capital whatever.

There is, therefore, no inexorable relationship between new investment and employment volume. Indeed, as previously pointed out, those nations having the smallest capital investments per worker tend to be troubled least by unemployment. It appears, therefore, that, if we are to discover the forces actually responsible for changes in employment volume, we must look elsewhere.

The Too-Low-Wage Lack-of-Purchasing-Power Theory of Unemployment

One of the favorite contentions of C. I. O. leaders is that unemployment is the natural aftermath of low-wage prevalence. They hold that, whenever this condition exists, there will not be enough "purchasing power" to cause a strong demand for finished goods. Without such a demand, it is obvious that production will languish, and, if it is slack, unemployment will, of course, result.

Sponsors of this theory all contend vigorously that an advance in wage rates increases the total "purchasing power" of the public and hence leads to more buying, which, in turn, brings about recovery.

Endorsement of this raise-wages-and-bring-prosperity theory is by no means confined to representatives of labor unions. This theory undoubtedly dominates the thinking of a large proportion of the American public. It has been the motive force leading to the adoption of such statutes as the National Industrial Recovery Act, and our minimum wage laws. Various writers on economics also subscribe to the thesis that raising wage rates increases "purchasing power."

High-Wage Policy

Many large employers evidently accept the same viewpoint, for they take great pleasure in boasting that they have always adhered to a "high-wage policy." With some, of course, such boasts may be mere bombast, but most of them are doubtless sincere, and the latter presumably firmly believe that, by paying top wage rates, they are benefiting both their employees and the public at large. Are they correct in this point of view? To answer this query, it is necessary to examine the facts and principles involved.

First let us consider whether it is feasible for a public-spirited employer to pay per unit of output wage rates higher than those paid by his competitors. Experience everywhere shows that the employer who does this is on the road to bankruptcy. If he fails, he evidently cannot longer benefit labor.

Yet some employers regularly pay average hourly wages higher than those paid by their competitors. What is the explanation of this situation? The answer is that the employer who persistently pursues such a "high-wage policy" is able to do so solely because he employs only the more efficient workers — discharging all of the less competent. From the standpoint of the latter class, the "high-wage policy" is, therefore, likely to appear anything but beneficent!

An occasional employer is able to pay wage rates exceeding those paid by his competitors because he has educated his employees, and has used great skill in "putting square pegs into square holes and round pegs into round holes." Such devices may make his employees unusually productive, and hence enable him to pay to his workers hourly wages far in excess of the rates paid by rival entrepreneurs.

It will be observed, however, that the cases just cited lend no support whatever to the theory that the mere paying of high wage rates benefits either employees or society in general. The truth is that, in time of depression, it is, strangely enough, not the employer who pursues a high-wage policy but, instead, the one who engages in a low-wage policy that is the true benefactor of the laboring class. In such periods, the best way to set the idle to work is to slash wage rates, for lower wage rates mean lower expenses of production, lower prices of products, and increased sales volume. Thus, if competition is at all keen, a cut in the wages of clothing workers will almost inevitably lead to reductions in the prices of clothing. Such reductions will give rise to increased sales of clothing, and hence it will be necessary to hire more clothing workers to replenish the stocks of merchants. More clothing will be turned out, sales will increase, employment will rise, and the wage total for clothing workers will expand.

Therefore, paradoxical though it may seem, in time of depression, a lowering of their wage rates normally increases the spending power of the working class as a whole at a little later date. Since the cutting of wage rates automatically increases the spending power of the employer, there is a double tendency for wage reductions to take a nation out of a depression.

But what about the hypothesis that the raising of wage rates increases "purchasing power" — that higher wage rates mean more money for workers to spend, and that more spending money means more buying of goods?

Wages and Purchasing Power

Those taking this position can support it by turning to Columns A and C of Table XXVI. The figures there presented show that, in 19 out of the 26 yearly periods covered, changes in hourly earnings were accompanied by corresponding changes in the net volume of new spending power.

In reality, however, this similarity in direction of movement is not at all due to any tendency for rising wage rates to enlarge the total volume of "purchasing power." On the contrary, the concurrence of movement results from the fact that, as new spending power expands, the demand for goods in general is strengthened. This growing demand for the *products* of labor of course causes the demand for *labor* to increase, and the price of labor to rise. The higher hourly earnings are, therefore, the RESULT of the increased productiveness induced by enlarged spending power, and are in no way the CAUSE of the increase in spending power.

What the proponents of the high-wage doctrine generally overlook is the fact that wages do not fall down from heaven, but must be paid by the employers. Therefore, when wages are advanced, every increase in the "purchasing power" gained by the wage recipients is, momentarily, exactly offset by a dollar decrease in the "purchasing power" of the employers. Hence, the raising of wage rates has not the slightest tendency to increase the total net volume of new spending power.

When confronted with this obvious fact, the advocates of higher wages usually parry by contending that the wage increases will be paid out of funds hoarded by the employers. However, Table XV shows that the hoarding hypothesis is contrary to fact. That a transfer of spendable funds from one class of the population to another — for example from employers to employees — cannot increase the aggregate of spending power, was well illustrated by the complete failure of the National Industrial Recovery Act either to increase the volume of employment or to promote recovery.

There certainly is no more logic in assuming that raising wage rates increases "purchasing power" than there is in assuming that raising the prices of groceries will increase "purchasing power." On the basis of the purchasing power argument, the higher prices for groceries ought immediately to increase the incomes of grocers and enable them to buy more goods and thus stimulate business activity, enlarge the national income, and increase employment. Of course, if this principle were true in the case of grocers, it would also apply in the case of everyone else who sold anything. The whole theory is so manifestly absurd that it is amazing to find that any person trained in economic science has ever been guilty of giving it credence.

Wage Rates, Prices, and Sales Volume

Not infrequently, those who assert that raising wage rates enlarges "purchasing power" take the position that increases of wage rates will be passed on to the buyers of the products turned out by the labor in question. They say that the physical volume of sales will not be reduced inasmuch as the purchasers of the goods will have had their incomes increased by the wage advance. They hold that the ultimate effect of the wage increase will be to raise the price level, and that there will be no tendency to reduce the physical volume of buying.

However, it has been shown in earlier chapters that arbitrary changes in the prices of selected groups of goods have little tendency to affect the altitude of the price level, for pushing up the price of one good usually causes the prices of others to fall — and *vice versa*. Normally, however, if the price of a good is raised by decree, the good's volume of sales is diminished. It follows that the notion that increased prices, produced by higher wages, can be passed on to consumers without diminishing consumption, and thereby reducing production and employment, is completely fallacious.[2]

Spending Power and Employment Volume

Previous chapters have presented evidence indicating that practically all radical changes in total sales volume — and hence in employment — are the results not of changing supply or changing desires, but rather of

---

[2] That this is true can be demonstrated algebraically. It seems certain that, in any period in which products are flowing steadily from producers to consumers, the volume of direct or consumption goods marketed will approximately equal the quantity produced in the same period. It follows that, as a rule, the total value of goods produced in *Period i,* (the average time interval between successive receipts of income) will approximately equal pq (the quantity q, it will be remembered, being the number of physical units of consumption goods bought in *Period i,* and p being the average price paid for such units). But if m equals the amount of cash in the possession of consumers in *Period i,* and if f equals the fraction of that cash spent for consumption goods, then evidently, as previously noted, $q = \dfrac{fm''}{p}$. Furthermore, as pointed out earlier, $m'' = kM''$, the quantity k presumably being a constant; and $p = \dfrac{P}{O}$, the quantity O representing the index of optimism. Hence, evidently, $q = \dfrac{fkM''}{\dfrac{P}{O}} = \dfrac{fkOM''}{P}$. It follows that any increase in the denominator, P, must cause q, the volume of consumption goods sold, to shrink, unless the increase in P is offset by a proportional increase in the numerator of the fraction. Since there is no reason to believe union or governmental action resulting in the forcing up of wage rates, and hence of the prices of the products of labor, has any tendency to increase f, k, O, or M'', the quantities comprising the numerator of the fraction, the conclusion is inevitable that the arbitrary raising of wage rates reduces q — the quantity of goods bought, cuts down production, and causes unemployment.

changing ability to buy. Once more, therefore, the evidence makes it clear that, if we seek the cause of fluctuations in employment and unemployment, it behooves us to note the movements which have occurred in the net volume of NEW spending power, for, as brought out in the previous chapter, it is this net volume of new spending power which primarily determines the aggregate wage bill of the nation.

Table XXVI

THE ACTUAL TOTAL VOLUME OF FACTORY EMPLOYMENT COMPARED
WITH THE TOTAL VOLUME AS COMPUTED FROM RECORDS OF NET
NEW SPENDING POWER AND AVERAGE HOURLY EARNINGS

Year	A Net New Spending Power[a] (Billions)	B Factory Wage Bill as Computed from Net Volume of New Spending Power[b] (Billions)	C Average Hourly Earnings of All Factory Workers[c]	D Employment Volume Billions of Hours Computed B ÷ C	E Employment Volume Billions of Hours Actual[d]	F Percentage Error of Estimate $100\frac{D-E}{E}$
1920	$65.70	$9.23	$0.606	15.23	19.15	−20.5
1921	53.13	6.77	.524	12.92	13.88	−6.9
1922	59.42	7.92	.494	16.03	16.56	−3.2
1923	66.83	9.27	.541	17.14	18.94	−9.5
1924	68.79	9.57	.562	17.03	16.77	+1.6
1925	71.09	9.96	.561	17.75	17.84	−0.5
1926	71.64	10.02	.568	17.64	18.14	−2.8
1927	74.67	10.54	.576	18.30	17.60	+4.0
1928	76.91	10.92	.579	18.86	17.71	+6.5
1929	78.60	11.21	.590	18.98	19.00	−0.1
1930	71.15	9.74	.589	16.54	15.05	+9.9
1931	56.91	7.00	.564	12.41	11.70	+6.1
1932	42.47	4.24	.498	8.51	8.56	−0.6
1933	44.60	4.62	.491	9.41	9.90	−4.9
1934	55.60	6.68	.580	11.52	11.03	+4.4
1935	60.71	7.63	.599	12.74	12.59	+1.2
1936	69.80	9.33	.619	15.07	14.50	+3.9
1937	67.21	8.82	.695	12.69	15.59	−18.6
1938	65.00	8.37	.716	11.69	11.41	+2.5
1939	72.62	9.79	.720	13.60	13.95	−2.5
1940	83.65	11.83	.739	16.01	15.38	+4.1
1941	100.31	14.96	.814	18.38	20.20	−9.0
1942	138.50	22.17	.924	23.99	24.59	−2.4
1943	161.78	26.54	1.014	26.17	29.70	−11.9
1944	178.07	29.58	1.065	27.77	28.60	−3.1
1945	177.50	29.43	1.097	26.83	25.81	+4.0
1946	166.61	27.29	1.190	22.93	21.93	+4.6
						Av. 5.5

[a] See Table XVI.
[b] See Table XXIV, Column D.
[c] See U. S. *Survey of Current Business*, 1940 Supplement, p. 44, and March issues for later years. Data are taken from the reports of the National Industrial Conference Board.
[d] See Table XXV, Column F.

Table XXIV shows clearly what the forces are that determine the total factory wage bill. It does not require a knowledge of advanced mathematics to make it clear that, if both the total of wage payments and the average wage rate per hour are known, the total number of hours worked can be calculated by dividing the wage total by the average hourly rate. In view of the facts revealed by Table XXIV, it follows that, if the net volume of new spending power, and the average factory hourly wage rate are both given, one ought to be able to approximate rather closely the total number of hours

CHART II

COMPARISON OF ACTUAL WITH EXPECTED VOLUME OF EMPLOYMENT IN ALL FACTORIES IN THE CONTINENTAL UNITED STATES▼

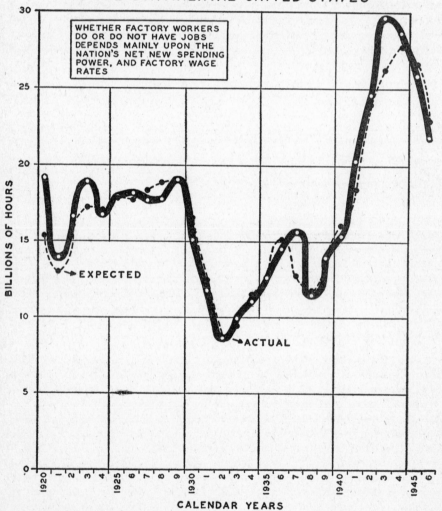

WHETHER FACTORY WORKERS DO OR DO NOT HAVE JOBS DEPENDS MAINLY UPON THE NATION'S NET NEW SPENDING POWER, AND FACTORY WAGE RATES

▼FOR DATA, SEE TABLE XXVI, COLUMNS D AND E

of employment which the factories of the nation can furnish. Such an approximation appears in Table XXVI.

Comparison of Calculated with Actual Employment Volume

In Table XXVI and Chart 11, the volume of factory employment, as estimated on the basis of net new spending power and average hourly earnings, is compared with the volume indicated by the data on the actual number of workers employed and the actual average number of hours worked per week. The degree of divergence between the estimated and actual figures is surprisingly small. It will, indeed, be observed that, in but three of the twenty-seven years covered, are the errors larger than 10 per cent, and in but one year are they as large as 20 per cent. For the entire period, the average error is only 5.5 per cent. When one considers the fact that the actual volume of factory employment must be the resultant of thousands of forces, it is most surprising to find that, in this field, two forces — the volume of new spending power and the average rate of earnings — dominate the situation to such a marked degree.

The conclusion to be drawn from Table XXVI and Chart 11 seems, therefore, to be that, in general, the volume of employment in a nation is determined almost entirely by two forces:

1. The net volume of new spending power
2. The average rate of pay

Legislation Inimical to the Working Class

Unfortunately, reformers and those responsible for legislation both here and abroad have been entirely unfamiliar with the relationship just stated. In their endeavors to improve the condition of the working class, they have, therefore, dealt with symptoms rather than with causes, and have secured the enactment of legislation which has brought disaster not only to wage earners but to the world at large. There seems indeed to be no logical way of escaping the conclusion that the relatively efficient members of the laboring class have suffered far more from the well-intended but misguided activities of the "friends of labor" than they have from any machinations on the part of the enemies of labor.

It is, for example, the former group who are responsible for the existing provisions in our Social Security laws, which prevent elderly workers from receiving the pensions for which they have paid unless they retire from work and thus curtail their incomes. This restriction was presumably put into the law at the behest of persons so ignorant of fundamental economic principles that they believed that, when an elderly person worked, he took away a job from a younger man or woman. Had such "friends of labor" been familiar with the fact that, whenever a worker's product is sold, the sale creates new spending power which, in turn, is soon used to buy goods and generate further production, they would not have desired to prevent able-bodied elderly persons from working, producing, and thus adding to their own and the national income.

Unemployment Insurance

Of all the laws enacted at the behest of the "friends of labor" for the "benefit" of the working class, probably the most disastrous from the standpoint of the laborers have been those providing for unemployment insurance. During the entire period between World War I and World War II, British workers suffered heavily from the effects of such legislation. The currency inflation accompanying World War I raised the British price level very sharply, and wages participated in the increase. After the war ended, the price level fell, but the British labor unions were strong enough to hold wage rates at inflated war-time levels. Had it not been for unemployment insurance (popularly known as the dole), such wage-rate maintenance would not have been feasible, for the idle would have found it impossible to subsist, and would, therefore, have marketed their labor at the best prices obtainable. Under such circumstances, England would not have been compelled to endure a twenty-year depression, with one to two millions of potential workers idling away their time while they lived on public largess.

The situation in Germany after its post-war deflation much resembled that in England. Vast numbers of erstwhile workers drew unemployment insurance while they loafed. Had public support been unavailable, they would have been compelled to go to work for such wages as the employers could have afforded to pay. Without this multitude of discontented idle, the probabilities are that Hitler's demagogic appeals would have fallen upon deaf ears; Hitler would never have risen to power; and millions of workers of many nations would have lived peaceful lives instead of dying on the battlefields or being blown to pieces by bombs.

That Americans generally need to master the elementary principles of economics is shown by the fact that our legislators entirely fail to understand that the disbursement of doles to the idle was one of the prime factors responsible for World War II. Therefore, they proceed to imitate the British and Germans by enacting unemployment insurance laws. The basic truth that ought to be drummed into the mind of each lawmaker is that *unemployment insurance insures unemployment.*

Americans have come to believe that it is a duty of government to protect its citizens against undue hardship. This end can be accomplished without resorting to payments for loafing. If government always stood ready to furnish industrious workers with jobs, but insisted that relief work be somewhat more strenuous than private employment, that no able-bodied relief recipient put in less than 60 hours per week, and that the hourly pay should never be more than two-thirds as great as that prevailing in private industry for like work, the government could not justly be charged with disregarding the welfare of its citizens. Yet it is safe to say that, with these rules enforced rigidly, the task of providing emergency jobs would never burden government seriously.

Minimum Wage Laws

Other glaring evidences of economic illiteracy on the part of the "friends of labor" are the State and Federal minimum wage laws. Such legislation while it may, in an occasional case, represent nothing but an empty gesture, often spells pauperization for large groups of formerly self-supporting and self-respecting citizens. Unfortunately, however, the effects of minimum wage laws are commonly hard to detect.

Suppose, for example, that the legal minimum hourly pay of makers of work clothes is increased from 40 to 65 cents. The demand for such garments is relatively inelastic. It may therefore happen that few of these garment workers will lose their jobs. What the "uplifters" responsible for the legislation overlook is that every additional dollar paid for work clothing lessens by one dollar the ability of the purchasers to buy other things, for since the total net new spending power of the nation was not increased by the new statute, the purchasers of work clothing will necessarily curtail their purchases of something else. If they buy less jewelry, makers of jewelry will lose their jobs, and neither they nor their employers will have the faintest suspicion that the minimum wage law was responsible for the falling off of orders and consequent unemployment. The fact which should be re-

CHART 12

THE VARIED EARNING POWERS
OF POTENTIAL WORKERS

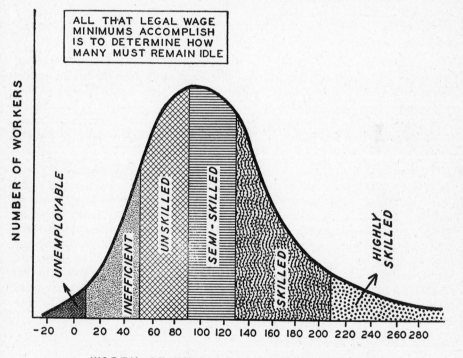

ALL THAT LEGAL WAGE MINIMUMS ACCOMPLISH IS TO DETERMINE HOW MANY MUST REMAIN IDLE

NUMBER OF WORKERS

UNEMPLOYABLE
INEFFICIENT
UNSKILLED
SEMI-SKILLED
SKILLED
HIGHLY SKILLED

-20 0 20 40 60 80 100 120 140 160 180 200 220 240 260 280

WORTH OF SERVICE IN CENTS PER HOUR

membered is that, if a minimum wage law really results in advancing the wages of a class of employees, it almost inevitably causes workers somewhere to lose their jobs.

The implicit assumption commonly underlying minimum-wage legislation is that all workers are approximately equal in productiveness, but that some are unlucky, and draw poor jobs; hence they need protection. In reality, of course, potential workers vary tremendously both mentally and physically. Some are so inefficient that no employer would have them around his shop. Others are worth a mere pittance. Some can earn enough to support themselves, but not enough to support a family. Others have earning powers ranging all along the scale, a few running into the higher brackets. The situation is represented by Chart 12. The wage scales indicated are purely hypothetical, applying only to a particular time in a given nation.

If, under the assumed conditions illustrated by Chart 12, the wage minimum is set by statute at 50 cents per hour, it will force the "inefficient" group to become parasites instead of producers. If the minimum is raised to 90 cents per hour, all the unskilled will lose their jobs. A wage minimum of 130 cents would throw out all the semi-skilled — and so on. It follows that, by raising its wage minimums, any nation can augment to any extent desired the numbers who must be either supported by charity or left to starve.

The notion that legislation is necessary to make wage rates advance as industrial productivity moves forward is highly erroneous. Wage rates forge ahead almost automatically whenever labor becomes more productive. The principal forces making industry more productive are:

1. Investment of more capital per worker
2. Invention of better ways of doing things
3. Education of the workers

The only sound procedure for getting higher wages for labor is to strengthen those forces. They constitute real keys to prosperity.

In this chapter, we have dealt with the forces determining the total volume of employment. We shall next consider why the volume of employment fluctuates so persistently and extensively.

Chapter XVII

FLUCTUATIONS IN EMPLOYMENT

Year to Year Changes in Employment Volume

Table XXVI and Chart 11 show for the manufacturing industry the LONG-TIME relationship existing between net new spending power, wage rates, and employment volume. Table XXVII, by contrast, compares the YEAR-TO-YEAR changes in these same variables. In dealing with SHORT-TIME changes, it seems superfluous to distinguish between the total of new spendable funds and the disposable fraction of such funds, hence the changes noted are in the total figures.

The quantities entered in Column C of Table XXVII indicate the excess of percentage changes in spending power over percentage changes in average hourly earnings. It will be observed that, in all but five of the twenty-six years covered, the respective signs of the items in Columns C and D are the same. This means that, in general, changes in the volume of employment in the manufacturing industry depend upon the relationship between the percentage changes in net new spending power and the percentage changes in average hourly earnings. In 20 of the 26 years covered, the movements were in accordance with one of the following five rules:

1. When the percentage increase in new spending power was greater than the increase in average hourly earnings, employment increased. Examples — 1923; 1925; 1928; 1934; 1935; 1936; 1940; 1941; 1942; 1943.
2. When new spending power increased and average hourly earnings fell, employment increased. Examples — 1922; 1933.
3. When the percentage drop in new spending power was greater than the drop in average hourly earnings, employment fell off. Examples — 1921; 1930; 1931; 1932.
4. When hourly earnings increased faster than new spending power, employment declined. Examples — 1924; 1945.
5. When hourly earnings increased, though new spending power was declining, employment shrank. Examples — 1938; 1946.

Moreover, the exceptions to these rules (found in 1926, 1927, 1929 and 1944) were characterized by movements in employment too small to be of great significance. Only in 1937 was there a marked departure from the expected behavior. In that year, employment rose when a decline was to be anticipated; but the collapse in employment in 1938 made up for its failure to drop in 1937. Apparently, this was merely a case of the resulting effect being delayed long enough to fall into the next year's record.

Cyclical Movements in New Spending Power, Hourly Pay, and Employment

Table XXVIII and Chart 13 have been constructed to compare not the year-to-year, but rather the cyclical fluctuations of average hourly earnings and net new spending power. The evidence presented shows that the correspondence between cyclical movements is even closer than is the correspondence between year-to-year changes.

Chart 13 shows (upper half) that, in every instance in which the solid

Table XXVII

YEAR TO YEAR PERCENTAGE CHANGES IN NET NEW
SPENDING POWER, HOURLY EARNINGS, AND
THE VOLUME OF FACTORY EMPLOYMENT

Year	Percentage Change from Preceding Year in			
	A	B	C	D
	Net New Spending Power [a]	Av. Hourly Earnings [b]	A–B	Aggregate Hours of Employment [c]
1921	−19	−14	−5	−28
1922	+12	−6	+18	+19
1923	+12	+10	+2	+14
1924	+3	+4	−1	−11
1925	+3	0	+3	+6
1926	+1	+1	0	+2
1927	+4	+1	+3	−3
1928	+3	+1	+2	+1
1929	+2	+2	0	+7
1930	−9	0	−9	−21
1931	−20	−4	−16	−22
1932	−25	−12	−13	−27
1933	+5	−1	+6	+16
1934	+25	+18	+7	+11
1935	+9	+3	+6	+14
1936	+15	+3	+12	+15
1937	−4	+12	−16	+8
1938	−3	+3	−6	−27
1939	+12	+1	+11	+22
1940	+15	+3	+12	+10
1941	+20	+10	+10	+31
1942	+38	+14	+24	+22
1943	+17	+10	+7	+21
1944	+10	+5	+5	−4
1945	0	+3	−3	−10
1946	−6	+8	−14	−15

[a] Computed from Table XVI, last column.
[b] Computed from Table XXVI, Column C.
[c] See Table XXV, Column G.

arrow was above the hollow arrow, employment rose (see broken arrows in lower half of chart); whenever the hollow arrow was above the solid arrow, employment fell. Thus when, between 1920 and 1921, net new spending power declined 19 per cent, while average hourly earnings dropped less than 14 per cent, employment fell off 28 per cent. On the other hand, when, between 1921 and 1929, net new spending power expanded by 48 per cent, while average hourly earnings rose only 13 per cent, the result was a 37 per cent increase in the volume of employment. *Here we have the explanation of that sweeping forward movement in industry which made the nation more prosperous than it had ever been before.*

The evidence presented in the preceding chapter makes it clear that, if all persons desiring employment were at all times willing to sell their services for the best prices obtainable, unemployment would not exist, for any amount of new spending power would buy all of the available labor supply. With full employment, production would be ample, and prosperity would tend to reign continuously. Depressions are, therefore, brought about by the inflexibility of wage rates — by their failure to drop when the net total of new spending power declines.

Table XXVIII

PERCENTAGE CYCLICAL CHANGES COMPARED FOR
NET NEW SPENDING POWER,
AVERAGE HOURLY EARNINGS,
AND THE
VOLUME OF FACTORY EMPLOYMENT

Period	Percentage Change in			
	A	B	C	D
	Net New Spending Power [a]	Average Hourly Earnings [b]	A−B	Factory Employment Volume [c] (Billions of Hrs.)
1920–1921	− 19	−14	− 5	− 28
1921–1929	+ 48	+13	+ 35	+ 37
1929–1932	− 46	−16	− 30	− 55
1932–1937	+ 58	+40	+ 18	+ 82
1937–1938	− 3	+ 3	− 6	− 27
1938–1943	+149	+42	+107	+160

[a] Computed from data in Table XVI, last column.
[b] Computed from data in Table XXVI, Column C.
[c] Computed from data in Table XXV, Column F.

The figures in Table XXVIII for the period 1929 to 1932 well illustrate this principle. When, in that three-year period, new spending power dropped 46 per cent and wage rates declined but 16 per cent, the immediate result was that factory employment shrank 55 per cent. For similar reasons, great declines in employment occurred in the mining and railroad industries.

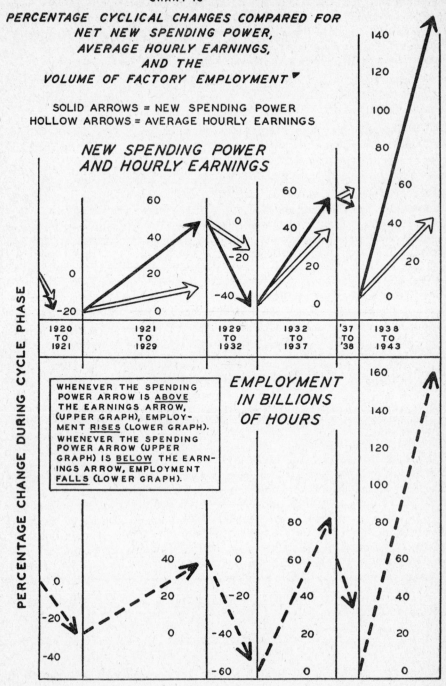

CHART 13

PERCENTAGE CYCLICAL CHANGES COMPARED FOR
NET NEW SPENDING POWER,
AVERAGE HOURLY EARNINGS,
AND THE
VOLUME OF FACTORY EMPLOYMENT ▼

SOLID ARROWS = NEW SPENDING POWER
HOLLOW ARROWS = AVERAGE HOURLY EARNINGS

NEW SPENDING POWER
AND HOURLY EARNINGS

| 1920 TO 1921 | 1921 TO 1929 | 1929 TO 1932 | 1932 TO 1937 | '37 TO '38 | 1938 TO 1943 |

PERCENTAGE CHANGE DURING CYCLE PHASE

WHENEVER THE SPENDING
POWER ARROW IS ABOVE
THE EARNINGS ARROW,
(UPPER GRAPH), EMPLOY-
MENT RISES (LOWER GRAPH).
WHENEVER THE SPENDING
POWER ARROW (UPPER
GRAPH) IS BELOW THE EARN-
INGS ARROW, EMPLOYMENT
FALLS (LOWER GRAPH).

EMPLOYMENT
IN BILLIONS
OF HOURS

▼FOR DATA, SEE TABLE XXVIII, COLUMNS A, B, AND D

The net outcome was that the American public was led to believe that *laissez faire* had failed, and that it was therefore necessary to substitute for it a regimented economy. Hence, even though we escaped internal violence, wage-rate rigidity in the face of sharply declining spending power brought about an extensive revolution in our basic economic institutions.

After 1932, however, new spending power expanded — rising 58 per cent by 1937. Since hourly earnings rose but 40 per cent, the volume of employment spurted forward, increasing, in fact, by 82 per cent.

Eventually, however, average hourly earnings moved ahead slightly while spending power dropped a little. The result was that, between 1937 and 1938, employment declined by 27 per cent.

The great advance in new spending power occurring after 1938 was largely brought about by bank-deposit expansion arising from Federal borrowing. Since, during the War, the Government restricted upward movements in wage rates, the net result was the greatest rise in employment taking place during the twenty-four years covered by our study. By 1943, employment was 160 per cent above the 1938 level.

The Key Ratio

Thus far, we have compared for corresponding periods the respective percentage changes in net new spending power, average hourly earnings, and employment volume. A simpler, and in some ways more effective, way of analyzing the relationships involved is to deal with the ratio of one to the other. This ratio may be expressed in terms of the fraction

$$\frac{\text{Net new spending power}}{\text{Average hourly earnings}}.$$

Table XXIX and Chart 14 compare year-to-year percentage changes in the size of this KEY RATIO with percentage changes in the volume of employment. A study of this table and chart shows that, in all but four of the twenty-six years covered, changes in the size of the KEY RATIO produced corresponding changes in the volume of employment. Moreover, in two of the four years in which the expected result did not materialize, the percentage changes in the size of this ratio were too small to be of much significance. While no definite relationship between the size of the change in the KEY RATIO and the size of the change in the volume of employment is apparent, it may be said that, in a broad way, the figures in Table XXIX indicate that the percentage change in employment tends to be about double the percentage change in the KEY RATIO.

The facts thus far set forth make it abundantly clear that the prosperity of a nation is commonly bound up with that ultra-important ratio

$$\frac{\text{Net new spending power}}{\text{Average hourly earnings}}.$$

Any serious decline in the numerator, unaccompanied by a corresponding fall in the denominator of the fraction inevitably brings about unemployment, depression, and discontent. It may even lead to revolution. On the other hand, a rise in the size of the KEY RATIO ordinarily means more employment, more production, and hence more prosperity.

Public Employment as a Cure for Unemployment

At the time when World War II was drawing to a close, leaders of both major parties were agreed that, if mass unemployment developed, it was the

Table XXIX

YEAR TO YEAR PERCENTAGE CHANGES IN THE RATIO OF NET NEW
SPENDING POWER TO HOURLY EARNINGS COMPARED WITH
PERCENTAGE CHANGES IN THE VOLUME OF FACTORY EMPLOYMENT

	A	B	C	D	E
	Actual		Ratio of New Spending Power to Average Hourly Earnings		
Year	Net New Spending Power [a] (Billions)	Av. Hourly Earnings [b]	The Key Ratio (A ÷ B)	Percentage Change from Preceding Year in the Key Ratio	Percentage Changes in Employment [c]
1920	$65.70	$0.606	108.4		
1921	53.13	.524	101.4	−6	−28
1922	59.42	.494	120.3	+19	+19
1923	66.83	.541	123.5	+3	+14
1924	68.79	.562	122.4	−1	−11
1925	71.09	.561	126.7	+4	+6
1926	71.64	.568	126.1	− [d]	+2
1927	74.67	.576	129.6	+3	−3
1928	76.91	.579	132.8	+2	+1
1929	78.60	.590	133.2	+ [d]	+7
1930	71.15	.589	120.7	−9	−21
1931	56.91	.564	100.9	−16	−22
1932	42.47	.498	85.3	−15	−27
1933	44.60	.491	90.8	+6	+16
1934	55.60	.580	95.9	+6	+11
1935	60.71	.599	101.4	+6	+14
1936	69.80	.619	112.8	+11	+15
1937	67.21	.695	96.7	−14	+8
1938	65.00	.716	90.8	−6	−27
1939	72.62	.720	100.9	+11	+22
1940	83.65	.739	113.2	+12	+10
1941	100.31	.814	123.2	+9	+31
1942	138.50	.924	149.9	+22	+22
1943	161.78	1.014	159.5	+6	+21
1944	178.07	1.065	167.2	+5	−4
1945	177.50	1.097	161.8	−3	−10
1946	166.61	1.190	140.0	−13	−15

[a] See Table XVI, last column.
[b] See Table XXVI, Column C.
[c] See Table XXVII, Column D.
[d] Less than 1 per cent.

duty of government to step in and employ the idle. However, in making such pronouncements, they took it for granted that it was easy for government to increase the total volume of employment. In nearly every instance, the fact was overlooked that, unless the government creates new circulating medium, it can add nothing either to total new spending power or total employment. Every dollar which it takes from taxpayers or non-bank bond buyers lessens by exactly the same amount the ability of these citizens to buy the products of industry and to supply labor with jobs.

It is of course true that, if, in time of depression, a government could and did hire a billion dollars worth of labor at 50 cents per hour, when, nominally, "going rates" in industry were $1.00 per hour, it would actually increase the volume of employment in the nation.

CHART 14

YEAR TO YEAR PERCENTAGES OF CHANGE IN
THE KEY RATIO
COMPARED WITH
PERCENTAGE CHANGES IN THE VOLUME OF FACTORY EMPLOYMENT▼

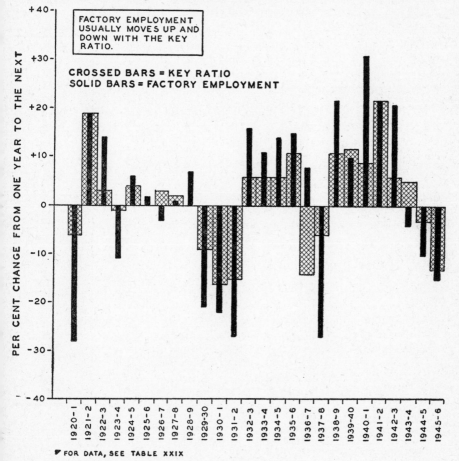

FACTORY EMPLOYMENT USUALLY MOVES UP AND DOWN WITH THE KEY RATIO.

CROSSED BARS = KEY RATIO
SOLID BARS = FACTORY EMPLOYMENT

▼ FOR DATA, SEE TABLE XXIX

As a rule, however, political pressure prevents any government from hiring labor below the "going rate." Commonly, indeed, it pays rates materially higher than private employers can afford to pay. The net result is that, when it takes a billion dollars from taxpayers or bond buyers, it is likely to reduce instead of increase the total volume of employment. Therefore, governmental attempts to bring about recovery through public spending are usually doomed to failure unless they are accompanied by the creation of new circulating medium. Such creation commonly involves what is known as "deficit financing," that is, it either increases the debt of the government to the banks, or expands the volume of paper money. However, as previously emphasized, both of these processes raise prices and thereby undermine the real value of money, bank deposits, notes, mortgages, bonds, and life insurance, thus destroying the savings of the thrifty. Hence, they must be regarded as dangerous stimulants to be administered only on prescription.

Wage Rates and Wage Totals

Practically everyone takes it for granted that a raise in wage *rates* will increase the total wage *income* of the wage workers. However, as a matter of fact, an *arbitrary increase* in wage rates usually *reduces* the total income of the laboring class. This is true because, when employers raise wage rates, the normal result is to increase the prices of the products of the labor in question. Since the advance in wage rates has not enlarged the net volume of new spending power in the hands of the public, an increase in the prices charged for the products means that fewer units of goods can be marketed, hence production will tend to decline. But declining production means less employment, and a reduced volume of new spending power.

To most people, the statement that higher wage rates may mean reduced incomes for the wage workers of course sounds paradoxical. The reason that the average man so considers it is that he fails to distinguish clearly between wage rates per hour or per piece and annual earnings. High wage rates, accompanied by much part-time work and widespread unemployment, usually mean that the total wage bill for all workers in the nation is abnormally low. In general, that wage total will be largest which is the result of wage rates which are not so high as to cause any considerable volume of unemployment.

The matter may be summed up thus: Rising wage rates bring prosperity to the working class only when the upward movements in these rates are the resultants not of arbitrary increases at the behest of monopolies or government, but when they are the outcomes of increased productivity on the part of industry. When wage rates are forced up faster than the advance in net new spending power, unemployment results, and this always spells hard times for the wage workers affected.

How this works out in practice is illustrated by the data in Columns A and B of Table XXIX. The figures there presented show, for example, that when, in the 1936–1937 period, the labor unions, backed by Government, pushed up average hourly earnings from $0.619 to $0.695, even though total new spending power was declining, the result was an employment drop in the next year amounting to 27 per cent. Table XXIV shows that this decline forced the factory wage bill down from $10.11 to $7.74 billions. The advance in wage rates therefore reduced the factory workers' total take-home pay $2.37 billions in a single year.

Clearly, the factory operators would have prospered far more had they again acted as they did in the 1920 to 1921 crash. At that time, the labor unions were too weak to prevent wage rates from falling. Therefore, a year after the drop in new spending power from $67.84 in 1919 to $53.13 in 1921, average hourly earnings declined from $0.606 in 1920 to $0.494 in 1922. The net result was that, between 1921 and 1923, employment volume rose from 13.81 to 18.94 billions of hours, and, in the same period, the factory wage bill climbed from $7.45 to $10.15 billions.

It follows, then, that any wage-rate increase which outruns the normal rising trend of net new spending power tends to bring on depression.

It is not exaggerating to say that, in the years 1930 to 1940 inclusive, factory operatives, by succumbing to the lure of the high-wage-rate sirens, lost potential wages amounting to some forty to fifty billions of dollars — a sum sufficient to have provided each worker with a $5,000 house.

Having analyzed the data pertaining to new spending power, wage rates, employment, and total earnings, it may be well now to outline the ways in which the relationships of these factors affect the welfare of nations.

How National Debacles Develop

The typical sequence of events which has, in recent decades, brought disaster to various nations, is as follows:

1. The currency is inflated, with the result that wage rates and other prices rise sharply.
2. Inflation is followed by deflation.
3. Labor unions, backed by such governmental aids as relief payments and unemployment insurance, prevent wage rates from falling, but other prices collapse.
4. Employers are unable to pay the inflated wage rates to any but the most competent employees, hence the less efficient are discharged.
5. The resulting unemployment produces serious economic and political disturbances.

As noted in the last chapter, this sequence of events gave Britain a twenty-year-long depression, and led Germany along the path which brought about World War II.

The Four Ways of Escaping from Depression

On the basis of the facts compiled, it appears that, when a nation is in the throes of depression, there exist four ways — and four ways only — by which it can free itself from the engulfing morass. It can escape by

1. Lowering wage rates faster than new spending power shrinks

2. Lowering wage rates and increasing or keeping constant new spending power
3. Keeping wage rates constant but increasing new spending power
4. Increasing wage rates but increasing new spending power still more rapidly

Any re-employment plan other than one of the four just stated has no chance of being successful, and hence may well be likened unto "sounding brass or a tinkling cymbal."

The last of these four ways is the one which, in recent years, has been most favored by American politicians. The labor unions demand ever higher wage rates — and the labor unions have votes. The net volume of new spending power can always be increased, to any extent desired, either by printing paper money or by creating deposits through borrowing from the banks. However, as we have repeatedly shown, the evils resulting from such inflation may be even more serious than are those connected with unemployment.

As brought out above, changes in the KEY RATIO or fraction, $\frac{\text{Net new spending power}}{\text{Average hourly earnings}}$, determine whether a nation is to move from prosperity to depression, or *vice versa*. As a rule, in those cases in which prosperity has suddenly given way to depression, the initial trouble-maker has been the *numerator* of the KEY RATIO or fraction. It appears, therefore, that, unless that numerator can be stabilized, there is little hope of assuring continued prosperity for the nation. The possibility of stabilizing net new spending power will be discussed in the next chapter.

Chapter XVIII

SPENDING POWER CONTROL

Factors in the Problem of Assuring Prosperity

It now seems clear that the problem of those who seek to maintain employment, national productivity, and prosperity at levels roughly as high as those prevailing from 1942 to 1947 resolves itself into the following two components: —

1. How can the KEY RATIO or fraction $\dfrac{\text{Net new spending power}}{\text{Average hourly earnings}}$ be kept from declining?
2. How can the savings of the thrifty be protected from the destructive results of inflationary price rises?

Unless these two goals can be achieved, it appears that we might as well resign ourselves to the continuance of an inefficient, bungling, fascist economy.

Inflation as a Device for Assuring Prosperity

Obviously, the simplest method of preventing a decline in the size of the fraction $\dfrac{\text{Net new spending power}}{\text{Average hourly earnings}}$ is to follow the Keynesian prescription and increase the numerator to whatever extent is necessary to keep pace with any increases in the size of the denominator. The person favoring this procedure can refer to Tables XXVIII and XXIX to support his position. These tables show that, between 1938 and 1943, average hourly earnings in factories rose from $0.716 to $1.014, an advance of 42 per cent. In the same period, however, net new spending power increased from $65.00 to $158.65 billions, an expansion of 144 per cent. The net outcome was that factory employment jumped 160 per cent. The resulting increase in production enabled us to carry on a major war without materially curtailing civilian consumption. This was, indeed, an amazing achievement. On its face, it seems to prove conclusively the correctness of the Keynesian position.

Nevertheless, certain weaknesses inhere in this formula for success. That such is the case will become increasingly evident if the labor unions continue to push wage rates higher and higher. True, as was demonstrated during the early part of World War II, inflation, if sufficiently vigorous, may make new spending power outrun the wage-rate advances, and if many people are idle, rapidly enlarge the volume of employment, and hence of production. As long as production increases, the growing volume of trade may offset the growth in the volume of circulating medium, and hence the price level may not rise materially. However, the process of employment expansion must inevitably stop when nearly all persons really desiring jobs have been absorbed into the working force. Thereafter, it is ordinarily impossible to counterbalance the effects of inflation by increasing production.

Price Control by Government

During and after World War II, those responsible for the fiscal policies of our own and other governments decided that it was possible, by use of a system of price controls, to neutralize the effects of inflation. In the United States, this task was assigned to the Office of Price Administration. Price ceilings were placed upon most essential goods used by consumers, and upon most raw materials.

What those responsible for the program did not understand was that holding down the prices of certain goods automatically makes other prices rise. As pointed out in an earlier chapter, the national income normally equals the value of the goods turned out in the productive process which generated that income. During World War II, inflation was going on at a rate of some $20 billions per year. This, of course, strengthened the demands for goods of all kinds. The retention at pre-War levels of the prices of necessities meant that the production of necessities would not rise in response to the enhanced demand; hence shortages developed all along the line, and rationing was instituted. Since total new spending power was far in excess of the aggregate value of necessities available, it was relatively easy to induce people to use part of their surplus spending power to buy War bonds. In this way, price-ceilings did assist in financing the War. However, had the Government, after full employment was attained, followed the sound procedure of levying taxes sufficient to cover its expenditures, more bond sales would have been unnecessary, and, at the close of the conflict, there would have been no huge war debt to threaten the security of the thrifty.

To the extent that the excess new spending power generated by inflation was not "mopped up" by sales of War bonds, it was spent for unrationed goods such as furs, jewelry, diamonds, entertainment, real estate, and securities. Huge sums were diverted to the "black markets." Thus price regulation accustomed a large proportion of the inhabitants to law breaking.

In general, as pointed out in an earlier chapter, the tendency of price fixing is to make people buy things they want less instead of things they want more. Commonly, it shifts demand, materials, and man power from necessities to luxuries. With a given total of spending, price regulation is not likely to make P, the general price level, lower than it would be if there were no regulation. If part of the market is not covered by price ceilings, the increases in the unregulated prices, coupled with the higher prices paid in black markets, will completely offset the lower prices prevailing in the regulated markets. Thus, in the United States during and after World War II, while regulated prices were rising 30 to 40 per cent, the prices of stocks roughly doubled, those of diamonds trebled, and costume jewelry sold at nine times the pre-war level. The average of all prices, including those of real estate, labor, and goods sold in the black market, as well as commodities commonly quoted, was doubtless about the same as it would have been had there been no O.P.A.

The Folly of Deficit Financing

The attempt to nullify by price regulation the effects of deficit financing and resulting inflation is more than futile, for it encourages lawlessness and wastes the time and energy of the regulators — men and women who ought to be engaged in productive activities. After the new spending power created by inflation has set to work the nation's available working force, further inflation will make the general price level climb upward, regardless of all of the endeavors of officialdom to hold it down. But, as prices rise, the real values of all claims to money shrink. The result is that holders of such monetary claims as insurance policies, bonds, mortgages, bank deposits, and annuities see their savings gradually fade away.

To those who believe in the sacredness of property rights, such confiscation of the proceeds of thrift is, of course, anathema. Furthermore, such a process of confiscation, if carried on persistently, has an effect which can scarcely be ignored even by those who care nothing for the ethical issues involved — it gradually eliminates the tendency to accumulate monetary claims, and, as pointed out in an earlier chapter, such accumulation is, in progressive regions, the customary method of amassing capital, and if new capital is not provided, economic progress stops.

Those who contend that government must use "deficit financing" to whatever extent is necessary to provide "full employment" will presumably insist that an adequate supply of new capital can be provided by government. Rarely, if ever, do they suggest that, to get such capital, the government tax its citizens. Instead, they generally assume that the government will secure by "deficit financing" the funds needed to pay for new plant and equipment. In practice, such "deficit financing" is likely to mean borrowing from the banks — in other words, deposit currency inflation.

The net result of having government furnish the new capital needed by industry is, therefore, to speed up the process of robbing the thrifty. Furthermore, whenever government furnishes the capital required for industrial expansion, government almost inevitably comes to control the industries of the nation — in other words — state socialism gradually displaces private enterprise.

Past experience indicates that, in nations following the primrose path of inflation, one of two things happens:

1. The inflation may continue until it reaches the explosive stage. The economy then blows up, and is rebuilt from the foundations. This happened in Germany after World War I, and in Hungary after World War II.
2. A conservative government uses drastic measures to stop inflation. Such was the case in France under Poincaré.

When the latter course is followed, the mere cessation of inflation reduces the volume of net new spending power. Thus, if, in 1942, the United States Government had suddenly stopped inflating the currency, Table XVI shows that net new spending power would have been curtailed by more than $21 billions. Unless such a shrinkage in inflation had been offset by an increase in the realized national income, it would, of course, have resulted in a net decrease in total new spending power, and any such decrease would have tended to reduce the volume of buying and hence the volume of production in the nation, thus causing unemployment. That the mere stopping of the process of creating new circulating medium may throw business into a "tail spin" shows what a dangerous stimulant inflation is.

The Problem of Controlling Net New Spending Power

The fact has been emphasized that the only way to prevent periods of mass unemployment is to prevent shrinkage in the size of the KEY RATIO, $\frac{\text{Net new spending power}}{\text{Average hourly earnings}}$, and that the only way to protect the savings of the thrifty is to prevent price-level increases. However, such increases are usually caused by the numerator of the fraction expanding at a relative rate exceeding the proportional growth in the national production total. Clearly, therefore, any program for sustained prosperity must involve control of the *net volume of new spending power.*

It will be remembered that this quantity is the algebraic sum of the realized national income and any *change* in the volume of circulating medium. The first of these components — the realized national income — is by no means easy to control. It is dependent not only upon such things as habits, customs, weather, and wars, but, as we have seen, is largely determined by the volume of employment, which, in turn, is the resultant of the past ratio of new spending power to average wage rates. That segment of the numerator of the fraction which is readily controllable by governmental action is, therefore, *the change in the volume of circulating medium.*

The Hard Money, Laissez Faire Thesis

It must be admitted that many able economists believe that the wisest monetary policy for the nation to pursue is to define a fixed weight of gold as a dollar, and leave the rest to *laissez faire.* However, most of those taking this position either ignore or gloss over the fact that we experimented with this policy for most of the century preceding 1933, and that the results were decidedly unsatisfactory. During this period, the price level fluctuated widely, and many serious depressions occurred.

As we have seen, booms and depressions are usually caused by oscillations in the volume of net new spending power, and such oscillations are commonly the resultants of changes in the volume of circulating medium. These changes are caused either by governmental printing or retiring of money, or by the banks expanding or contracting deposit volume. Hence, if governments could be stopped from issuing new money to pay their bills, and if commercial banks could be prevented from enlarging or reducing their respective deposit volumes, a prime cause of depressions of the modern type would be eliminated. Therefore, to make their position sound, those advocating monetary *laissez faire* ought to insist upon a constitutional amendment abolishing both the right of the government to expand credit money volume, and the privilege of banks to have outstanding demand "deposits" in excess of their holdings of monetary metals. In other words, they should demand that the nation be placed upon a strictly "hard money" basis.

The general tendency in recent years has, of course, been to depart further and further from such a basis. One of the arguments in favor of establishing the Federal Reserve System was that the world's gold supply was not keeping pace with the growth in the world's volume of trade, and that, therefore, credit money was needed to make good the deficiency. Another reason for demanding such a central banking system was to make our money supply elastic. In reality, of course, the system has produced a money supply which stretches when it ought to contract, and contracts when it ought to expand.

Since, as a matter of fact, expansion in the world's joint supply of gold and silver would, apparently, have been able to keep pace with the growth in trade volume, our economy might have made satisfactory progress if we had never had either credit money or banks. However, both are highly convenient instruments. Both are thoroughly woven into our economy. It, therefore, appears to be more feasible and more desirable to subject them to national control than to abolish them.

Logical Basis of Monetary Control

It seems clear, however, that there is no hope of attaining enduring prosperity, unless we do establish scientific control over the total supply of money and bank deposits. Only by establishing such over-all control can we hope to avoid such pernicious interferences with economic liberty as price fixing, wage fixing, priorities, material allotments, production control, profit control, and rationing, and, by contrast, approach as closely as feasible to pure *laissez faire* and individual liberty.

Instead of fluctuating erratically, the volume of circulating medium should expand at approximately the same relative rate as the increase in the physical productivity of the nation as a whole. Such expansion would make it keep pace both with the growth in population and with advances in per capita productivity. But is it feasible to prevent those erratic variations in new spending power which give rise to booms, depression, and not infrequently catastrophic debacles in national economies?

It seems certain that this question must be answered in the negative in the case of any nation which permits its fiscal authorities to pay governmental expenses by directly or indirectly expanding the nation's stock of money and deposit currency. As long as our Government persists in printing money or borrowing from commercial banks in order to secure funds to pay interest on its bonds, to finance public works, or to pay current expenses, it is impracticable, in a free economy, continuously to maintain sound economic policies. In other words, unless the Treasury can be stripped of all money-issuing powers, the quest for sustained prosperity is likely to remain as futile as that of looking for the pot of gold at the end of the rainbow. This principle is just as applicable in war time as in peace time. What our nation needs is a constitutional amendment so drawn as to prevent the Federal Government from using its money-creating powers to finance its expenditures.

The Logic of Borrowing to Finance War

Many will, of course, hasten to assert that, without power to borrow freely from the banks or to print paper money, no government could conduct a successful war. Moreover, most people firmly believe that, by borrowing, the burden of the war can partly be thrust upon future generations. However, as pointed out in an earlier chapter, neither borrowing from the banks nor borrowing from other domestic lenders postpones to the future any part of the cost of a war. Every bit of equipment used, every ton of supplies for the army or navy must come from current or past production. Every dollar of the expense must be subtracted either from current income or from accumulated savings.

The very important point which is commonly overlooked is that, when a government uses either monetary or bank deposit inflation to pay its expenses, it is really levying a hidden tax on every holder of money, bank deposits, notes, mortgages, bonds, or life insurance, for the inflation slowly but persistently diminishes the value of every dollar represented by such claims or instruments. Most of the owners of these instruments think that they are escaping with relatively light tax payments. Few of them realize that they are being subjected to heavy "capital levies" — that they are thus helping to pay for the war while it is going on.

As previously noted, all that can, in reality, be postponed to the future is the settlement of the question as to which class of the population shall in the future be required to transfer funds to which other class of the population. The sound policy is to do the apportioning while the war is on — to distribute the burden among the citizens in the way that then seems most appropriate. This procedure leaves no debt problem to be wrestled with after the war ends.

Since inflation normally arouses but little popular resentment, it usually appeals to politicians and fiscal authorities as being a convenient way of meeting war expenses. However, inflation, by raising prices, increases the war expense as measured in dollars, and hence enlarges the amounts which the Treasury must raise.

Public Finance and "Pay-as-You-Go"

As a matter of fact, the pay-as-you-go method of financing a war would secure for the citizens as a whole an average scale of living somewhat higher than they would be able to enjoy if the war were financed by borrowing, for, since there would be no inflation, there would be neither need nor excuse for price controls. Their absence would make available for more useful duties an army of workers who, in the presence of inflation, would be engaged in price regulation. Still more important would be the higher rate of productivity which would exist were there no price-control fetters to hamper industry and lessen output. Furthermore, it would prevent any decline in the general purchasing power of the dollar, and hence there would be no surreptitious filching away from the thrifty of the wealth which they had accumulated in the form of monetary claims.

The feasibility of paying for a war primarily out of the proceeds of taxation depends largely upon the fact that it is possible to collect from producers very heavy excise taxes, and to compel employers to withhold from employees sizable fractions of the pay to which they are entitled under their contracts. Since such large collections are feasible, it is possible to prevent tax receipts from lagging far behind governmental expenditures.

No Federal fiscal policy can be considered sound unless it provides that, when the fiscal authorities find that additional funds are needed, they are under the necessity of presenting to Congress easily intelligible plans for raising the desired amounts, and unless it also specifies that the levies provided for are to be neither camouflaged nor hidden. Any proposed procedure for taxing away savings should be subject to hearings by Congressional committees, and debate on the floor of Congress.

The Need for a Monetary Authority

Since it is not feasible to eliminate undesirable changes in new spending power unless the volume of circulating medium can be prevented from fluctuating erratically, it is clear that any feasible plan for stabilizing the numerator of the KEY RATIO, $\dfrac{\text{Net new spending power}}{\text{Average hourly earnings}}$, must place complete control of the supply of money and demand deposits in the hands of some scientific, non-partisan, responsible body which may conveniently be referred to as The Monetary Authority.

It has sometimes been suggested that the Federal Reserve Board act in this capacity. Were this suggestion followed, it would be necessary almost to reverse the Board's interpretation of the chief duty which the Federal Reserve Act imposes upon the Board — namely that of accommodating the needs of business. The Board has always assumed (doubtless correctly) that this mandate means to accommodate the *demands* of business. As we have seen, business demands most credit in times of undue optimism — the very time when, from the standpoint of furthering long-time prosperity, credit extension should be most discouraged. Since the Federal Reserve System has grown up in this tradition, there is much to be said against placing monetary control in its hands. The sole duty of the Monetary Authority should be to stabilize the price level — in other words, to keep the value of the dollar constant.

The next question to be considered is what such an Authority having ample powers could do to prevent undesirable fluctuations in the volume of circulating medium, provided that the Federal Government renounced all right to use currency inflation as a means of obtaining revenue. It may be well, at this point, to emphasize again the fact that, without this proviso, scientific monetary control is impossible.

Monetary Control Procedure

One of the first duties of The Monetary Authority would be to decide upon a definite criterion which would enable it to determine whether or not the circulating medium was contracting or expanding unduly. Various gauges are available. The most dependable seems to be an index measuring changes in the total value of a huge imaginary basketful of goods representing the average annual output for the nation as a whole of all important standardized products.

This basket would not contain such intangibles as securities, for fluctuations in their values would not affect the command of the dollar over the necessities or comforts of life. It would not contain units of labor, for these are not products, but are, instead, means used in the productive process. The contents of the basket would, however, represent not only direct goods, such as food or clothing, but also indirect goods, such as livestock, raw materials, fuel, and minerals. The basket would necessarily contain only standardized goods, for it would be impossible to measure the extent of price changes applicable to other goods. The quantities of standardized goods would, however, be so adjusted as to represent similar non-standardized goods. Each good in the basket would be priced in one or more of the leading markets for that good.

Let us assume that The Monetary Authority began operations on January 2, and that, at that time, the basketful of goods was worth $40.0 billions. Let us suppose further that, on February 1, the value of the basketful had increased, and stood at $40.3 billions. This increase would indicate that the volume of circulating medium was increasing faster than was warranted by the volume of trade, and that, therefore, the purchasing power of the dollar was diminishing, with the result that the savings of the thrifty were being nibbled away. Under such circumstances, what, if anything, could The Monetary Authority do to prevent this process from going further?

A time-honored device for preventing commercial banks from expanding loans and deposits too freely in time of optimism is to raise the rates at which the central bank will rediscount eligible notes tendered by the commercial banks. Thus, if a member bank which is lending money at six per cent finds that it must pay eight per cent to replenish its reserves at the Federal Reserve Bank, it is likely to stop building up its reserves, and, when its reserves have fallen to the legal minimum, it must stop lending. It appears, therefore, that one method which The Monetary Authority could use to stop increases in the price level would be to require the Federal Reserve Banks to raise their rediscount rates.

Irving Fisher and a number of other economists have concluded that the best way to prevent commercial banks from enlarging, in times of optimism, their demand deposit totals is to require all such banks to maintain at all times 100% monetary reserves against all demand deposits. Were this condition imposed, The Monetary Authority, by limiting the amount of pocketbook money outstanding, could control absolutely total demand-deposit volume. Professor Fisher would initiate this plan by permitting the commercial banks to exchange for money enough of their existing assets to cover all demand deposits outstanding at the date when the plan was initiated. This arrangement would prevent the inauguration of the plan from inflicting on the banks any loss in earning power.

A third method of preventing demand deposits from expanding unduly in times of optimism would be to place restrictions upon prospective borrowers. For example, brokers might be required to increase margin requirements. Sellers of goods on the instalment-payment plan might be required to curtail the percentage of credit extended. Thus, in depression periods, a

20 per cent down payment might be permitted, while, in boom times, an 80 per cent minimum might be enforced.

It seems quite certain that a Monetary Authority, equipped with proper powers, could, by use of the devices just mentioned, prevent any undesired *rise* in the price of the imaginary basketful of goods pictured above. Would it be equally feasible to prevent a *decline* in the price?

If banks were required to keep 100% monetary reserves against their demand deposits, and if The Monetary Authority retired no money in times of pessimism, when demand for loans slackened, a depression could not, as in the past, be brought about by a contraction in the volume of circulating medium.

Let us suppose, however, that in such a period, because the 100 per cent reserve plan was not in operation, because of a tendency on the part of the public to build up cash reserves, or because of any other reason whatever, the total value of the hypothetical basketful of goods fell from the standard $40.0 billions to $39.5 billions. How could The Monetary Authority prevent a diminution in the flow of money around the circuit, and a consequent lessening of production? How could it restore the value of the basketful to the $40.0 billion standard? In brief, how could it prevent a depression from developing?

Ample experience shows that the lowering of rediscount rates at the Federal Reserve Banks could *not* be depended upon to prevent new spending power from shrinking. As someone has put it, pushing on the lines doesn't make the horse go. When the public is pessimistic, the number of persons who are both considered satisfactory as credit risks and who desire to borrow is relatively small. Similarly, the number of those who are both able and willing to buy goods on the instalment plan is much smaller than was the case when optimism was the rule. Obviously, therefore, The Monetary Authority could scarcely be expected to control successfully the net volume of new spending power unless it utilized a procedure which would operate as effectively in times of pessimism as in times of optimism.

The "Open Market" Device

Fortunately, there is available a very simple device which, apparently, fulfils this requirement. All that is necessary to stop a shrinkage in the volume of net new spending power is to exchange newly-issued paper money for government bonds, gold, or silver. To arrest an unwanted increase in spending power, the process would be reversed, the bonds, gold, or silver being exchanged for paper money, which would be retired as rapidly as it was acquired. This process represents one type of "open market operations."

Its workability depends upon the fact that every addition to the circulating medium increases net new spending power; every subtraction does the reverse. By contrast, bonds and unminted gold and silver do not circulate, and have practically no effect upon either the volume of new spending power or the price level.

The advantage of this plan of control would be that it would impose no restrictions upon the freedom of action of either producers or consumers.

What it would do would be to offset the anti-social effects of over-optimism and over-pessimism. Thus if, in times of undue pessimism, the paying off of loans at the commercial banks decreased demand deposits by a billion dollars, and caused the value of the hypothetical basketful of goods to fall from the standard $40.0 billions to $39.5 billions, The Monetary Authority would issue a billion dollars of new paper money and use it to buy in the open market government bonds or precious metals. Under our present banking arrangements, the recipients of this money would, as a rule, deposit it in banks, thus increasing the bank deposit total by a billion dollars. The contraction in spending power brought about by pessimism would, therefore, be entirely offset by the action of The Monetary Authority, and there would be no shrinkage in net new spending power and hence no tendency for industry to go into a tailspin.

In most cases, the sellers of the bonds or precious metals would use the proceeds of the sales to buy other securities or commodities. This buying would tend to make prices rise, and hence the value of the basketful would move up toward the $40.0 billion mark. If, because of hoarding by some of the sellers, it failed to reach that level, The Monetary Authority would merely buy enough more bonds or precious metals to achieve the desired result. Hoarding could, therefore, interfere in no way with maintenance of adequate new spending power. The larger the amount of Federal bonds purchased in the open market, the less would be the interest charge which the Federal Government would be called upon to meet, so, the more bonds bought, the better it would be for the taxpayers. By making some of its bond issues callable, the Federal Government could eliminate any possibility that, in an extensive bond-buying campaign, it might be compelled to pay unduly high prices for its bonds.

The banks receiving the monetary deposits might use the money either to replenish their respective reserves at the Federal Reserve banks, or to buy securities. If they pursued the latter course, the impetus of their buying would be added to that of the bond sellers, and would therefore accentuate the tendency to push the price level higher.

Next let us suppose that, in a period of optimism, widespread borrowing from commercial banks increased deposits and net new spending power by one billion dollars, and thereby drove the value of our hypothetical basketful of goods from $40.0 billions up to $40.5 billions. The Monetary Authority would then proceed to sell in the open market to non-bank investors either precious metals or a new issue of callable Federal bonds of a type not usable as collateral for bank loans or available for bank purchase. All money or deposits received for the precious metals or bonds should be placed in a special fund which should never be drawn upon unless and until the value of the hypothetical basketful of goods fell below $40.0 billions and necessitated renewed buying of bonds or precious metals. The process of impounding money and deposits should be continued until the resulting reduction in the net volume of new spending power forced down to $40.0 billions the value of the hypothetical basketful of goods.

This method of controlling the net volume of new spending power and the price level has the following desirable features: —

1. It is simple and automatic, and does not require repeated action on the part of Congress or the general public to make it work effectively
2. It does not interfere in any way with business customs, free competition, free enterprise, or *laissez faire.*
3. It does not increase the public debt. Thus when, in time of depression, a government exchanges its bonds for money or deposits which it impounds, it acquires new assets equal in value to the new debt which it has created. On the other hand, if it exchanges its bonds for funds to pay for public works, boondoggling, or relief, it gets itself ever deeper into debt, and it accumulates no assets which can later be used to pay off the debt. Similarly, when a government exchanges its paper money for work, it accumulates no assets which can, whenever necessary, be used to retire the paper money. If, however, it trades paper money for gold, silver, or bonds, it is in a position to retire the paper money without levying taxes for that purpose. To levy taxes is likely to be politically non-feasible.
4. The sale of precious metals or bonds during the boom furnishes The Monetary Authority with the funds needed to pay for the precious metals or bonds, which it will necessarily buy when the next recession appears.

On the basis of the facts presented, it seems that, from the economic standpoint, it is a relatively simple matter to control the net volume of new spending power. Since such control would benefit greatly almost all classes of the population, it appears that the chief obstacles preventing the installation of such controls are ignorance and inertia. Unfortunately, both of these are hard to overcome.

Red Herrings

Those opposing national control of spending power and the price level usually do not meet the issue fairly, but, instead, draw red herrings across the trail. One of their common subterfuges is to demand international stabilization of the exchanges and of the price level. Careful statistical investigation shows that even very large fluctuations in international exchange rates have had no noticeable tendency to lessen the volume of international trade.[1] It is obvious that there is practically no chance of establishing a sound international currency. Talk of international control of prices is therefore usually merely a dust-throwing device.

Keeping All Currency Redeemable in Precious Metals

In the past, however, international balances have usually been settled either in gold or silver. Since this custom has proved both workable and convenient, it is desirable that any sound national monetary system be tied to one or both of these metals. Inasmuch as the United States is a large producer of each of these metals, it seems desirable to make all of our money redeemable in either gold or silver at the option of the owner of the money. However, the amount of gold or silver payable for a paper dollar ought not to be determined arbitrarily, but rather should be based upon the respective

---

[1] See the article by the present writer in the *Journal of the American Statistical Association* for June, 1935, pp. 387-395. Later extensive research also shows that variations in exchange rates have surprisingly little influence upon the volume of trade between nations.

current commodity values of gold and silver in the markets of the world. If, according to our assumption, the hypothetical basketful of goods was worth $40.0 billions when the control plan was inaugurated, whatever weight of gold would thereafter exchange in the open market for the basketful of goods ought to be worth $40.0 billions. Similarly, whatever weight of silver would buy the basketful in the world's markets ought to be worth 40 billions of dollars. To assure the continuous maintenance of this value relationship, all that would be necessary would be for The Monetary Authority to vary the respective prices which it would pay in paper money for gold or silver. If its reserves of either precious metal became inadequate to assure prompt redemption of paper money on demand, the price of that metal would be advanced sufficiently to replenish the reserve. If reserves of the metal became superabundant, the price would be lowered. Redemption of paper money in gold or silver would always be on the basis mentioned.

Maintenance of a Stable Price Level

The probabilities are that, with this arrangement in force, the respective weights of gold and silver obtainable for a paper dollar would remain comparatively stable, but either might drift slowly upward or downward as mines were discovered or exhausted, or as new mining processes were developed. The value of the dollar in terms of commodities in general would remain unchanged month after month, year after year, and decade after decade. Inflation and deflation would be forgotten. Public utility rate regulation would be simplified. Long-term contracts such as life insurance policies could be entered into with confidence. The thrifty would no longer need to be beset by the fear that their savings would disappear. And, if average hourly earnings rose no faster than average hourly productivity, the KEY RATIO or fraction, $\dfrac{\text{Net New Spending Power}}{\text{Average Hourly Earnings}}$ would not shrink, and hence periods of mass unemployment would disappear. If war could be avoided and undue increases in population prevented, the nation could look forward with confidence to a long period of sustained and gradually increasing prosperity.

The Big If

Unfortunately, confidence in this roseate prospect is greatly shaken by the presence of one of the "ifs" just mentioned — "if average hourly earnings rose no faster than average hourly productivity." Clearly, if the ratio of the denominator to the numerator of the fraction should increase, the size of the KEY RATIO would decline, and unemployment and depression would almost inevitably result. Whenever labor has virtual political control of the nation, is there any likelihood that it will refrain from pushing up wage rates faster than any increase which may occur in the volume of net new spending power? Under such conditions, is it at all probable that, if net new spending power shrinks, labor will consent to a proportionate reduction in average hourly earnings? Unless labor can learn on which side its bread is really buttered, there is little likelihood that prosperity can be maintained. Therefore, the most menacing of all economic difficulties confronting the American people today is undoubtedly the labor problem. Can it be solved? That is the question to be discussed in the next chapter.

Chapter XIX

THE ROAD TO LABOR PROSPERITY

Does the United States Have a Labor Problem?

Since, in the United States, wage workers constitute the largest segment of our gainfully occupied population, their welfare is rightly regarded as constituting the best single measure of national prosperity. It is, therefore, not surprising that, throughout the nation, "The Labor Problem" has long been a popular subject for discussion.

But, to the mythical man from Mars, it would seem strange that the United States could have any serious labor problem. In pre-war days, to get as much in the way of food and clothing as the typical American could obtain by an hour's labor, the Britisher had to work two hours, the German or Frenchman three hours, the Russian or Italian four or five hours, and the Hindu or Chinaman even longer. Yet, even the last-mentioned earned enough to keep body and soul together.

As shown in an earlier chapter, restriction of our birth rate has prevented population from pressing unduly upon our great store of natural resources; our men of genius have made amazing discoveries and inventions; and our thrifty people have saved great quantities of capital and thus made it possible, by providing education, research, power, and equipment to utilize effectively these products of genius. The result has been a remarkable increase in the volume of goods produced per hour of labor. As previously noted, those who work for wages and salaries, rather than those who have saved the capital, have been the chief beneficiaries of this increase in output. Thus the index of *real* factory wages per hour rose from 100 in 1850 to 203 in 1890, to 305 in 1929, to 446 in 1940, and to 515 in April, 1947 — a rate of progress far eclipsing anything ever experienced previously or elsewhere in the history of the world.

This tremendous increase in average real hourly earnings enabled members of the working class to choose between more income and more leisure. As the rising standard of living reduced the birth rate and thereby cut down the size of the average family, they began to question seriously the desirability of working the 60 to 70 hours per week which had been the custom of their ancestors for countless generations. Wisely, they decided that they wanted more leisure. Since the length of the working week is of far more consequence to the employees than to the employers, the latter yielded gradually to demands for fewer hours. In 1850, the factory worker averaged 69.0 hours of work per week. By 1890, his working time had dropped to 60.0 hours per week; by 1914 it had declined to 51.5 hours; and in 1940 it was down to 39.4 hours per week — only 57 percent as long as the working week of 1850. At present, the tendency seems to be to make the standard something like 40 hours.

Despite the fact that the average present-day factory worker has taken out so much of his gains in leisure that he works but little more than half as many hours per week as did his counterpart in the early days of the Republic, the real weekly wages of the man with a steady job are now at least 2½ times as large as were those prevailing a century ago.

Even in a bad depression year like 1932, with all its short working-time and unemployment, real annual earnings for all persons ordinarily making their livings by working in factories averaged probably some 40 per cent higher than did the real annual earnings of the same class a hundred years earlier.[1] Today the average railway worker and the average factory worker are each paid more than a dollar and a quarter per hour. Even unskilled road builders receive nearly a dollar per hour. Few members of the nation's labor force earn less than twice a subsistence wage. Normal working time has been reduced to 40 hours per week. Employers vie with one another in providing safe, comfortable working conditions. How, under such circumstances, is it possible to say that the United States still has a labor problem? Strangely enough, however, the fact remains that a labor problem really does exist. What is it?

Our Present-Day Labor Problem

The only labor problem of moment at the present time is this: *How can manual and clerical workers be taught to understand and strive for their own welfare?*

The educated workingman believes, of course, that he is fully aware of where his interests lie. He has been taught by labor leaders, by most writers in periodicals, and by nearly all so-called "labor economists" that only by the formation of powerful labor unions which will represent him in collective bargaining can he hope to secure his fair share of the products of industry, and be assured of steady employment. This point of view is generally endorsed by the public, hence Congress has enacted such laws as the Clayton Act and the Wagner Act which permit and encourage labor unions to engage in conspiracies in restraint of trade and to monopolize the market — practices which are severely punished if engaged in by employers. Congress and the State legislatures have also passed minimum wage laws and granted public compensation to the unemployed. Most workers have not the slightest doubt that such statutes actually protect them against untoward economic conditions and the greed of unscrupulous employers. But the facts set forth in earlier chapters prove that these assumptions are almost diametrically opposed to the truth. As we have seen, labor monopolies have shown no ability whatever to increase labor's share in the value added by manufacture — to get a larger fraction of net new spending power [2] — to make real hourly wages advance faster than production. Collective bargaining, strikes, labor wars — all of these combined rarely, if ever, secure for labor returns as large

---

[1] More detailed information concerning changes in the earnings of factory workers is given in an article by the present writer entitled *Raising the Workingman's Scale of Living.* It is a publication of the Committee for Constitutional Government.

[2] Between 1933 and 1939, the per cent of unionization among all employees in the United States increased from 8 to 20 per cent. By 1945, it had grown to 36 per cent. (See the present writer's study entitled "Unions and the Workingman's Income," published by the Committee for Constitutional Government.) Yet, as Tables XIX and XXI and Charts 8 and 9 in Chapter XV show, labor's share in the nation's product has shown no tendency to grow larger.

as it would receive without any turmoil if it insisted upon free competitive bargaining by each individual for himself.

What labor monopolies, collective bargaining, strikes, minimum wage laws, and unemployment insurance have really accomplished is to cut down production, throw millions out of work, reduce total payrolls billions of dollars in a single year, discourage thrift, and promote inflation, lawlessness, and riots. It follows that what labor sadly needs is protection against its "friends"!

Fallacies Afflicting the Working Class

The problem of how to get the typical workingman to realize on which side his bread is really buttered is anything but a simple one, for his mind is thoroughly imbued with a choice collection of the economic fallacies heretofore discussed. For example, he usually believes that his interests are in conflict with those of his employer, not understanding that, when profits rise, wage payments rise; when profits fall, wage payments fall.

Most wage earners take it for granted that the raising of wage rates increases "purchasing power," and thus stimulates business, for it never occurs to them that, if higher wage rates are paid, they reduce the spending power of the employers to the same extent that they increase the spending power of the employees. They also either ignore the fact that higher wage rates, by increasing the expenses of production, almost inevitably raise the selling prices of products and hence reduce the volumes of sales, or else they make the false assumption that such price advances can be passed on to the consumers without cutting the volume of buying.

The Real Interest of the Employees

If they generally realized that, without abundance of saving to provide large amounts of capital per employee, there would be no opportunity for the worker to secure either higher wage rates or a shorter working week, the typical wage worker would be extremely anxious to encourage capital formation, and hence would vigorously oppose taxation of savings. However being ignorant of the relationship existing between saving and the progress of the working class, he is likely to endorse tax measures which virtually confiscate the incomes of those who accumulate the bulk of the capital.

Since most working class families are anxious to get full returns from their social security payments, and since they do not want the real value of either their savings-bank balances or their life insurance policies to diminish, those knowing their own interests would oppose inflation. This would mean that, since they would want the price level to remain constant, they would always demand that government finance its expenditures by taxation, rather than by borrowing from the banks.

Since the prime economic interest of the working class is to have full opportunity for employment at the best wage rates obtainable, the workers, if sufficiently well informed, would insist that no action be taken which would make average hourly earnings increase relatively faster than the slow upward trend in the volume of net new spending power, for they would know that a diminution in the size of the Key Ratio, $\dfrac{\text{Net New Spending Power}}{\text{Average Hourly Earnings}}$, would spell unemployment and reduce their annual incomes. If they understood all these things, the future outlook for the average American laboring man would be rosy indeed.

As stated at the beginning of the chapter, the welfare of the working class dominates the welfare of the nation. But the welfare of the working class is dependent primarily upon keeping wage rates properly coordinated with net new spending power. It follows, then, that whoever rules the wage rates of the nation holds that nation's welfare in the palm of his hand. By raising wage rates unduly, he can throw millions out of work, paralyze industry, and bring about dire depression. By lowering wage rates he can re-employ the idle, make the factories hum, increase the national income, and replace despair and misery with confidence, hope, and prosperity.

Paradoxically enough, the more that labor battles for higher pay, the more meager are the annual earnings of the working class. Unfortunately, those who pose as the champions of labor, and who often really believe that they are labor's chief benefactors, have been prone to push wage rates up along a gradient steeper than that representing the increase in production. This procedure has brought to the wage-working class the curse of unemployment and the bane of poverty.

If employees really understood that the share of the value product of any given industry which labor gets or can get is practically constant, comes to labor almost automatically, and cannot be increased by any amount of bargaining, battling, or legislating, they would oppose bitterly all moves which would reduce production and hence diminish their own incomes. Instead, they would cooperate vigorously with their employers to reduce waste, maximize output, and thereby increase their own earnings.

Experience of the Lincoln Electric Company

The experience of the Lincoln Electric Company (a concern making arc-welding machines and electrodes) shows what amazing results may be attained when such a policy is continued over a period of years. In that corporation, the employees now own most of the stock. Their representatives sit with those of the management in an Advisory Board and make recommendations concerning the problems of the enterprise, and the management nearly always finds it feasible and desirable to accept those recommendations.

Every effort is made to get each employee placed in the type of work for which he is best adapted. Whenever feasible, work is paid for on a piece rather than on a time basis. Great care is exercised in seeing that piece rates are fair, and, once set, they are never reduced to offset increased proficiency on the part of the workers. At the end of the year, workers are given bonuses, the sizes of the payments being based upon their respective efficiencies, and upon the profitableness of the company's operations.

Mr. James F. Lincoln, the President of the Company, says that, since

1933, the policies just cited have resulted in the following remarkable achievements:

1. The hours of direct labor required to manufacture a 200 ampere welding machine have been *reduced from 60 to 16.*
2. The hours of direct labor required to manufacture a ton of 3/16 inch Fleetweld No. 5 electrode have been *reduced from 12 to 2½.*
3. In a period in which the prices of other manufactured products have, on the average, risen about 33 per cent, the selling prices of these Lincoln Electric products have been *reduced* thus:
   (a) Arc-welding machines from $560 to $200
   (b) Electrode, per pound, from 12 cents to 5.7 cents.
4. The growth in the average output per worker has been *more than twice* as great as the growth in the average output per worker in all plants producing electrical machinery.
5. Dividends per share of Lincoln Electric stock have been *trebled.*
6. The average annual pay of the Lincoln Electric worker has *risen from $1250 to more than $5800.*

Mr. Lincoln ascribes these results mainly to the fact that the employees have been cooperating to increase rather than to restrict output, and have learned how to use their respective abilities effectively. He holds that both of these things have been developed by educating employees to understand what their own interests really are, by giving them genuine incentives to increase output, and by dealing fairly with them at all times. Observation leads him to believe that the combined intelligence of any group of workers is usually much superior to the wisdom of the typical supervisor who directs their operations. A major problem of management is how to utilize this combined knowledge.[3]

Experience has amply demonstrated that the Wagner Act, which its sponsors fondly believed would usher in an era of labor peace, has really made certain the frequent recurrence of industrial civil war. Since no amount of collective bargaining or striking increases labor's share in the net value product of industry, what this war between management and labor has really accomplished is to take billions of dollars out of the pockets of the wage workers, and to reduce the real incomes of the stockholders and the public at large. Neither labor nor management can hope to make full use of their opportunities until they pattern their actions after those of the Lincoln Electric Company, and act as partners, which they really are, rather than as enemies.

The Need for Wage Flexibility

One of the obstacles preventing cooperation between labor and management and cutting down efficiency of operations, has been the attempt to maintain a wage system based upon fixed payments per hour. As we have seen, mass unemployment is usually the result either of forcing up wages faster than the increase in productivity warrants or of keeping wage rates rigid in a period when net new spending power is declining. Basically,

[3] James F. Lincoln, *Lincoln's Incentive System,* Chaps. I to VII

therefore, the labor problem of today is how to get the laboring class to understand that it can never be steadily prosperous unless it adopts a policy which will make wage rates flexible — which will adjust them to changes in the aggregate of net new spending power.

Recently, labor has been demanding not only fixed wage rates, but a guaranteed annual wage. However, no employer can safely guarantee steady employment to all his workers unless he can prevent serious declines in his volume of output. He cannot prevent such declines unless he can vary his sales prices to meet changes in the demands for his goods. He cannot thus vary his selling price for a good unless he can, at the same time, vary his wage cost per unit of output. Obviously, what is needed is a contract providing for flexible wages. To secure the maximum possible stability in the annual incomes of both employers and employees, a flexible wage system should be substituted for the present rigid wage system.

The Fixed-Wage Illusion

One of the prime reasons why we have a labor problem is that someone, sometime and somewhere, invented the notion that employers ought to pay to their employees the same wage rates year in and year out, during good times and bad, and that, by so doing, labor would not suffer when hard times appeared. This plan has never worked out as expected. In most cases, after depression has persisted for sometime, wage rates have been cut. In those instances in which wage rates have been maintained, labor has suffered far more severely because of lack of employment than it would have suffered from wage cuts. Since, after all, it is the annual wage, and not the wage rate which is of interest to labor, maintenance of fixed wage rates has brought nothing but hardship to the laborers.

The more the wage problem is studied the clearer it becomes that the way to secure the needed flexibility and to avoid depressions is to abandon the illusion that labor can shift to capital the risks of industry, and frankly recognize the fact that, willy-nilly, employers and employees are partners in enterprise and must together share its burdens and enjoy its fruits. Once they accept this view, they can readily so arrange things as to increase annual wages, to increase annual profits, and to avoid endless bickering over wage rates.

The Unit Wage System

The way to accomplish these obviously desirable results is to make wages, salaries, and dividends not nominally fixed, but frankly variable. Instead of receiving a fixed contractual sum each year, each of the partners in production should be given an equitable share in the *distributable income* turned out by the enterprise. The term *distributable income* represents the balance remaining out of gross revenues after the corporation has covered the cost of depreciation, materials, supplies, tools, power, taxes, insurance, rent, royalties, interest, and similar fixed charges.

To see how this flexible system would work, let us take as an example the case of a corporation the accounts of which are balanced monthly. Let us, for the sake of simplicity, assume that employer and employees agree to maintain for the time being the *status quo,* and let us therefore define as one unit that amount of labor or capital which yielded $1.00 in the calendar month just preceding the installation of the new plan. Thus, if, in that month, common labor had been receiving 50 cents per hour, a unit of common labor would be two hours' work. If skilled mechanics had been paid $1.00 per hour, one hour's work of a skilled mechanic would be counted as one unit. If the salary of the president of the company was $2,000 a month, 1/2000 of a month's work by the president would constitute one unit. The unit system would apply to piece work also. If, for example, a coatmaker had been getting $1.00 for the stitching of a coat, this piece of work would be designated as one unit of labor. If a share of the stock of the corporation had been paying dividends of $3.00 per year, or 25 cents per month, a share would be designated as one-quarter of a unit; in other words, it would take 4 shares of stock to constitute a unit. The sizes of all units would remain unchanged until the contract was modified.

Let us suppose that the contract was signed at a time when business was somewhat below normal and times were improving. In such a case, the contract might well provide that all distributable income above $1.10 per unit should be carried to reserves to meet contingencies. Employees' reserves could be set aside to help pay wages or salaries in bad years. Stockholders reserves might be either invested in plant, or held to augment dividends in lean years.

Let us assume further that, in some particular month after the signing of the contract, the numbers of units of labor and capital employed were as designated in the first numerical column of Table XXX and that the distributable income available for employees and stockholders was $129,600 or $1.35 per unit. Under such circumstances, the apportionment of income to the various classes would be as shown in the later columns of the table.

Table XXX

**APPORTIONMENT OF DISTRIBUTABLE INCOME
UNDER THE UNIT SYSTEM**
(In prosperous month)

	Total Number of Units in Class	Disbursed Amount ($1.10 per unit)	Carried to Reserve ($0.25 per unit)	Distributable Income
Operatives....................	60,000	$66,000	$15,000	$81,000
Clerical Staff.................	12,000	13,200	3,000	16,200
Administrative and Technical Staff.......................	3,000	3,300	750	4,050
Officials.....................	2,000	2,200	500	2,700
Total for Employees..........	77,000	84,700	19,250	103,950
Stock.......................	19,000	20,900	4,750	25,650
Total....................	96,000	$105,600	$24,000	$129,600

The employees would receive in the given month $84,700 in wages and salaries, the stockholders would get $20,900 in dividends, and $24,000 would be carried to the various reserves.

Now let us suppose that some time has elapsed, that the nation is passing through a severe depression, and that the distributable income for a calendar month has fallen to $80,000. Let us also assume that, in the interim, 20,000 shares, that is 5,000 units, of new stock have been sold to investors, and that the working force has been increased. With these conditions, results might be as shown in Table XXXI.

Table XXXI

APPORTIONMENT OF DISTRIBUTABLE INCOME
UNDER THE UNIT SYSTEM

(During a depression)

	Total Number of Units in Class	Total Distribution to Class
Operatives...	78,000	$52,000
Clerical Staff......................................	12,000	8,000
Administrative and Technical Staff....................	3,600	2,400
Officials..	2,400	1,600
Total for Employees................................	96,000	64,000
Stock...	24,000	16,000
Total..	120,000	$80,000
Total Distributable Income.........................		$80,000

With $80,000 of distributable income, and nothing carried to reserves, it would be possible to distribute only $0.66⅔ per unit. Employees would receive $64,000, *in toto,* and the stockholders would get $16,000 in dividends. Money wage rates per hour or per piece would therefore all be off a third from the rate prevailing at the time the contract was signed. Dividends per share would likewise be off a third. However, retail prices would be relatively low, hence the 66⅔ cents per unit might buy nearly as much in the way of goods as the $1.00 per unit received when the contract was negotiated. Furthermore, if the operatives felt that they could not live on the reduced wages, or the stockholders considered higher dividends imperative, they might vote to draw upon their reserves accumulated during years of prosperity. The reserves should be definitely the property of the classes for whom they were laid aside, and the directors of the corporation should have no power to shift reserves from one class to another.

The adoption of this flexible wage system would obviously spell the end of contracts for fixed wage rates. In the future, all disputes between employers and employees would hinge on the question of how much of each class of labor and how much stock was to be counted as one unit. Common laborers might fight to get their unit reduced from 2.0 hours to 1.8 hours, while leaving the units for other classes of labor unchanged. All labor might unite to force up from 4 to 5 the number of shares of stock counted as one unit. The new system would offer no hindrance to collective bargaining between an employer and his employees. It would, however, make it unnecessary to revise wage contracts frequently, for neither fluctuations in the general price level nor the ups and downs of business would make revisions imperative. However, it would doubtless happen from time to time that the rate of pay for a given grade of labor in one plant would run consistently lower than the rate of pay for similar labor in another plant in the vicinity. In such a case, it would be imperative for the plant paying the lower wage to reduce the quantity of that specific kind of labor counted as one unit. Were this not done, the enterprise could not retain its required supply of this category of employees. To make the plan work smoothly, a permanent simple arrangement for making adjustments in the relative sizes of the units should be agreed upon in advance by the employer and employees.

What the Unit Wage System Would Accomplish

Were the terms of a collective bargaining contract those shown in the example, it would follow that the employer turning out a product the demand for which was elastic would have an excellent chance of preventing sales from falling off when demand slackened, for he could safely reduce his selling prices. Such price cuts would of course be likely to reduce wage rates as well as dividends, but there would be little danger of employees quitting, for, at such times, it would not be easy to find other jobs. Furthermore, all employees would know that their wages would automatically advance as soon as business picked up, hence they would not be anxious to shift to other concerns not offering this safeguard.

If the employer could stabilize sales volume, he could also stabilize employment. The larger the percentage of employers thus stabilizing production, the smaller would be the fluctuations in the demands for goods in other industries. Therefore, if this plan of wage payment were installed in industries producing goods the demands for which were elastic, the heretofore highly fluctuating demands for such goods as steel, locomotives, and machine tools would become far more stable than was formerly the case.

Were this unit system of wage payments widely adopted, it seems probable that, in most industries, the satisfactory employee could count upon his job continuing month after month and year after year, and he would know that he would always receive wages, though, in some months, the wage rates would be higher than in other months. With this plan for bringing about flexibility in wage rates and prices in operation, the fluctuations in wage rates would presumably rarely be larger than 10 or at most 20 per cent. This would be in striking contrast to the situation existing at present in which the workers' wages tend to drop suddenly from a 100 per cent basis to a zero basis, and, frequently, to remain there for months.

Under this new type of contract, the stockholders could also count upon receiving dividends each year, but the amount of the dividends would vary from time to time. To the average stockholder, however, it would be far more desirable to have some income arriving each quarter than to have *large* dividends occasionally, and *no* dividends at other times.

Since, under this plan, workers could scarcely avoid realizing that their pay depended upon the volume of goods turned out, loafing would be frowned upon by fellow workers, hence production would increase markedly. This fact, coupled with steady employment, would give to the average employee in the average year wages much higher than he would receive under the present system. The stockholder would also, for like reason, receive, on the average, dividends materially larger than he had previously enjoyed.

Fortunately, in appraising the usefulness of a wage system geared to the value of the product, it is not necessary to rely entirely upon deductive reasoning, for the Nunn Bush Shoe Company of Milwaukee has been operating on such a basis since 1935. According to Mr. H. L. Nunn, president of the concern, and also according to employees of the company, the plan has been remarkably successful both in stabilizing employment and in promoting harmonious relations between the employer and the employees.

One should be careful to avoid confusing a plan of this type, which may correctly be referred to as *A Partnership for Prosperity,* with profit-sharing arrangements. The latter have commonly proved unworkable because, while workers are always ready to share profits, they are usually reluctant to share losses. The *Partnership for Prosperity* is also almost entirely unrelated to plans which promise to workers fixed or minimum annual salaries regardless of the state of business. Plans of the latter type are likely to collapse as soon as a severe depression occurs, for, under such conditions, continuance will probably spell bankruptcy for the employer.

As long as industry generally retains its present system of fixed money wage rates, while, at the same time, labor organizations are powerful enough to control the labor market, it seems improbable that the leaders of such organizations can resist the pressure from their members to fight steadily for even higher hourly pay. They will, therefore, tend to push up wage rates faster than the growth of net new spending power warrants. Hence, unless the flexible unit system can be substituted for existing contracts calling for fixed money wages, there appears to be little likelihood of avoiding mass unemployment, and little prospect of assuring continuing prosperity.

Chapter XX

THE KEYS

Why the Road to Prosperity Has Not Been Followed

The thesis advanced in the first chapter of this book is that the road to sustained prosperity is not a figment of the imagination, but has been thoroughly surveyed and is entirely passable. However, before all seventeen gates along this road can be opened, the correct key for each must be found and used. Experience shows that the task of securing these keys has thus far baffled those charged with responsibility for the nation's welfare and progress. The prime reason for this situation is that the true keys are buried in a huge mass of false keys. These false keys are commonly referred to as economic fallacies.

The following fallacies have been gleaned solely from the discussions in the preceding chapters of this book. Therefore, this list must not be thought of as including all of the common errors by which economists are beset, but it does show that such misconceptions are very numerous. For the convenience of the reader, the numbers of the fallacies have been made to correspond to those of the chapters in which they are mentioned or discussed.

Trouble-Making Fallacies

I   A. That our economic mechanism is too complex for anyone to understand, and that it is beyond anyone's ability to keep it running smoothly.

      B. That freeing enterprise from all restrictions will insure full employment and prosperity.

      C. That our people cannot have both security and opportunity, but must choose between them.

      D. That, without governmental control of industry, we cannot maintain reasonably full employment.

      E. That any effective governmental interference with *laissez faire* means regimentation, and serious limitation of freedom of enterprise.

II   A. That, everywhere, improved methods of production have made the problem of getting enough to eat one which affects only a few nations in exceptionally bad years.

      B. That "living on a subsistence level" means occupying a "cold-water flat," wearing clothes that are frayed or out of style, getting steak only occasionally, and going to the movies but once a week.

      C. That our own ancestors seldom suffered from severe poverty.

      D. That Malthus was an ill-informed and short-sighted harbinger of evil who foresaw ills that never materialized.

      E. That, in any nation, one can increase food production almost indefinitely by modernizing agricultural methods.

F. That the world is big enough to support comfortably a population much larger than that now existing.

G. That modern methods of agriculture have greatly increased the productivity of the average acre of farm land.

H. That the growth in the world's food supply has far outstripped anything that Malthus considered possible.

I. That our productive skill is now so great that it is relatively simple to keep production growing faster than any probable rate of population expansion.

J. That, today, any nation can long have a high birth rate and yet remain prosperous.

K. That a family enjoying an abundance of comforts and luxuries necessarily has a high standard of living.

L. That a family in dire poverty necessarily has a low standard of living.

M. That improving methods of production and thus increasing the prosperity of a nation or class necessarily raises its standard of living almost immediately.

N. That there exists any other force which exerts as much control over the welfare of a nation as does the average standard of living of its inhabitants.

O. That inventions, ingenuity, thrift, free enterprise, and abundance of natural resources would have made the United States prosperous even if our ancestors had not raised their standards of living, thus reducing the birth rate.

P. That the fact that Manhattan Island is densely populated and prosperous proves that population density might be greatly increased elsewhere without markedly impairing the prosperity of the people.

Q. That the Malthusian principles of population are not applicable to today's conditions, and that the population problem is no longer troublesome.

R. That capital accumulation may successfully offset the ruinous results of a high birth rate.

S. That improved sanitary and health measures reduce the death rates of countries having low standards of living.

T. That loans to enable low-standard-of-living foreign nations to mechanize their industries would make their inhabitants more prosperous or lower their death rates.

U. That heavy emigration from nations having low standards of living and high birth rates would lessen the populations of those countries.

V. That in low-standard-of-living, high-birth-rate regions the poverty of the masses is to any noticeable extent due to heavy taxation, church tithes, or high rents imposed by oppressors.

W. That, in such regions, the condition of the poor would have been alleviated to some extent had the wealth and income of the favored few been distributed among the masses.

X. That, in such regions, the concentration of wealth and income in the hands of the few has tended to prevent progress.

Y. That it is unnecessary to give much attention to the conservation of our natural resources — the assumption being that the future will provide for itself.

Z. That environment is almost as influential as heredity.

III
A. That governmental planning of industrial activity is something relatively new.

B. That socialism and communism are inherently almost identical.

C. That Russia, under Stalin, has a communistic system.

D. That, under the competitive system, businessmen produce for profit rather than for use.

E. That it is possible for any managed economy to fit production to the wants of the citizens.

F. That any managed economy can attain the efficiency of one operating under *laissez faire.*

G. That a planned economy is likely to choose competent, honest, and efficient men to control the industries of the nation.

H. That a government can engage in price fixing without hampering production.

I. That, in the United States, freedom has been diminished but little.

J. That limiting profits in competitive industries does not necessarily lessen production, and may be necessary in war time.

K. That, under free competition, very high profits mean that the customer has been overcharged.

L. That, in business, profits are almost universal and losses relatively rare.

M. That, as long as reasonable returns on investment are permitted, profit limitation does not seriously retard industrial progress.

N. That most of the benefits of efficient large-scale enterprises accrue to the owners of these enterprises.

O. That progressive taxation of corporate profits is sound public policy.

P. That, during the "Thirties," the competitive machine broke down.

Q. That, in the United States, manufacturing and merchandising have largely come under the control of giant corporate monopolies.

R. That any governmental limitations on *laissez faire* are unwarranted.

IV
A. That goods can be produced by human beings, unaided by Nature.

B. That the value of paper money depends solely upon the possibility of redeeming it in gold or silver.

C. That a bank has in its vaults or tills the depositor's money.

D. That, in the main, commercial bank deposits originate through the act of depositing money in a bank.

E. That bank-deposit inflation is less dangerous and destructive than is monetary inflation.

F. That, money performs no functions that are really essential to the existence of a modern economy.

V
A. That, once money is saved, the retention of the saved funds is a simple and almost automatic process.

B. That, by investing in Government bonds or other very high-grade securities, one can almost eliminate any danger of losing his savings.

C. That, for any given nation or group, the gross volume of saving is an index of the net volume of saving.

D. That thrift necessarily produces net savings.

E. That net saving is always the result of thrift.

F. That an increase in net worth, as reported by an expert accountant, necessarily indicates the existence of any real net saving.

G. That all social saving enlarges the nation's stock of tangible goods.

H. That hoarding *necessarily* results in involuntary saving by persons other than the hoarder.

I. That large private saving necessarily results in large social saving.

J. That an increase in the total amount of bank deposits, money, and savings bonds on hand in a nation indicates real net saving on the part of the inhabitants taken as a whole.

K. That it is possible to measure net saving by considering changes in assets while ignoring changes in liabilities.

L. That the act of paying off a debt constitutes saving by the debtor.

M. That, during World War II, the people of the United States accumulated a huge volume of unspent real net savings.

N. That it is possible to approximate closely the net volume of real saving in the United States.

O. That the 1930–1940 depression period was characterized by an unusually large volume of saving.

P. That the nation may suffer because of "over-saving" and over-capacity of plants.

Q. That "over-saving" is a cause of depression.

R. That saving is the opposite of spending.

S. That, as an individual's income increases in size, the proportion which he spends tends to diminish.

T. That spending lessens the wealth of the spender.

VI
A. That saving always equals investment.

B. That property is equivalent to real estate.

C. That capital is equivalent to wealth.

D. That a bond is never capital.

E. That a corporation's bond is part of its capital.

F. That the purchase of any durable good necessarily constitutes an investment.

G. That, when a government spends vast sums for naval vessels, airplanes, parkways, and public buildings, it is increasing the investing total for the nation.

H. That all private investing goes to buy tangible goods.

I. That all investing is necessarily socially beneficial.

J. That invested capital tends to reproduce itself almost automatically.

K. That the gross volume of investing is an index of the net volume of investing.

L. That the vanishing of our frontier lessened seriously our opportunities for investing.

M. That the slowing down of population growth tends to bring about economic stagnation.

N. That the decline in investing which occurred after 1929 was caused by the maturing of our economy.

O. That the volume of investing cannot be maintained without the development of new industries.

P. That old industries require little new capital.

Q. That the appearance of new industries is necessary if prosperity is to be maintained.

R. That, at any time and place, there is any absolute amount of opportunity for investing.

S. That a high volume of investing is necessarily accompanied by low interest rates.

T. That interest rates are dominated solely by the *supply* of loanable funds.

U. That interest rates depend wholly upon either the supply of or the demand for capital.

V. That, without additional capital, increasing employment is impossible.

W. That overcrowded, poverty-stricken countries have more unemployment than prosperous nations.

X. That, with interest rates at zero, saving would be ample to assure rapid progress.

Y. That encouragement of investing is a device which is likely to be effective in extricating a nation from depression.

VII   A. That the depression of the "Thirties" was characterized by the accumulation of great stores of idle money.

B. That "liquidity preference" leads to underinvesting and hoarding.

C. That high "liquidity preference" tends to increase the average liquidity of investments.

D. That compulsory investing of all "idle funds" would lessen the supply of such funds.

E. That, during the "Thirties," either "lack of confidence" or "liquidity preference" was responsible for the scantiness of investing in new securities.

F. That persons with small incomes furnish a large proportion of the net savings accumulated in the nation.

G. That, under the competitive capitalistic system, high taxes on the prosperous classes are compatible with rapid industrial advancement.

H. That very high tax rates do not conflict with the institution of private property.

VIII A. That an abundance of natural resources per capita will necessarily make a nation prosperous.

B. That the bulk of the rewards of thrift go to those who do the saving.

C. That an increase in output per worker usually indicates that the worker himself is more productive.

D. That wage rates can be increased materially without an increase in the supply of capital per worker.

E. That the average workingman knows how to promote his own interests.

F. That the short working week now generally prevailing is a gain brought about by the organization of labor.

G. That the high pay now enjoyed by American workers is the result of efficient bargaining by labor unions.

H. That responsibility for the relative inefficiency of British industry lies primarily with her capitalists.

I. That, through public spending, a nation's prosperity may be enhanced.

J. That doles and unemployment insurance benefit the working class.

K. That a "cyclically balanced budget" is a workable fiscal device.

L. That an unbalanced budget is necessary in time of depression and in war time.

M. That if, during World War II, the Federal Government had balanced its budget, the people's scale of living would have been lowered.

N. That, by borrowing, our Government placed upon future generations part of the burden of paying for World War II.

O. That heavy Governmental spending, if for laudable ends, does not threaten the existence of private enterprise.

P. That, since we owe it to ourselves, a huge public debt does not endanger the nation's welfare.

Q. That progressivity in tax rates usually benefits the poorer classes of the population.

R. That maintenance by government of low interest rates is usually socially desirable.

S. That governmentally-managed social security systems always benefit the masses of the people.

T. That our present Social Security set-up is fair and reasonably satisfactory.

U. That government should leave wholly to private initiative arrangements for protecting individuals against emergencies and the vicissitudes of life.

V. That an increase in the per capita supply of capital is not a prerequisite to economic progress.

IX A. That, before 1933, the purchasing power of the dollar was reasonably stable.

B. That, as a rule, "demand deposits" are originated by depositing money in banks.

C. That, during World War II, the O.P.A. prevented inflation from making much headway.

D. That an individual's demand for goods is closely related to the supply of circulating medium which he possesses.

E. That monetary data for the period of the depression indicate any marked tendency toward hoarding.

X A. That the validity of the equation of exchange is in some way connected with the validity of the quantity theory of money.

B. That the *equation* of exchange does not necessarily balance precisely.

C. That failure to balance the equation of exchange by substituting statistical estimates implies that the equation is faulty.

D. That the term "general price level" refers solely to the prices of tangible commodities.

E. That the arbitrary lowering of the prices of goods of one kind has no tendency to raise the prices of other goods.

F. That changes in the price level always parallel changes in the volume of circulating medium.

G. That changes in the volume of circulating medium have little tendency to affect the price level.

H. That the causal relationships in the equation of exchange never vary.

I. That, in the absence of inflation, increases in industrial operating expenses can, in general, be passed on to customers.

XI A. That, if we reverted to a back-to-nature economy, our present population might still exist in relative comfort.

B. That money is not an essential part of the nation's productive mechanism.

C. That the velocity of circulation of money and deposits is independent of the velocity of circulation of other goods and the nature of the prevailing industrial structure.

D. That the velocity of circulation always tends to vary inversely with the supply of circulating medium.

E. That a decrease in velocity of circulation necessarily indicates that hoarding is going on.

F. That velocity of circulation exerts a causal influence upon business activity.

G. That because velocity varies greatly, the stabilization of the price level by varying the currency supply is impracticable.

H. That artificial devices for speeding up velocity may help to extricate a nation from depression.

I. That advertising and "buy now" campaigns may aid in bringing about business revival.

J. That forcing people to spend for consumption goods is a policy which might be used effectively to stimulate business, increase employment, and benefit the nation.

XII   A. That hoarding is necessarily anti-social.

B. That the free spender benefits the rest of society more than does the "tightwad."

C. That hoarding is usually illogical.

D. That, in the United States, hoarding has led to under-investing or has brought about depression.

E. That the average family has very small cash reserves.

F. That spending is the opposite of saving.

G. That, during the "Thirties," total spending was far smaller than total national income — in other words, that hoarding was then extensive.

XIII   A. That demand is the same as purchasing power.

B. That intensifying the want for a good is equivalent to intensifying the demand.

C. That ability to buy necessarily makes demand.

D. That demand tends to approximate a man's stock of ready cash.

E. That lowering the price of a good increases the demand for it.

F. That a feasible device for getting a nation out of depression is to persuade each producer to lower the selling prices of his products.

G. That demands for consumption goods and demands for speculative goods have similar limits.

H. That production necessarily creates demand.

I. That currency inflation creates no genuine demand for goods.

J. That going without goods in war-time creates a great pent-up demand for goods.

K. That disbursement by government of money secured by taxation or by selling bonds to individuals increases total demand.

L. That a war, financed on a pay-as-you-go basis, would increase the total demand for goods.

M. That the total demand for goods can be increased by advertising.

N. That lending by the United States to foreign nations of money raised by taxation or borrowing from individuals increases the total demand for American products.

O. That the size of the national income can be increased by making resolutions concerning what it must be.

XIV   A. That the national income is the sole source of new spending power.

B. That reducing the total of indebtedness to banks is sure to cause depression.

C. That borrowing to buy is never an economically unsound practice if all amounts borrowed are paid when due.

D. That a heavy curtailment in the total volume of buying implies widespread hoarding.

E. That governmental buying necessarily lessens the volume of private business.

F. That governmental buying, not supported by deficit financing, can stimulate private business in general.

G. That, without deficit financing, government can increase employment by engaging in a public-works program.

H. That agricultural prosperity, important as it is, dominates the prosperity of the nation.

I. That the factory wage total governs agricultural prosperity.

XV A. That high pay for those at work necessarily spells prosperity for the working class.

B. That *costs* of production and *expenses* of production are identical.

C. That unionization, collective bargaining, and strikes have increased labor's percentage of the value product of industry.

D. That real wage rates per man hour can be increased without increasing physical productivity per man hour.

E. That industrial output represents primarily the product of current labor.

F. That, under the competitive capitalistic system, it is possible for industry to get the services of capital without paying for the accumulation of the capital.

G. That the total earnings of wage workers can be increased without increasing the nation's volume of net new spending power.

H. That, in a period in which the nation's total of new spending power is not increasing, wage increases can be "passed on to the consumer."

I. That PRESENT income is dependent upon PRESENT production.

J. That, in practice, a nation's prosperity ever increases in a period when employment volume is declining markedly.

K. That forces other than wars or crop failures would cause business depressions if all workers and other producers sold their services and products at the best prices obtainable.

XVI A. That resolutions that we must have "full employment" necessarily lessen the amount of unemployment.

B. That it is easy to determine at least approximately when employment is "full."

C. That the amount of unemployment is affected but little by the volitions of the potential workers.

D. That it is possible to measure the volume of unemployment in a nation.

E. That, in the United States, the concentration of wealth and income in the hands of the few has been steadily increasing.

F. That inequality in wealth and income leads to depression and unemployment.

G. That overproduction is one of the causes of depression and unemployment.

H. That lowering wage rates reduces purchasing power, and raising wage rates increases it.

I. That a high-wage policy benefits the wage-working class.

J. That, in time of depression, employers who cut wage rates injure the working class, while those who maintain wage rates benefit the working class.

K. That the effect upon purchasing power wrought by raising wage rates is any different from that produced by raising the prices of groceries.

L. That when pensioners are required to stop working they make more jobs for other people.

M. That "social security," as administered in the United States today, is based upon sound actuarial principles.

N. That unemployment insurance is a remedy for unemployment.

O. That unemployment insurance is not much of a menace to the social weal.

P. That it is possible, by enacting minimum wage laws, to raise the average level of wages.

Q. That an effective minimum wage law does not necessarily produce unemployment.

R. That it is possible, by wage manipulation, to legislate upward the level of real wages.

XVII A. That the depression of the "Thirties" was evidence that *laissez faire* and free enterprise had failed.

B. That, if the government refrains from inflating the circulating medium, public works programs have any tendency to increase employment.

C. That raising wage rates almost certainly increases wage totals.

XVIII A. That, since inflation brought us out of the depression of the "Thirties," inflation ought to be used whenever unemployment becomes a serious problem.

B. That it is possible, by using price controls efficiently, to overcome any adverse effects resulting from inflation.

C. That price controls can be used effectively without hampering production noticeably.

D. That a government can engage in price fixing without encouraging lawlessness, and generating "black markets."

E. That price fixing is consistent with freedom of choice on the part of buyers.

F. That, in the United States, it is possible, by using price ceilings, to prevent the general price level from rising as far as it would otherwise go.

G. That having government provide capital for industry does not endanger free enterprise.

H. That the mere stoppage of inflation has no tendency to bring about a recession in business.

I. That, without control of the net volume of new spending power, it is practicable, with existing price rigidity and a free country, to maintain prosperity for any long period of time.

J. That a fixed metallic monetary standard guarantees stability of business activity.

K. That elasticity in a currency supply guarantees stability in business activity.

L. That stabilization of the price level is possible while the government is allowed to pay its expenses either by printing money or borrowing from the commercial banks.

M. That government could not conduct war successfully were it forbidden to inflate the circulating medium.

N. That inflation lessens the burden of war upon the finances of the richer sections of the population.

O. That no tax system can be devised which is capable of financing fully a major war.

P. That it would be impracticable for any Monetary Authority to prevent fluctuations in the price level.

Q. That the "100% reserve" plan, if applied to the commercial banking system, would promote inflation.

R. That, by lowering their rediscount rates sufficiently, the Federal Reserve Banks can induce borrowing, and hence prevent a contraction of the volume of deposits in commercial banks.

S. That, if many people engaged in hoarding, open market operations would not be effective in increasing the total supply of spending, and thereby raising prices.

T. That, unless one can prevent public sentiment from becoming pessimistic, depressions are inevitable.

U. That open market operations and public spending programs have similar weaknesses.

V. That no one nation can, by itself, stabilize its price level — international action being essential to stability.

XIX A. That the labor problem in the United States is how to prevent the laboring man from being oppressed by ruthless employers.

B. That working-class members today are not much more prosperous than were their forebears.

C. That most workingmen really know what their own interests are.

D. That most of the friends of labor have any conception of the steps necessary to benefit the laboring class.

E. That the interests of the employer commonly conflict with those of his employees.

F. That heavy taxation of the wealthy benefits the laboring class.

G. That we are likely to achieve sustained prosperity before we get general wage flexibility.

H. That there is much likelihood of securing sustained prosperity until the custom of paying wages at fixed rates per piece or per hour is generally abandoned.

I. That any employer, while paying fixed wage rates per piece or per hour, can safely enter into a contract guaranteeing steady annual wages for all his employees.

J. That the flexible unit wage system is applicable to but a small fraction of industry.

Keys to Pandora's Box

Some of the false keys in the heap within which the keys to prosperity are to be sought merely open the way to paths leading nowhere. Others, however, are, instead, veritable keys to Pandora's box. Among such are the following fallacies:

1. That, in making plans for future world welfare, it is safe to ignore the population problem.
2. That the quality of the population is a matter concerning which the public does not need to concern itself.
3. That people must steel themselves against their inherent desires for security, and think only of opportunities for advancement.
4. That individuals be allowed to shift to others the burden of providing for them and their families in time of misfortune or unemployment.
5. That unemployment insurance legislation safeguards the interests of labor.
6. That the sacredness of private property and freedom of contract are not essential to the nation's welfare, and hence that it is not a prime function of government to protect either.
7. That governmental measures resulting in the leveling down of wealth and income are beneficial to the poorer classes of the population.
8. That measures should be taken to keep profits in competitive industries down to "reasonable" levels.
9. That heavy taxation of saving and of inheritances can be indulged in with impunity.
10. That forced spending or investing of cash balances held by individuals is socially desirable.
11. That it is unnecessary for a government to balance its budget every year — cyclical balancing being sufficient.
12. That government has no legitimate functions in connection with the nation's economy.
13. That regulation of the supply of circulating medium is unnecessary.
14. That government can establish a price and wage structure superior to that produced by free competition.
15. That regulation of wages and other prices is compatible with freedom.
16. That minimum wage regulations may improve the lot of the less efficient members of the working class.
17. That, in order to assure full employment, government must control the activities of industry.
18. That government can finance, control, or operate industry effectively.
19. That monopolies representing persons having low or moderate incomes may safely be allowed to operate without restraint.

THE SEVENTEEN KEYS TO PROSPERITY

All the preceding chapters of this book have been devoted to describing the keys to prosperity with sufficient care and detail to enable the reader to distinguish them from the false keys, and especially from the keys to Pandora's box. The time has now come to list in order the keys to prosperity. By their aid, it is possible to unlock all of the gates and allow the nation's motor caravan to move ahead along that smooth sweeping turnpike, gently rising and uninterrupted by any sharp hills or declivities, which constitutes the road to sustained prosperity. Here is a list of the 17 keys which have been described:

1. Prevention of war — an end which cannot be attained without the establishment of a really effective world government.
2. Prevention of any undue population pressure upon the supply of material resources available to the nation.
3. Conservation of natural resources.
4. Maintenance of the quality of the population.
5. Forcing of the thriftless to insure themselves and their families against the untoward vicissitudes of life.
6. Preservation of freedom of movement from place to place within the nation. This includes the right to go to one's place of employment without molestation, and to receive the full protection of government while so doing.
7. Guarantee by government of the right to acquire, hold, dispose of, and bequeath private property. This includes the duty of government to use all means at its disposal to prevent the unlawful seizure or destruction of private property.
8. Freedom of contract, and guarantee by government of the sacredness of contracts made. Freedom of contract includes the right to sell one's services and other goods where and when one pleases at the best prices obtainable.
9. Freedom of investment and private enterprise.
10. Encouragement of invention.
11. Protection of the thrifty from confiscation of their savings by taxation and otherwise.
12. Avoidance of governmental deficits, in bad years as well as in good years.
13. Prevention of either inflation or deflation of the volume of circulating medium.
14. Governmental adjustment of the net total volume of spending power to the extent necessary to prevent any considerable changes in the general price level.
15. Withdrawal of government from the ownership, administration, or control of the operations of construction projects, farms, factories, banks, insurance funds, and transportation facilities.
16. Prevention by government of oppression of the public by either capitalistic or labor monopolies.
17. Substitution of provisions for flexible wage rates instead of fixed wage rates in contracts between employers and employees.

It is undoubtedly true that the national economic motor caravan can move ahead even if some of the keys are not found and hence some of the gates remain locked, for there are by-passes around most of the gates. The detour trails are, however, rough, rugged, and, in many cases, almost impassable. For example, the road leading around Gate 1 runs through a swamp and the one around Gate 2 ends in an impenetrable jungle. If we really wish our nation to progress smoothly and steadily along the upward gradient, we must find and make use of all seventeen of the Keys to Prosperity.

FINIS

INDEX

Ability to pay, 132
Absolute level of prices, 109–11
After-tax income
    and security flotations, 68–74
    apportionment of, 74–75
Agricultural activity
    relation to
        new spending power, 158–160
American Revolution, 22

Bank
    deposits, 29–32, 89–99, 105, 145–153
    investments, 91–94
    loans, 91
    notes, 30–33
    reserves, 95
        100%, 206
    runs, 95–98
Bank credit, 29–33, 145–156
    contraction
        causes depression, 150–152
        reason for, 150
    stoppage of expansion, 150
Banks
    assets, 91–94
Birth rates, 7–16
    differential, 15–16
Black Death, 8
Black markets, 200
Bonds and price-level control, 207–210
Borrowing
    causes depressions, 151
Borrowing by
    government, 31–33, 40–43, 90–94, 145–147, 200–205
    individuals, 40, 91, 145, 148–151
        restrictions on, 206–207
Budget
    cyclically balanced, 82
    need of balancing, 82–85, 203–205
    planning, 205
    unbalanced, 81–84, 200–202
Buying
    potentials, 139
    volume of, 139

Cameralism, 17–18
Capital
    formation
        related to tax rates, 76, 84
    private, 52
    relation to
        natural resources, 12
        prosperity, 12

    social, 46
    supply per wage worker, 78–80
Cash
    reserves, 109–111, 124, 127–128
Cathedrals and poverty, 14
Certificates
    gold and silver, 30–32
Charlatans, economic, 2
Checks on population growth, 8
Chrysler, Walter, 25
C. I. O., 161–162
Circuit flows, 126
Circulating
    credit, 29–33, 105
    medium, 32–33, 61, 89–102, 105–110, 118, 132, 146–147, 203, 205–210
Circulating medium
    control of volume, 205–210
    relation to
        business cycles, 202
        demand, 132
        idle money, 64–65
        open-market operations, 207–210
        physical output, 203
        price level, 100–101, 103–110, 119–123, 205–210
        security flotations, 61
Circulation of
    goods, 113–115
    money and credit, 113–131
Clayton Act, 212
Collective bargaining, 212–213
Colonies, American, 9, 17, 21–22
Combining unit, 103
Committee on Economic Accord, 34
Communism, 18–19
Compensation of employees, 97–98
Competition
    abandonment of, 21
    characteristics of, 19
    free, 12, 22
Consumers
    demands of, 137–138
    power of, 24–25
Consumption
    opposite of saving, 49
    relation to
        demand, 137
        spending, 129–131
Costs, real economic, 161
Credit
    bank, 29–33, 206
    circulating, 29–33